THE UNCONSCIOUS
AND
EDUARD VON HARTMANN

THE UNCONSCIOUS
AND
EDUARD VON HARTMANN

A HISTORICO-CRITICAL MONOGRAPH

by

DENNIS N. KENEDY DARNOI

MARTINUS NIJHOFF / THE HAGUE / 1967

PRINTED IN THE NETHERLANDS

Ohne Ideen kann kein Mensch leben, da jeder Mensch notwendig irgendwelchen Zielen zustrebt.

Johann Fischl, Idealismus. . . . [1]

---

[1] *Idealismus, Realismus und Existentialismus der Gegenwart* (Graz: Verlag Styria, 1954) Vorwort, p. V.

CONTENTS

INTRODUCTION

No man can live without ideas, for every human action, internal or external, is of necessity enacted by virtue of certain ideas. In these ideas a man believes; they guide his actions, and ultimately his whole life. Study of these ideas and principles is one of the distinctive tasks of the history of philosophy. But were we to restrict the field of interest of the history of philosophy to a mere detached academic "cataloguing" of past ideas, the history of philosophy itself would have joined long ago the interminable line of barren catalogued ideas. The study of the wisdom of past ages, however, is very much alive. Not only is it alive, but in the words of Wilhelm Dilthey: "What man is, he learns through history."[1] Thus, the culture of every generation is inevitably related, whether thetically or antithetically, to the previous one, and the political and economic struggles of any present are always the consequences of an earlier and perhaps even fiercer battle of ideas.

It is imperative to know the history of the philosophies that nourish the present if we wish to know ourselves and the world about us. The Socratic call to self-knowledge is as indispensable a condition of a truly human existence today as it was in the fifth century B.C. Whenever man has refused to abide by this principle, the price of his folly has been enslavement to some external force and the debasement of his essential dignity as man. The greatest disease of Western culture today is the fact that Western man has forgotten to meditate. He senses the reason for the decline in creative activity and for the lack of Western political initiative, which threaten the very foundation of Western culture, in the fact of self-alienation on the part of the Western man. The beginnings of a hopeful return from our present fatal state of self-alienation to the security of self-recognition must be from that rational discipline which through the scrutiny of internal connection between

1 As quoted by Fischl, *op. cit.*, p. 23.

human thinking and progress is capable of holding up to man the mirror of self-knowledge. Thus, a sincere study and an unbiased presentation of those great ideas which in some way and to some extent influenced the course of humanity are the foremost tasks of the historian of philosophy.

The study of the history of philosophy will be delusive unless we study actual men in the concrete circumstances in which they lived and which influenced their intellectual and psychological formation. In the course of the present work we intend to make it clear that we do not accept an abstract idea-history in the sense of the Hegelian determinism but rather a history of ideas that are conceived, developed, and thought out by men of flesh and blood with definite personalities and characters of their own. It is obvious that at least a brief survey of the cultural background and immediate surroundings of any philosopher is both indispensable and helpful in understanding and evaluating a system in question. Without the knowledge of individual characteristics and prevailing cultural trends, we would be so much poorer in placing into its proper perspective the differences, for instance, between Socrates' philosophy and Aristotle's, between Augustine's and that of Thomas Aquinas, between Leibniz's and Kant's, or between Schopenhauer's and von Hartmann's. Although both component elements, the psychological and the historical, or if we prefer, the subjective and objective, are of essential importance in understanding and evaluating properly the intellectual outlook of a philosopher, we must also bear in mind that the prevalence of the objective elements does not always vouch for the greater objective value of the system itself. If this is true *in abstracto*, it is much more so in the case of the philosopher who is the object of the present treatise, Karl Robert Eduard von Hartmann.

This study of the philosophical system of von Hartmann owes its origin to a twofold consideration. First, the work aims to give a comprehensive and unified presentation of von Hartmann's doctrine based on his metaphysical first principle, the unconscious. Such an undertaking seems to be warranted on the basis of the fact that in contrast to historical studies in other languages, no one single work in English philosophical literature is dedicated in its entirety to such a study.[1] This is not to say that there are no works in the English language dealing with von Hartmann's doctrine, for at the end of the last and in the early

---

[1] We have listed in our bibliography all the major works we found in the course of our research concerning von Hartmann's philosophy in German, French, Spanish, Italian, and Hungarian.

part of the present century there appeared sporadic works treating some aspects of his prolific philosophical activity, especially his pessimism and the notion of the unconscious.[1] What is still lacking is a single work presenting his metaphysical *Weltanschauung* in its comprehensive totality and the application of such a metaphysics to the various fields of human activity. Such a work is further warranted by the fact that any study prior to the completion of his life-task necessarily had to content itself with a fragmentary view of von Hartmann's system because of his constant change and development in thought. Thus, in evaluating his philosophy and integrating it properly into the progressive flow of human ideas, his later corrective, or rather modifying works, must be taken into account. This task obviously could not have been done by his contemporary critics. Therefore, if von Hartmann's philosophical position is better defined and more clearly integrated with the past as a result of this work, one of the aims has been achieved and all efforts are compensated for.

The second reason for this study is a sense of historical exactness. This historical exactness refers primarily to the genesis and manifold application of the term unconscious. It is beyond the scope of this treatise to enter into the various psychological implications of the unconscious as it is adopted and employed by the different schools of psychoanalysis, psychophysics, psychovitalism, or psychologism. Nor is its intent to establish a direct line of descent of Freud's *es-Unbewusste* and Jung's *Kollectiv-Unbewusste* from von Hartmann's *Das Unbewusste*. Endeavor is focused upon the task of showing that any later application and meaningful usage of the term takes its origin from von Hartmann's philosophy. In spite of the fact that von Hartmann labors hard to furnish the unconscious with an impressive genealogy, this work maintains that he is the first philosopher to work out a system of thought based upon the metaphysical principle of the unconscious. Thus the possibility of employing the term meaningfully in any other related philosophical disciplines especially in epistemology, psychology,

---

[1] Francis Bowen, *Modern Philosophy, from Descartes to Schopenhauer and Hartmann* (New York: Scribner, Armt. Co., 1877), pp. 429–480 deal with von Hartmann's philosophy in general; Samuel Butler, *Unconscious Memory: a Comparison between the Theory of Dr. E. Hering and the "Philosophy of the Unconscious" of Dr. E. von Hartmann* (London and New York: A. C. Fifield, 1880) (2d ed.; New York: E. P. Dutton Co., 1910); Ernest Dare, *Religion of the Future* (London: W. Stewart and Co., 1886). It is the second part of von Hartmann's *Religion des Geistes* (Berlin: Carl Dunker, 1882); A. Kenner, *The Sexes Compared* (London: Swan Sonnschein Co., 1895); Edgar Saltus, *The Philosophy of Disenchantment* (Boston: Houghton, Mifflin Co., 1885), ch. V. analyzes the pessimism of von Hartmann; Alfred T. Schoefield, *The Unconscious Mind* (New York: Funk and Wagnalls Co., 1901); James Sully, *Pessimism: a History and Criticism* (London: Henry S. King and Co., 1877).

and ethics, finds its final justification in von Hartmann's metaphysics. If the questionable distinction of being the "father of systematic pessimism" is Schopenhauer's, the title of the "father of systematic philosophy of the unconscious" must be reserved for von Hartmann.

In order to show how this twofold purpose of the book is achieved, it has been thought helpful to give a brief exposition of the arrangement of the work. Chapter I gives a background of the elements making up von Hartmann's mental formation, personal as well as social, practical as well as theoretical. Chapters II to V concentrate upon the systematic development of his metaphysical system of concrete monism of the unconscious. Since the key to the understanding of every philosophical system depends on the knowledge of its method and epistemology, Chapter II gives a brief outline of von Hartmann's method and noetic principles. Chapter III shows the practical application of these principles in the pursuance of the discovery of the metaphysical noumenon. This discovery is conducted in three stages: in the study of nature, in the study of man, and in the reciprocal activity of will and idea, whose dualism is "sublated" in the monism of the unconscious. Chapter IV concentrates upon further clarification of this notion by giving von Hartmann's division, definition, and properties of the different kinds of unconscious. Chapter V follows von Hartmann in giving the historical genesis of the notion itself as he allegedly found its express or implied usage in philosophy, literature, aesthetics, history, and the natural sciences. Chapters VI to VIII study in general the practical consequences of the application of the metaphysical unconscious to various fields of human activity. The first investigation in Chapter VI leads to an analysis of the value of life wherein the value judgment is found to be negative and impels von Hartmann to make a pessimistic evaluation of life. Chapter VII concerns itself with the ethical aspect of human life which through the different stages of its evolution culminates finally in acting for man's highest purpose, the deliverance of the absolute from its transcendental misery. This aim finds its ultimate realization in the new religion of the unconscions, wherein all attain their sought after salvation in their unity with the unconscious asbolute spirit, as shown in Chapter VIII.

This study seeks to be more then a mere exposition of von Hartmann's philosophical system. Our ideal in learning is not simply an analysis of new trends of troughts solely for the sake of amassing further information, but rather to show new applications of truth, and come closer to a more comprehensive vision of reality. Thus, any new truth will be trustworthy to the extent that it measures up to the unchangeable principles of reason and understanding. If phylogeny is a true mirror of the progress of the human mind, it is also equally a true mirror of the unchangeable aspect of this mind, the forever enduring, therefore, manifestly natural exigency of the mind that its demand for its proper object be fulfilled in as simple an act as possible. The recognition of this natural "givenness" of the unifying tendency of the human intellect and the necessity of finding the true universal principle that satisfies this craving of the mind for unity and order are the primary and indispensable requisites of any true philosophy. The discovery, through genuinely scientific procedure, of an intelligible principle that in some way pervades all the objects presented to the mind, thereby remaining in living contact with the real, yet, at the same time transcending them all, is a task that no philosophy can shun if it wants to remain a philosophy worthy of its name. To the extent that any philosophy measures up to this universal need of the human mind, we accept it to be true philosophy, and to the extent any system ignores it or contradicts it, we must label it an inadequate or contrary philosophy to the natural inclinations of the complete human agent. This is the basic criterion adapted in this critical study of von Hartmann's philosophical system.

We find the purest recognition of this natural yearning of man's soul for an ultimate principle, and the most genuinely dedicated rational endeavor to attain it, in the classic tradition of an ontocentric self-reflective realism. Aristotle conceives true philosophizing exactly in this manner. According to him, philosophy consists in the fulfillment of a natural desire for scientific knowledge, the culminating point of which is the contemplative possession of the absolute.[1] The knowledge of the mere immediate objects of our experiences cannot satisfy this natural yearning of the intellect, since a penetrating analysis of their inner nature will disclose only their basic insufficiency and unintelligibility. Their being consists in being related and they become intelligible in the light of the term of their relation. The more they resemble this term, the more they are, the more intelligible they become. Thus, their "relatedness" unveils what is proper and intimate to them: their dependence on the divine being. The knowledge of the insufficiency of the self and of the objects of its immediate experience, leads to the knowledge of the "other" *par excellence*, of the supreme transcendent. Man's center is not here below, but elsewhere; it is beyond the limited; it is

[1] *Metaph.* I, 1. 980a 23ff.

not in his nature, but above his nature.[1] The whole of Aristotelian metaphysics witnesses to the presence of the eternal transcendent in the individual delivered to the fluctuations of time. Although the manner of this divine presence in temporality remains an unsolved enigma in Aristotle, yet this trans-historical, transcendent view of man and the world about him is, in the purest philosophical traditions of Greek wisdom, perhaps an inarticulate, but irrepressible yearning for the supernatural that makes Aristotelianism a genuinely human philosophy of life in the widest connotations of the term.

St. Thomas at once envisions the universally true and lasting values as well as the failings attributable to individual imperfections in the philosophy of Aristotle. He also starts from what is evident in our immediate experience of the visible and tangible world, in fact from what is most self-evident of all; namely, that something exists, that there is an "other," that there is being. To this basic, self-evident premise he ultimately resolves all subsequent conclusions.[2] From this starting point, denial of which necessarily entails the rejection of rationality, he then proceeds to unravel all its implications according to the rigorous method of *propter quid* reasoning, the most truly scientific type of thinking possible.[3] He also finds, like Aristotle, that this causal inquiry in its culminating, final resolution aims at the eternal transcendent being – God himself. At this point, St. Thomas succeeds in resolving the Aristotelian riddle of the presence of the eternal in the temporal, of transcendent act in concrete becoming, by showing that God, the transcendent principle of order, communicates through his efficacy, his governing laws to the natural-teleological order of individual things.[4] With the aid of the principle of relation, which is the metaphysical basis of the principle of order, St. Thomas reasons with absolute certitude to the existence of a personal God. With this step he has eliminated the shortcomings of the Greeks, who gained no certain knowledge as to the existence of a personal God, and consequently were unable to solve the mystery of divine efficacy concerning material things. At the same time, he also solves the dilemma of his medieval contemporaries who found no rational answer for the supernatural self-revelation of God in the physical reality of this world. First, a consistently thought out and

---

[1] *Metaph.* I, 2. 982b 9–10. Cf. also A. E. Taylor, *Elements of Metaphysics* (London: Methuen and Co., 1952), 13th ed.; pp. XI–XII.
[2] *In Metaph.*, Prooem.; *De ente et essentia*, Prooem. *in Boeth. de Trinitate* VI, 1. ad 3, *De Ver.* 1 lc., *S. Th.* I, q. 5, a. 2c.
[3] *In* I. *Post. Anal.* lect. 17, no. 3, no. 5; *In Boeth. de Trin.* V, 1. ad 9m.
[4] *S. Th.* I. II, q. 91, a. 1.

systematically employed principle of order will bring about that harmony of opposites which fulfills the yearning for unity of the entire ancient world as well as Western speculation.

The same problem besets modern man and philosophy, since it is basically a human problem, but with the all-important difference that modern man, rejecting all contact with the historical past, pretends to be his own beginning and wholly independent of any divine order. The result is a chaos of existentially more or less bankrupt theories and opinions. The inner insufficiency of any anti-transcendentally orientated philosophy is an open admission of an existential poverty that leaves a gnawing hunger in the heart of man and plunges him into disorder.

Would not a rationally founded and transcendentally directed outlook on life be the answer to our existential hunger? Is it then really so strange and untimely to see the advantages of a philosophy that is meta-empirically directed though based on principles gained through the rigorous method of scientific inquiry?

From this all-important fact of rationally established existence of a supreme personal being, a properly existential philosophy takes its origin. Henceforth, the particular problems and enigmas disclose their importance, not in their isolation but rather in their metaphysical connection as organic parts of the whole designed by God. The recognition of this truth furnishes material for the construction of a philosophical bridge from natural truth to a personal God, and from a personal God back to the destiny of individual men as this destiny faces them in their personal lives. This principle of proper perspective or order is an intrinsically active, living principle. It not only welcomes every new discovery, every ascertained insight into the mysteries of nature, and every scientific enrichment and fulfillment of the inquiring spirit, but all these are actually the existential realization of its own development. The more perfectly the detailed design of this order is revealed, the greater is the recognition of its rationality, greater is the glory of its creator, who cannot call the parts of this universal pattern into being without arranging them simultaneously in an orderly fashion. Thus, only an existential philosophy of order can be perennial, yet young, of lasting value, yet forever growing. Scientific progress endangers it not the least; in its existential outlook it is continually rejuvenated as it progresses, while its own progress serves as a dynamic source of inspiration for any future discovery. We find this inner vitality and magnetic vigor to be the secret of its ability to establish a timeless dialogue with men in every historical period. This timelessness, universal humanity, and reassuring sanity are the appeal for us of a being-centered reflectively self-critical philosophy, as it progresses through the ages, from Aristotle to Edith Stein, and to its still laboring students. It is not a blind submission nor mental slavery that binds us to these faithful custodians of all lasting human values, but rather the joy of possession of the attained and the promising gratification of the attainable that directs our searching mind toward them. We heed and welcome the directives and findings of every sincerely committed and unbiased questioner of truth and the mystery of being. Historical boundaries are no handicap in this common human enterprise, for each dedicated lover of wisdom is but the momentary voice of the perennial longings of all generations. A-historism is a chimera for man, but neither are we slaves to an unquestioning awe of the achievements of the past. To investigate it in the spirit of freedom, and to render its views of reality in terms of our own need and quest of being is the ideal we endeavor to follow. We find in this intellectual atmosphere a genial simplicity where there is no sceptic hesitation regarding the existential commitment, no equivocity, no ambiguity of speech cultivated, for beyond loosely employed terms half-truths are hidden, and half-truths are all-destructive of man and his values. A mind nurtured along these lines will have the assurance of acquiring the most efficacious means against the greatest ill of our day and against the abandonment of an encompassingly realistic thinking; namely, thinking in being.

United with the past in our common love of being, and professing a mental affinity for the basic principles of a being-centered critically reflective realism, we enter the gates of the new philosophy of concrete monism.

Shall here also the eternal quest for being receive an unprejudiced hearing and treatment for its own sake? Will the philosophy of the unconscious also employ an equally rational procedure, or is it so inescapably the product of its time that it cannot divorce itself from the stigma of its impact? Does it bear the unmistakable marks of the historical period of its origin: the unreserved admiration of the idea of evolution, and the romanticist fascination by the mythical, by the search for the "absolute absolute," professing its attainment preferably in some unknowable, irrational noumenon? And, as a result, are we left in the dark as to the true value of human existence in an existentially given and teleologically ordered plan for the totality of reality by a supreme, personal, intelligent Being?

In order to resolve these questions and contrast our own position with that of von Hartmann, there has been added a critical evaluation of the problem treated in each respective chapter, to the extent this criticism seemed desirable and helpful in viewing the question objectively. This has been done with the hope that giving an immediate answer to the established position of von Hartmann on the basis of its merits, we shall avoid the indictment of bias and prejudice against him. Finally, for a comprehensive evaluation of his entire system, there has been added a concluding chapter wherein we endeavor to relate it once more to the past, show its significance for the successive historical periods, and on this basis sum up its objective merits in aiding and promoting a more penetrating knowledge of reality.

CHAPTER I

VON HARTMANN'S LIFE. HIS RELATION TO KANT, SCHOPENHAUER, HEGEL AND SCHELLING

... in order to throw more light on the meaning of certain philosophical movements, we have resorted to significant episodes in the lives of their authors. I wish I could have done it more often, for the biography of a philosopher is of great help in understanding his philosophy. ...[1]

Gilson's opinion could hardly be applied with greater truth to any philosopher than to von Hartmann. Without the knowledge of certain relevant data in his life it would be impossible to attempt a proper evaluation of his philosophy. Some events in his life seem to be so decisive and so deeply affecting his intellectual development and character-formation, that without knowing von Hartmann the man, we cannot understand von Hartmann the philosopher.

Eduard von Hartmann was born in Berlin on February 23, 1842, the only son of a Prussian army officer.[2] After completing his studies in the classics, modern literature, and the natural sciences, he was graduated from the Friedrich Werder gymnasium in 1858. He was a retiring student, having very few friends, hating all "oppressive" discipline in school, and despising the "consecrated" authority of his teachers.[3] In these early years of his mental formation, he had already displayed a liking for the arts, particularly music and painting, as well as for mathe-

---

[1] Etienne Gilson, *The Unity of Philosophical Experience* (New York: Chas. Scribner's Sons, 1954), p. 300.

[2] The main sources for von Hartmann's life are his autobiography, *Mein Entwickelungsgang*, written at the end of 1874 and published as the first study in Part A of the *Gesammelte Studien und Aufsätze* (Berlin: Carl Dunker, 1876). Some references to his life are also found in the third volume of the *Philosophie des Unbewussten* (Leipzig: Hermann Haacke, 1890). My quotations refer mainly to these two works. For a detailed description of his life see Arthur Drews, *Eduard von Hartmanns Philosophisches System im Grundriss* (Heidelberg: C. Winter, 1906), 2nd ed.; pp. 1–70 and his *Das Lebenswerk Ed. von Hartmanns* (Leipzig: T. Thomas, 1907); Hans Vaihinger, *Hartmann, Dühring, und Lange* (Iserlohn: J. Baedeker, 1876); Theodore Kappstein, *Eduard von Hartmann* (Berlin: F. A. Perthes, 1907); Otto Braun, *Eduard von Hartmann* (Stuttgart: Fr. Frommann, 1929). The last two are in the series of Frommanns *Klassiker der Philosophie*, ed. by Richard Falckenberg (Stuttgart: E. Hauff, 1909).

[3] *Gesammelte Studien und Aufsätze* (Berlin: Carl Dunker, 1876), Part A, p. 15.

matics and the natural sciences. These latter played an important role throughout his entire literary career, and his philosophical outlook itself was decisively influenced, if not determined, by this uncommon inclination to the positive sciences.

Having completed his secondary education, young von Hartmann was undecided as to a profession. His choice was divided between music, painting, writing, and the professional pursuance of the natural sciences. He even thought for a while of taking up the systematic study of philosophy, but he quickly banished the thought. His reason for this foreshadows his dislike for professional philosophers who, in his opinion, "degrade philosophy to the level of a breadwinning study."[1] In the midst of his hesitations, he found that to follow in his father's footsteps would be the simplest solution to his problem. The military profession, he reasoned, would leave time for his favorite artistic hobbies, and as an officer, he would engage professionally in the study of mathematics and the sciences, thus developing all his talents according to his ideal of becoming a "whole man."[2] His thoughts were followed by action, and soon he was on his way to a brilliant military career. However, his expectations did not materialize, for a knee injury suffered earlier had worsened, and he was forced to give up his dreams concerning a military profession. In 1868 he submitted his resignation to his superiors, and later sadly remarked in his biography: "I was bankrupt in all that appears great and desirable to mortals, – bankrupt in all, save one thing: ideas."[3]

This somber confession is also an implicit admission of his inability to achieve anything better than mediocrity in his other endeavors. Von Hartmann had never felt that his musical compositions, paintings, writings, or poems were good enough to gain the approval of the public. In view of the adverse criticism, he became more and more convinced that the way determined by fate could not be evaded any longer, and with renewed enthusiasm he dedicated himself to the study of philosophy. The results of his devotion soon began to appear in the form of small works that culminated in the publication of his first and best known work, the *Philosophy of the Unconscious*.[4] The unexpected

[1] *Ibid.*, p. 16.

[2] *Ibid.*, p. 17.

[3] Wilhelm von Schnehen states that some of his drawings and oil paintings are in the property of the family. His musical compositions consist of a few songs and vocal duets and quartets; he also tried his talents in composing an opera of three acts. Inspired by Lope de Vega's *Star of Seville* he wrote the opera's libretto in five days but the work was never published.

[4] Von Hartmann composed two short treatises, *Reflection on the Mind* and *The Mental*

triumph of the work and the universal acclaim of its author, wholly unlike the reaction of Schopenhauer's first appearance before the public, established young von Hartmann among the literary notables of the day and launched him on a career that lasted for forty-two years and produced a list of works dealing with the most varied subjects.[1]

But the glory and fame that came in such a gratifying measure to the young author were not to remain lasting companions. As soon as the voices of adulation had ceased about the oddities of the new philosophy, the stern criticism of professional critics left only shreds of the entire work. Under their continuous attacks von Hartmann was forced to review the *Philosophy of the Unconscious*, but it is significant to note that none of these revisions affected any of the basic principles of the work. In his autobiography he states that:

Such revisions will never take place, since in the course of time I became more convinced of and more confirmed in these principles.[2]

None of his later works is a repudiation of his early philosophical beliefs, but are rather further developments and applications of these basic tenets to the various fields of human activity. In view of his stand, the critics' assaults became more and more intensified and finally culminated in a strange ostracism of von Hartmann as well as his works. His former literary adversaries ignored him completely, and this hurt him more than their previous sarcastic criticisms. This and a recurrence of his earlier physical disability forced him into semi-retirement, but his literary activity continued without interruption with an amazing productivity. He labored to develop an outline of a history of philosophy which he wished to write in his lifetime, but had not found sufficient time to complete it, since he died on Pentecost Day in 1906.

Before we discuss von Hartmann's philosophy on the basis of its merits, there is another aspect of his personality that demands our close

---

Activity of Sensation, in 1859 when he was only seventeen years of age. Prior to the publication of his main work in 1869 there were other minor literary endeavors completed, *Concerning the Value of the Intellect* and *Cognition Regarding Human Fate and Luck; On the Simple Root of the Principle of Sufficient Reason; On the Concept of the Infinite (and Null); On the Dialectical Method*, which was published only months before the *Philosophy of the Unconscious*, in May, 1868.

[1] The best-known critics of the day, Gottschall, Carrière, Lorm, and Scherr, hailed the young author and his work as the beginning of a new era in German philosophical literature, and recommended it enthusiastically to their readers. The copies of the first publication disappeared from the bookstores within a few months. Foreign countries hurried to obtain copyrights for translation. The universities of Leipzig and Göttingen offered him chairs of philosophy, and the Prussian Ministry of Culture invited him to the university of Berlin, but young von Hartmann declined the honor for reasons of health as well as his personal desire to remain uninfluenced by the official trends of the schools.

[2] *Op. cit.*, p. 45.

attention, for it influences to a great extent his attitude toward his predecessors. This is the indiscriminate admiration for the principle of organization and subordination, which he learned to respect and emulate in his early youth. He was born and brought up in a military milieu, and it was almost inevitable for him not to be affected by what he thought to be the most perfect manifestation of this principle: the Prussian military system. His words are a tribute of admiration for an organization, "wherein the strictest subordination serves as an indispensable means for the achievement of the intended end."[1] It proved to be a dangerous weapon in his hands. Such a principle may well be functional in a military organization, but it can hardly be employed as the only norm of criticism regarding the philosophical exposition of past systems without necessarily inflicting injustice on these systems. Yet in his unrestrained eagerness to establish the right to existence of his own metaphysical noumenon, the unconscious, von Hartmann saved no effort to mold, arrange, and organize the thoughts of his predecessors in such a way that in his interpretation they served only one purpose: to establish the need for the metaphysical foundation of the unconscious. Need for this new philosophy is most emphatically declared in his *History of Metaphysics*, where he states that the aim of any future philosophy must be:

To give a thorough revision of concrete-monistic pantheism according to the inductive method and the transcendental-real theory of knowledge; furthermore, to assume the absolute substantial subject of theism, without its consciousness, self-awareness, and personality into pantheism. Thus to prevail over one-sided panthelism as well as panlogism by means of two coordinated attributes of the (unconscious) substance, so as to bring the materialistic dependence of conscious intellectual operations upon organic functions to unlimited calculations. Finally, to allot the individual a more worthy and relatively more independent position than it has in the abstract monistic and materialistic pantheism, without, however, hypostatizing it.[2]

This is the program of the new philosophy and von Hartmann's philosophical creed, which will also serve as the guiding norm in the interpretation of his predecessors, particularly Kant, Hegel, Schopenhauer, and Schelling, all of whom will merely promote, in von Hartmann's hands, the logical necessity of the philosophy of the unconscious.[3]

---

[1] *Ibid.*, p. 18.

[2] *Geschichte der Metaphysik* (Leipzig: Hermann Haacke, 1899), vol. II, p. 99.

[3] In the following presentation of von Hartmann's exposition of Kant, Hegel, Schopenhauer, and Schelling the immediate sources are *Das Philosophische Dreigestirn des 19. Jahrhunderts*, published as section D in the *Gesammelte Studien und Aufsätze* (Berlin: Carl Dunker, 1876). *Schellings positive Philosophie als Einheit von Hegel und Schopenhauer* (Berlin: Otto Loewenstein, 1869); *Geschichte der Metaphysik*, especially vol. II (Leipzig: Hermann Haacke,

Von Hartmann's interpretation of Kant, which is relevant to this work, commences with an analysis of his *Kritik der praktischen Vernunft*, wherein he endeavors to reduce the duality of will and idea, by considering them as two attributes of God, i.e., the creator of the world of the things-in-themselves.[1] In doing so, Kant warns us to remove from these concepts all that may be reminiscent of human willing and cognition; namely, any eudemonological motivation of the will and the spatial-temporal restrictions of the cognitive process. Having removed these anthropomorphic notions from the divine volitional and intellective operations, Kant insists that:

... we have arrived at an intellect that *does not think*, (i.e. not in time, discursively and abstracting), but *knows intuitively*,[2] and we have arrived at a will that is directed toward objects whose existence cannot influence its own happiness.[3]

These words of Kant may full well receive their proper interpretation through the doctrine of analogy; however, von Hartmann eagerly seizes them and exploits them according to the demands of his own concrete-monistic position. The expressions "an intellect that *does not think*" yet "*knows intuitively*" can be understood, he contends, only in the light of the unconscious ideas, for intuition is the exclusive property of the absolute unconscious. Furthermore, these unconscious ideas form also the content of the Kantian divine creative will, according to von Hartmann, which regulates the world of noumena. Fully satisfied with the result of discovering the shadowy yet sufficient traces of the unconscious in the absolute noumenon of Kant, von Hartmann goes a step further and declares that the unconscious logical is a silent hypothesis throughout the Kantian system, and only in view of this hypothesis can we fully grasp the meaning of all Kant's endeavors.[4]

What is only remotely suggested by Kant, von Hartmann finds to be brought to the fore with much greater clarity and purposiveness by two of Kant's followers, Schopenhauer and Hegel. Their contribution

1899); 10th edition of the *Philosophie des Unbewussten* (Leipzig: Hermann Haacke, 1890), vol. III, introductory chapter I. *Mein Verhältnis zu früheren Philosophen.*

[1] Von Hartmann uses the Rosenkranz and Schubert, Leipzig; Baumann, 1838–1842, 12-volume edition of *I. Kants Sämmtliche Werke*, of which the VIIIth volume is the *Kritik der praktischen Vernunft*. The pagination hereafter refers to this edition. The present reference is made to vol. VIII, p. 281.

[2] From the verb "*anschauen*," which in Kantian terminology expresses the immediate comprehension of a given object in its complete distinctness without recourse to the aid of concepts and conclusions, cf. Rudolf Eisler, *Wörterbuch der philosophischen Begriffe* (Berlin: E. S. Mittler & Sohn, 1904), vol. I, pp. 41–47.

[3] *Op. cit.*, VIII, p. 282.

[4] *Philosophie des Unbewussten* (Leipzig: Hermann Haacke, 1890), 10th ed., vol. III, introductory chapter I. *Mein Verhältnis zu früheren Philosophen.*

to the development of the notion of the unconscious is to be praised, although von Hartmann can hardly forgive their fatal blunder of separating once more the mere attributes of the unconscious, will and idea, and thereby hypostatizing them.

In von Hartmann's analysis, Schopenhauer conceives the intellect in a purely materialistic manner, inasmuch as for him it is a mere product of the brain, and admits only the blind, unconscious will as the unique metaphysical principle. This narrow metaphysical outlook plunges Schopenhauer into the most extreme pessimism where there is no place for any ray of rational hope but only the expectation of personal annihilation in the bosom of Nirvana. For Hegel, on the contrary, there is the idea which, as the single metaphysical principle, dialectically evolves from its primordial unconsciousness to its full self-awareness. Any striving or drive (*Trieb*) is explained simply as the result of the dialectical self-evolution of the idea. This rational metaphysical outlook provides Hegel with an optimism that regards evil as a mere antithetical and transitory phase in the all-encompassing role of the rational.

Apart from showing the need for the unconscious, the critical study of the Schopenhauerian and Hegelian philosophical positions serves an additional purpose for von Hartmann. He intends to prove thereby also the inadequacy of any philosophy that is based on the absolute dichotomy of will and idea, and he hastens to make a plea for the need of their unification as two "coordinated attributes of the (unconscious) substance."[1] Von Hartmann professes to have found the realization of this need, at least in outline form, in Schelling's last philosophical creed, the "positive." It forms the subject of Schelling's final work, *Introduction to the Philosophy of Mythology*,[2] and von Hartmann gives a detailed critical exposition of it [3] with the purpose of using Schelling's positive philosophy as the immediate introduction to his own system of thought.[4]

At the outset of the *Introduction to the Philosophy of Mythology* [5] Schelling performs a valuable service for von Hartmann by proving the

---

[1] Cf. footnote 2, p. 13, above.

[2] *Schellings Sämmtliche Werke*, ed. by his son K. F. A. Schelling, (Stuttgart: J. G. Cotta, 1856–61). The first division consists of 8 volumes, the second division of 4 volumes. The present quotation refers to div. II., vol. I, pp. 57–58.

[3] *Schellings positive Philosophie als Einheit von Hegel und Schopenhauer* (Berlin: Otto Loewenstein, 1869).

[4] The following is a brief summary of Schelling's positive philosophy by von Hartmann on the basis of his *Schellings positive Philosophie*. Von Hartmann's source for the critical exposition of this work is the above quoted collected edition of Schelling's writings edited by his son. Cf. footnote 2 above.

[5] *Schellings Sämmtliche Werke*, div. II, vol. I, pp. 58 ff.

basic insufficiency of Hegelian panlogism as well as Schopenhauerian panthelism, thereby confirming von Hartmann's claim of the need of their coordinated unification. Contrary to its pretensions, Schelling states, the Hegelian idea is never proved to explain more of reality than the mere logical contents in the essence of things. Even at the summit of its dialectical fulfillment, the absolute idea remains as remote from reality as at the beginning of its logical process. Regardless of the spatio-temporal dimensions of the dialectical process, the idea can never step out of its own sphere; it is forever hopelessly entangled within its own monolithic nature out of which there is no bridge to reality, no possible escape into the realm of existence. The logical idea can never achieve more than to account for the "whatness" or essence of things. All it knows is the conceptualized substitute of the thing, but never the thing itself, thus remaining irredeemably a one-sided, negative philosophy.

On the other hand, there is in any existentially given phenomenon or experience more than the mere content or idea of the thing. It contains its nature that is knowable, accessible to the intellect, plus something that is outside the realm of the intelligible, therefore, irrational and inaccessible to the intellect.

In the eternal fact of self-revelation, as we now perceive it in the world, everything is under rule, in order, and in form; but beneath all this, at the basis of things, there is always the ruleless, as if ready to break through once more; nowhere does it appear obvious that order and form were the primary original states, it seems rather as if the primary ruleless (irrational) has been brought to order (to rationality). This is the incomprehensible basis of reality in things, the never soluble remainder, which can never, not even through the greatest efforts be dissolved by reason, but it remains eternally in the beyond.[1]

In this unknown and unknowable, this irrational basis of reality, which gives the "that" or existence of things whose "whatness" or essence is determined by the intellect, we must recognize the will.

No real existence is conceivable without a closely qualified willing. That something is, therefore, the existence of a certain thing is recognizable by the fact that it affirms itself, and that it excludes everything else from itself, resisting all that seeks to destroy its existence. ... But resistance lies, properly speaking, only in willing; will is the power of resistance, and the only unconditionally resistance-capable in the world, consequently the properly "unconquerable."[2]

Since this will is alogical it is not bound to any intellect. Moreover, it is the only alogical we know; consequently, we may call it "the alogical."

Thus far Schopenhauer is correct, so Schelling holds, but he then

---

[1] *Ibid.*, div. I, vol. 7, pp. 359–360; div. I, vol. 8, p. 212.
[2] *Ibid.*, div. I, vol. 1, p. 218.

commits the unforgivable mistake of making this blind, unenlightened will the sole metaphysical principle of his philosophy. The will is empty and objectless without the idea, for the idea places the "whatness" of willing. An empty willing which wills nothing but to will, and yet cannot will because it does not know what to will, and does not know what willing is, is a mere struggling and blind urge for existence, without ever being able to arrive at it alone. It is a dark, senseless process within the will, a wicked striving, a mad merry-go-around, which can never lead to an end, for its cycles return eternally like the puppets in a harlequinade.

Schelling sums up the criticism of Hegel and Schopenhauer in the following statements: Hegel has expounded the standpoint of panlogism and Schopenhauer the theory of will-pantheism, each of them providing a system in the most consistent one-sidedness of their principle, thus making obvious what such a principle in its isolation can do and cannot do. Their inadequacy of explaining reality in their separate adaptation proves clearly that they postulate each other as supplements, and that the two must be sublimated into a higher unity. This union cannot be a mere fusion of the two principles; they must be united with the firm insistence upon their distinctive character.

Schelling finds the union of these two principles in the absolute substance, or God, in whom all possible perfections reside. Neither the idea nor the will is self-explanatory, for one cannot exist without the other; therefore, they cannot subsist independently. Thus, they are not substance. "They themselves are not substances, but merely the attributes of the One supra-actual."[1] "We have one substance with two attributes, consequently we do not state that there is $1 + 1 + 1$, rather, that there is only the One, i.e., the Substance."[2] This substance is not without its attributes, but it is above its attributes; it is more than the mere union of these, prior to these. Each of the previous principles is inadequate in its isolation. This new principle, being the unity of the two, is the one as well as the other, and therefore, not one-sided any longer. This substantial identity, or this identical substance of the first and second principle, viz., will and idea, can be represented by the symbol A^3.[3]

[1] *Ibid.*, div. II, vol. 1, p. 222.
[2] *Ibid.*, div. II, vol. 1, p. 235.
[3] A or A_1 or A^3 is Schelling's symbol for the absolute, or absolute spirit, A^1 is defined by him as the pure possibility of being, i.e., the will; A^2 is the pure object, something which is in no way a subject, i.e., something which cannot do anything, but is only presentation or idea. A^3 is therefore, the unity of will and idea, or the absolute spirit. Cf. *Gesammelte Studien und Aufsätze*, p. 718.

Henceforth von Hartmann takes over the criticism of Schelling's own absolute identical substance in his characteristic exoteric and arbitrary interpretation.

For Schelling the absolute identical substance in his positive philosophy is the personal triune God of Christianity; this even von Hartmann could not deny. Nevertheless, he goes back to Schelling's earlier philosophy, particularly to his philosophy of identity, to mold the notion of this absolute substance according to his own fancy and needs. Despite Schelling's explicit statements to the contrary, von Hartmann states that Schelling has not forsaken his earlier pantheistic position in his last or positive philosophy.[1] But in order to substantiate this judgement, no direct proof is adduced from Schelling himself, rather von Hartmann brings in his own interpretation of pantheism. According to it pantheism means neither "everything is God," nor "all is God," but "God is all," wherein "all" includes the world as well as God.[2] Furthermore, von Hartmann identifies pantheism with monism, and this identification will help him in making the Schellingian terms denoting the oneness of God, such as "God is the One," "God is the only One," "the individual One who is also All," expressive of pantheistic unicity.[3] The only explanation for this abuse of Schelling's expressions is a reference to Schelling's rejection of an empty, inefficacious theism, the product of shallow rationalism, according to which God is one only externally, since he has no other gods beside him. But Schelling rejects only this "in-itself-divided god" of rationalism, and defends against it a monotheism in which God is also intrinsically one. Thus von Hartmann is by no means justified in insisting further that this monotheism is in itself pantheism. Not even the fact that Schelling attributes a distinct personality to this absolute substance alters the matter for von Hartmann, since he believes that Schelling only warns against that kind of pantheism in which, as in the substance of Spinoza or in the idea of Hegel, God is the "*blindly* (necessarily) *existent* and the not capable of non-existence." In other words, von Hartmann persists, Schelling has rejected only the kind of pantheism in which God must *eternally, necessarily*, and *blindly will*, but by no means the kind in which the absolute can eventually be delivered through willing, and thus ultimately return to non-willing and to non-existence.[4]

There is no defense against this tendentious adaptation of Schelling's

---

[1] *Ibid.*, p. 720.
[2] *Ibid.*, p. 721.
[3] *Schellings Sämmtliche Werke*, div. II, vol. 1, p. 174.
[4] *Op. cit.*, p. 722.

doctrine of the absolute, personal substance in the service of the new philosophy. Von Hartmann proceeds with a single-minded purposiveness to reach the predetermined goal of his philosophical creed, "... to assume the absolute substantial subject of theism, without its consciousness, self-awareness, and personality into pantheism." In further realization of this aim, he has another objection to Schelling's eviscerated, depersonalized notion of substance that has become nothing more than a remote substrate of unconscious manifestations in von Hartmann's interpretation.

Von Hartmann holds [1] that Schelling's notion of A^3 is aprioristically established, and that it is abstract. We must remedy this by experimental verification to make it concrete. In complying with this demand of his own philosophy, he proceeds to observe the capacity of representative thinking of Schelling's A^3 in its phenomenal manifestations. But representative thinking presupposes consciousness, and von Hartmann holds that consciousness is the final culmination of organic function. Thus from the experimentally observable fact of phenomenal or organic consciousness, it is concluded that the primordial, pretemporal, and noumenal existence of A^3 is the state of the unconscious spirit which contains in itself its attributes of willing and thinking. We are told once more that the "unconscious spirit" is the mere corrected derivative of Schelling's "unconscious world-spirit" established in his philosophy of identity.[2]

The aim is finally achieved, and von Hartmann believes that he has shown the path and laid down the blueprints of the philosophy of the future. The task of this philosophy is twofold: in the realm of the noumenal, it must conclude to a spiritualistic monism; in the realm of the phenomenal, it has to restore again the proportion between the speculative and empirical aspects of philosophy.

As to the first task, Schelling has shown the right direction in his philosophy of identity by recognizing the absolute noumenon as the eternal unconscious. Hegel has pursued this principle further on the side of the unconscious logical idea, and Schopenhauer on the side of the unconscious alogical will. This unwarranted dichotomy is brought to a unity once more in Schelling's positive philosophy by the principle of the absolute spirit. Take away from Hegel's idea and from Schopenhauer's will the predicate of unconsciousness, and panlogism and panthelism will immediately and irrevocably relapse into theism. This

---

[1] *Ibid.*, p. 723.
[2] *Ibid.*, p. 724.

imminent danger threatens to ruin Schelling's positive philosophy, for he omits to proclaim energetically and unequivocally that the absolute noumenon is the eternal unconscious, as he does in his first system. Thus von Hartmann concludes to the need and the necessity of the philosophy of the unconscious.

As to the second task of strengthening and furthering the cause of philosophy by placing it upon natural-scientific foundations, von Hartmann believes with candid self-satisfaction that, even if he is not the only philosopher to attempt this aim, he certainly is the best of those who do so. In his own words:

I am the only philosopher who has undertaken this task simultaneously in an antitheistic and antimaterialistic manner, while all the others follow either the mechanistic view, which is presently the dominating one among our natural scientists; or they seek to adapt the data of the empirical sciences for the aid of the pre-Kantian Christian theism.[1]

Von Hartmann envisions his historical mission and significance by bringing to a close the circle of ideas of the great philosophical "tricomets" of nineteenth century Germany. By elevating the claim of each of these thinkers to the exclusive validity of their teaching, and placing them upon the level of the highest possible unity, he believes that he has purified their doctrines and has united the eternal truths in their teaching into a perfect and complete metaphysical principle of totality. This all-comprehensive principle is the principle of the unconscious which alone is capable of holding within itself in an organic unity the true core of its immediate predecessors. This principle, developed and established in an inductive way, alone contains satisfactory answers to all the enigmas of the noumenal as well as the phenomenal world, is the firm conviction of its founder.

---

[1] *Ibid.*, conclusion, pp. 724–729.

CHAPTER II

METHOD OF INQUIRY

Speculative Resultate nach inductiv-naturwissenschaftlicher Methode.

Eduard von Hartmann

Even a superficial acquaintance with von Hartmann's philosophy would sufficiently reveal his concern with the correct method of philosophical inquiry. This preoccupation can easily be understood if it is recalled that the nineteenth century felt the full force of the stormy controversy between the exact character of the natural sciences and the free, "mystical fancy" of romanticist thinkers. The influence of these different ideologies shows itself in philosophical literature as well where, in so far as method is concerned, the purely *a priori* and the purely *a posteriori* fought for exclusive recognition in the discovery of truth. This acute rivalry prompts von Hartmann to subject to particular scrutiny all possible methods of cognition.[1] In his last work on this problem in the first volume of the *System der Philosophie im Grundriss*, von Hartmann divides the different methods of cognition into four classes: 1) gnosis, or intellectual intuition, 2) dialectic, 3) deduction, 4) induction.[2]

None of these methods is accepted by von Hartmann in its traditional form and validity. His preference and usual procedure of resolving all differences into a unifying higher synthesis will be adapted here also in

[1] Von Hartmann dedicates a large part of his writing to a criticism of Hegel's dialectic. Thus his first publication *Über die dialektische Methode* (Berlin: Carl Dunker, 1868). In this treatise he also analyzes the methods of Plato, Aristotle, Kant, Fichte, and Schelling. In the *Philosophische Fragen der Gegenwart* (Leipzig: Wm. Friedrich, 1885), the real-dialectic of Bahnsen is criticized, while in the *Kritische Wanderungen durch die Philosophie der Gegenwart* (Leipzig: Wm. Friedrich, 1889), the mystical dialectic of Haller. In *Schellings philosophisches System* (Leipzig: Hermann Haacke, 1897), von Hartmann deals penetratingly with "intellectual intuition," so also in section B, chapter IX, of the *Philosophy of the Unconscious*. His most comprehensive exposition of method and theory of cognition is laid down in *Das Grundproblem der Erkenntnistheorie* (Leipzig: Wm. Friedrich, 1889), in the *Kategorienlehre* (Leipzig: Hermann Haacke, 1896), and in the *Grundriss der Erkenntnislehre* in his *System der Philosophie im Grundriss* (Bad Sachsa: Hermann Haacke, 1907), vol. I.

[2] *System* (Bad Sachsa: Hermann Haacke, 1907), vol. I, pp. 32–47.

dealing with the proper method of philosophical investigation. His plan is to carefully examine them all, weigh their advantages and disadvantages, and finally, collect their useful elements into the higher synthesis of his own "criticistic" method. In the following we intend to see how von Hartmann attains the proper method of the *Philosophy of the Unconscious* through the critical analysis of traditional methods.

Dialectic, the first method criticized, is discarded as wholly useless for philosophical knowledge. In his first published work: *Über die dialektische Methode*, von Hartmann attributes the origin of dialectic to Zeno of Elea.[1] Heraclitus developed it further, and from him the sophists took it into their own philosophy under the name of *eristic*. This same method was later perfected by Socrates and Aristotle. In modern times Hegel's name has become almost synonymous with dialectic, and he has given it an all-important application in his philosophical system. According to von Hartmann dialectic is the:

> ...Most venturesome, self-defeating attempt of a conceited and chimerical storming of heaven, which fancies to embrace with one grasp of its arms the entire universe; whereas, what it actually holds in its arms is nothing else but the ghost of its own imagination.[2]

It is a delusion to think that dialectic can bring forth any new, positive, and real content of knowledge. Whatever value it may seem to have, it snatches furtively from experience. This method is also fallacious in accepting the validity of the principle of contradiction only for the act of intellectual reflection, which takes the thesis and antithesis of the dialectical process apart and makes them self-reliant, while denying any value of the same principle for reason and its speculative synthesis. The principle of contradiction is under no circumstances invalid. Thus von Hartmann can see nothing but a "morbid perversion of the mind" in the dialectical method, which is wholly incapable of giving us real knowledge.

The method of gnosis or intellectual intuition owes its origin to Plato who set up the ideal of absolute cognition.[3] His method serves as the exemplar of all subsequent forms of philosophical intuition. Whenever men have striven for absolute cognition, this same method has been employed. Intellectual intuition partakes of the nature of mystical cognitive vision, and as such, it stands high above the rules of ordinary perception and association of ideas. It is the result of higher inspiration

---

[1] *Über die dialektische Methode* (Berlin: Carl Dunker, 1868), p. 3.
[2] *Ibid.*, p. 120.
[3] *System* (Leipzig: Hermann Haacke, 1907), vol. I, p. 32.

and of an exposure to the metaphysical all-spirit, in which the act of the intellect's participation in this vision is not realized consciously. It gushes forth spontaneously from the unconscious depths of the mind, although it is also capable of being awakened by suggestions, hypnosis, and ecstasy. As pure experience, its nature is of the ideal order; its noetic value is exclusively subjective. As ostensibly indirect experience or as means of experiencing trans-subjective phenomena, it is beyond control, thus it is useless as a source of cognition. Heuristically or didactically, it could be employed in the service of some other method, even if its own demonstrative value is nil. It sees and finds relations and aims which cannot be attained by purely systematic means, but the degree of probability of these findings must be ascertained by some other way. This kind of cognition is an unobstructed vision of genius, and it may supplement and complete some other method. If intuition is helpful in any of the sciences, it is much more so in philosophy, the final object of which, according to von Hartmann, is the attainment of the absolute, the ego, and the relation of the two, which can be comprehended only in a mystical beholding. In order to make this kind of cognition useful for philosophy, which, essentially and formally, is superior to any kind of purely rational knowledge, it must be methodically grounded and objectified by another method; namely, deduction.

Since Descartes this method has played a significant role in philosophy.[1] With its help, philosophers have striven continually to deduce the entire universe with mathematical certainty from the supreme principle of identity of thought and being. That this endeavor is doomed to failure is sufficiently evident in the philosophy of Hegel. The nature and the demonstrative value of deduction is completely misunderstood. It cannot conclude to any knowledge not already contained in its premises, and the premises in turn, receive their certitude only through previous inductions. If this were not the case, then philosophers claiming demonstrative value for their principles must have acquired them through some sort of mystical flight, which has no place in philosophy. According to von Hartmann, there is no value in mere rational demonstration, because there are no valid *a priori* judgments whatsoever, and, least of all, the synthetic sort. Purely speculative principles can have no probability coefficient, and can mediate, at best, only formal knowledge. In order to have real content, philosophy must begin with real principles which, in the final analysis, rest upon experience.

Thus it appears that only induction can furnish the empirical ma-

[1] *Ibid.*, p. 38.

terial, and with it, the starting point and necessary foundation for a realistic philosophical inquiry.[1] How much von Hartmann depends on induction can be seen by the subtitle of the *Philosophy of the Unconscious* which claims to gain "speculative results by employing the inductive method of the natural sciences."

According to its nature, induction proceeds from several particular judgments to a universal conclusion, without the circumferential content of the latter being exhausted by the former. Induction, therefore, is an incomplete and imperfect method of cognition, in that it can give us only problematically universal but by no means apodictically necessary judgments. Whether we apply this statement to the induction of causes (*Ursacheninduction*) or induction of laws (*Gesetzesinduction*) we are justified in either case.[2] For in the first alternative, the relationship between effect and cause can be ascertained only with greater or lesser probability in each individual case, and the value of the sum-total of all these judgments remains equally the same; namely, probability. In the second alternative, in the case of the induction of laws, the result is similar, for the universal law directing singular phenomena is merely surmised by the researcher in an intuitive visualization, which must be then tested as to its probability through methodical analysis. Thus all that induction can provide of itself in either case is mere probability.

This inner imperfection of the inductive method notwithstanding, von Hartmann is convinced that only that philosophy can have any real value which is built on experience. He finds his historical mission in the recognition of this fact, and he is determined to arrive at a metaphysical outlook of the world in spite of the empirical method. Von Hartmann recognizes an innate desire and natural want in man for metaphysical knowledge, and in his opinion if it is not built upon empirical data, metaphysics undoubtedly will degenerate into occultism and theosophy.

Philosophy (like any other science) also must be empiricism, inasmuch as it originates from experience, controlling its progressing steps by experience, and the higher its pyramidal construction of cognition seeks to reach the wider the empirical foundation must be prepared. ... In this sense even the last and highest peak of philosophy, metaphysics, must be empiricism, i.e., its pinnacles of speculation must rest upon empirical ground, in order not to be a groundless castle in the air.[3]

Since the inductive method is valid for all the sciences, it must be

[1] *Ibid.*, p. 43.
[2] *Ibid.*, p. 44.
[3] *Ibid.*, p. 19.

valid for philosophy also. These experiences supply the philosopher with the findings of the particular sciences, and he in turn, must fully employ them. He must possess the most extensive knowledge of all the experimental sciences so that he may base the foundation of his philosophy upon their findings. Empirical knowledge is indispensable for the philosopher, but it is only the beginning; the real task of the philosopher starts afterwards. For von Hartmann this special philosophical endeavor consists in elevating into a higher synthesis the advantages of all methods of cognition, and in doing so, he sets the stage for the construction of his own "criticistic" method.[1]

In view of the inner insufficiency of both methods, deduction, which cannot attain to objective reality, and induction, which cannot furnish metaempirical knowledge, the philosopher has the duty of employing both methods and of synthesizing the speculative principles in an inductive way with the highest available results of scientific observations. Only in this way can he bridge the gap between reality and the speculative principles as well as elevate subjective conviction into the order of objective truth. Induction must in a certain sense supply verification to deduction. Purely logical speculation may not contradict the facts, nor can empirical explanation ignore or reject the conclusions of logical speculation. From the synthesis of the two, we can gain that particular degree of certitude which alone is attainable by philosophy, according to von Hartmann.

Empirical or assertory certitude is possible for the philosopher only with regard to the facts of experience. Philosophical knowledge begins first with the analysis of the data of experience, and in the course of this analysis the philosopher leaves the ground of the simple certitude that is present at its source. On the other hand, apodictical certitude produces merely formal, not real knowledge. Hence, philosophy must renounce apodictical certitude if it wants to gain real cognition. In the objective-real sphere of the sciences, there exists nothing of absolute certainty, but there is nothing of complete uncertainty either. Everything is found to be more or less probable or improbable. The area of human cognition lies between these two limits, graded through the different degrees of probability. This probability can be mathematically calculated as to its proper degree when the cases in question lend themselves to analysis in a sufficient number; from which then those that are favorable to the phenomenon under consideration will be collected. This calculation of probabilities cannot be employed in the subjective-

[1] *Ibid.*, p. 58.

ideal sphere, according to von Hartmann; for any necessity in this order could be determined only extrinsically through transcendental causality. On the other hand, the calculation of probabilities is possible in the objective-real sphere on the basis of the hypothesis that, since in this order everything is causally determined, a chance of equal value can be extended to all occurrences, because the totality of the causes is unknown.[1] This hypothesis is justified when the sum of the constancy of a phenomenon permits the occurrence of one of its contraries. But the additional variable conditions, which determine the probability of one of these contrary occurrences, must be compensated for in a sufficiently large number of cases so that the anticipation of the occurrence of either phenomenon will be equally probable. The theory of probability first comes to full sovereignty in the metaphysical sphere because here it has only two alternatives of equal value. Since being is declared contrary to non-being, the question in this order is restricted to the relation of absolute willing to non-willing, and the chance of both occurrences is wholly equal.

Von Hartmann is gratified by the thought of having proved the claim of philosophy to the exact same degree of probability that is had by the natural sciences. When philosophy leaves the ground of observable facts in the course of its investigation of reality, then the possible loss of probability is counterbalanced by the greater width of its empirical basis. As to the summit of philosophy, metaphysics, it also must be satisfied with probability and renounce any hope of apodictical, absolute knowledge. Von Hartmann leaves us one consolation, however, in stating that metaphysical probability is greater than a fifty-fifty chance, greater, namely, than the probability of the other non-metaphysical possibilities.

Criticism, or the criticistic method is then the unity of empiricism, speculative inductivism, and probabilism, in which the immanent, positively creative critique and critical foresight joined with prudence has given the name to the whole method.[2]

The first observation to be made about von Hartmann's criticistic method is that its function is primarily negative. It shows the relativity of different epistemological viewpoints and attempts to resolve these differences in a higher synthesis. In von Hartmann's opinion, it supplements the Aristotelian dialectic and totally opposes the Hegelian dialectic of contradiction, which renders all cognition impossible. The Aris-

[1] *Kategorienlehre* (Leipzig: Hermann Haacke, 1896), p. 354.
[2] *Op. cit.*, p. 61.

totelian dialectic is an "art of trying and doing" which draws conclusions from the comparison of former systems, i.e., from their difficulties and contradictions, thus showing the probability of their singular position. This comparative analysis afforded Aristotle the opportunity to search for a higher synthesis. As a method of orientation and as a directive, this Aristotelian method of investigation is still useful. But in order to be an independent and direct path to cognition, it needs completion in the opinion of von Hartmann. This completion will apply not so much to the theoretical principles of Aristotle's method, but rather to its practical application to the historical realm.

This is a strange criticism from a philosopher whose historical analysis contains more speculation than pure historical facts. History is a logical scheme for von Hartmann, according to which the idea gradually enfolds itself, and historical description has only one rule to follow, i.e., the curve of development of the idea. Lacking a sense and appreciation for objective facts, he interprets and changes them around according to the demands of his arbitrary presuppositions. He sees only the idea in its dynamic self-realization, and this vision gives him a ready made definition of history, which will be strictly enforced in the interpretation of historical facts. Thus von Hartmann does not complete the Aristotelian dialectic; he merely changes it into a dialectic of the development of the idea.

He is equally unsuccessful in avoiding the basic fallacy of the Hegelian dialectic, the attainment of purely formal knowledge, which he criticizes so severely. Von Hartmann distinguishes his method from its Hegelian counterpart by the following three points: it is built on induction, it rejects the threefold partition of the dialectical process, and its moving force is not contradiction but the inner insufficiency of each single stage in the development of the idea. These differences will help us to understand, von Hartmann contends, how intuition as a complement to induction, can foresee the resolution of contraries and the flow of history although we are conscious only of single acts. Intuition is the participation in the knowledge of the unconscious absolute spirit, which embraces all future events in the present. But this interpretation is in contradiction to one of von Hartmann's own basic principles, according to which conscious knowledge is communicated to the absolute only after it has risen to consciousness in its phenomenal manifestations, viz., in man's consciousness. Prior to it there is no conscious knowledge in the absolute, nor meaningful intuitive vision of itself in which man can participate. On the basis of this axiom the absolute cannot possibly communicate any useful intuitive knowledge to man, thus intuition is of no real value to the phenomenal individual under these circumstances. It seems, therefore, that negative criticism is hardly an improvement over those methods it intends to complete and correct.

The positive aspect of the criticistic method is based on experience exclusively, and any speculative conclusion von Hartmann may infer from it will be equally measured by experience. But this is a fallacious position inasmuch as the greater cannot be measured by the lesser. The natural sciences deal with specifically similar things bound together by universal but changeable laws, whereas the mind approaches its objects in the metaphysical domain from their necessary and unchangeable aspects. Induction can conclude to universally valid judgments only if its conclusions are based on the completeness of its correctly selected premises, on the universal value of the causal principle, and on the primary axioms of thinking. But according to von Hartmann, the causal principle, as well as the norms of thinking, are inductively established. Their validity, therefore, cannot surpass with any kind of certainty the limits of the experimental sciences, consequently, they can claim, at best, only a probably universal validity. Thus the degree of certitude of induction, in von Hartmann's opinion, is the combined product of probability of the conclusion of induction and of the principle of causality, as well as the first principles of thinking, all empirically verified.

The preceding considerations indicate that von Hartmann gives a rather imperfect and inadequate exposition of induction as a method of cognition leading to the discovery of the metaphysical principle. Induction [1] in its complete view and total ramifications entails much more than a mere observation of facts, a computation of the possibility of a particular phenomenon's future occurrences and the determination of the probability coefficient expressing the degree of certitude the mind can attain in its efforts to know reality. In every contact of the mind with reality the primary datum attained is the kernel of all knowledge, i.e., being. That this apprehension of being is implicit and unrealized at the first instance of the cognitive operation, is no argument against the possibility of its development to its full ontological implications. Even if this *conceptio entis* in the case of empirical knowledge is about particular beings, any meaning and value this knowledge can have will

---

[1] It is helpful to recall in connection with this problem the distinction Aristotle, and following him, St. Thomas make between perfect and imperfect induction. Cf. *Eth. Nich.* VI. 3, 3; *Anal. Post.* I. 71, b9; *In Anal. Post.*, I. 1, n. 4; 17, n. 5.

derive from its relation to the mind's natural knowledge and possession of the notion of being itself, from the *conceptio entis qua entis,* inasmuch as the all-encompassing vision of being is the human mind's constitutive *a priori.*[1]

It is at this point in the process of human cognition that the total value of a philosophical system is decidedly determined. For if the full ontological implications of the simplest act of human cognition are neglected and ignored, there can never be a truly philosophical, metaphysical investigation of the real. It is understandable that a merely "scientific" method, induction in the sense of the natural sciences, refrains from a thematical treatment of the metaphysical implications of the question, but then it should not claim to gain "speculative results" which can guarantee a purely metaphysical explanation of reality.

Von Hartmann's inductive method, as he adopts it, is simply a one dimensional registration of observable phenomena, which precludes the possibility of fully comprehending them in their ontological significance. As long as his method remains such, it is in vain to think that by expanding the field of experimental observation the metaphysical value of these same phenomena will be strengthened. The value of a philosophical system does not depend on the width of its empirical foundation, rather on the depth and intensity of the intellect's penetration into the intelligibility of these phenomena. It is true that "the philosopher's task begins where the scientist's terminates," but this axiom of von Hartmann is nowhere accomplished in his own methodology. Although his criticistic method purports to be a unity of diverse inadequate methods, its manner of viewing reality, however, remains on equal level with those methods it criticizes. In its final analysis the criticistic method is a radical dispersion toward multiplicity and "in no way gathered into unity."[2]

To remain on this level of knowing reality is tantamount to disregard the intellect's natural desire for knowledge which is oriented toward the most intelligible and most unified knowledge of the real.[3] Only the recognition and actual realization of this truth will ensure the true value of empirical knowledge. Only in this ontological perspective of induction can we envision that it connaturally contains that toward

---

[1] ... *"nos ea quae addiscimus, ante in notitia habuisse." De Ver.* q. 10, a. 6. *"Scientia ergo praeexistit in addiscente in potentia non pure passiva sed activa, alias homo non posset per seipsum acquirere scientiam." Ibid.* q. 11, a. 1.

[2] *De Ver.,* q. 2, a. 2 ad 2.

[3] *In Met.,* Prooem.; *Ibid.* bk. XI, 1. 1; *S. Th.* I. II. q. 57, a. 2 ad 1.

which the intellect is naturally ordained as the ultimate aim of all its operations: the apprehension and vision of being as being.[1]

The transition from the knowledge of particular being to the actual possession of being as being, according to the mind of Aristotle and St. Thomas Aquinas, occurs through the abstractive operation of the intellect.[2] In view of the diversity of reality as attainable by the human intellect this abstractive process is completed through three distinct stages differentiated by the mind's gradual assimilation with the intelligible content of the real.[3] The consummation of this vision is that possession of the knowledge of being which discloses it as the fundamentally necessary and absolute aspect of the real whose knowledge leads to the first cause as the ultimate explanation of all reality.[4]

Such an encompassing view of reality will forever remain impervious to the inductive criticism of von Hartmann, and it is indeed "an illusion to suppose that he was winning this 'speculative' result by the inductive method of natural science."[5]

---

[1] S. Th. I. q. 85, a. 3; In Met. bk. I. 1. 2, n. 46.
[2] De Trin. q. 5, a. 1 and 3 ad 1; S. Th. I. q. 85, a. 1 and 2 ad 1; C. G. bk. II, ch. 96. Met., Prooem.; Phys. bk. I, l. 1.
[3] De Trin. q. 5, a. 3.
[4] S. Th., I. II. q. 66, a. 5, ad 4.
[5] Wilhelm Windelband, A History of Philosophy (New York: Harper and Brothers), vol. II, p. 647.

CHAPTER III

DISCOVERY AND REALM OF OPERATION OF THE UNCONSCIOUS

The vast material in the three volumes of the *Philosophy of the Unconscious* is amassed for the task of proving the existence of the unconscious in the macrocosm as well as in the microcosm. It is the book of books of von Hartmann's *Weltanschauung,* and even if some particular aspects expressed in this work may have been changed in the course of his later development, viz., certain views related to the philosophy of nature, it has always remained the guiding light and directive norm for his subsequent scientific and philosophical inquiries. In its essential outlook, it always serves for von Hartmann as the permanent font of his system of thought, and any later work called to deal in detail with the problems discussed and treated in his *opus magnum* must conform basically with the principles laid down here, whether in the field of cognition, philosophy of nature, metaphysics, psychology, religion, ethics, or aesthetics. In the following discussion we intend to acquaint ourselves with the content and purpose of this work, together with later works relevant to the same problems in order to establish the existence and to discover the field of operation of his metaphysical first principle, the unconscious.[1]

[1] In order to facilitate verification of quotations and avoid needless misunderstandings it is proper to state that the William C. Coupland translation (London: Kegan, Paul, Trübner and Co., Ltd., 1893) of the *Philosophie des Unbewussten* of von Hartmann does not contain all three volumes of the 10th edition (Leipzig: Hermann Haacke, 1890) of the same work. Coupland's translation is based on the ninth edition in two volumes. Although Coupland's translation is in three volumes, the third volume is merely the second part of von Hartmann's second volume of the *Philosophie des Unbewussten,* containing chapters XII, XIII, and XIV of this second volume. Thus when we refer to volume I and volume II it means Coupland's English translation; and volume III refers to von Hartmann's original third volume of the 10th edition of the *Philosophie des Unbewussten.* Actually this third volume is part of von Hartmann's *Ausgewählte Werke* (Leipzig: Hermann Haacke, 1885–1921), 2nd ed.; vol. IX, and contains the three Darwinistic writings, *Das Unbewusste vom Standpunkt der Physiologie und Descendenztheorie; Wahrheit und Irrtum im Darwinismus; Die Naturwissenschaftlichen Grundlagen der Philosophie des Unbewussten und die darwinistische Kritik.* Further references in this chapter are made to his collected essays on the philosophy of the unconscious: *Gesammelte philosophische Abhandlungen zur Philosophie des Unbewussten* (Berlin: Carl Dunker,

The first part of the first volume considers the realm of organic life, particularly the organic life of animals, and shows us the manifestations of the unconscious in this domain of the experimental sciences. Of the many surprises we must be prepared for, we receive one at the beginning of the first chapter, when von Hartmann, with a bold but unsubstantiated assumption, tells us that the fundamental and most primitive activity of the mind, willing, is by no means the exclusive property of man. There is only a difference of degree and not of kind between man and animals, he holds, and we must "cease to give ourselves an air of superiority" by assuming an essential difference; consequently, in the manifestations of animal operations and activity, we must clearly perceive a will. "The dog will not separate itself from its master; it wills to save the child who has fallen into the water; the bird will not let its young be injured... etc."[1] It would be of no avail to call these actions "reflex actions" in the ordinary sense of the word, i.e., involuntary reactions, von Hartmann contends, because they bear clearly the distinctive marks of voluntary actions, that is, emotion and consistency in carrying out an intention. Furthermore, the example of the decapitated frog shows us that in his motions there is an unmistakable evidence of non-reflective acts of will, which proves not only the presence of will in animal organism but also the dispensability of brain or brain consciousness for the execution of the actions of the will.

Numerous other examples will be brought up to prove that there are many independent wills spread throughout the entire living organism, and that the will only externalizes itself through the brain but by no means depends upon it for its existence and operation. Cerebral consciousness attests to the animal's self, but the many different detached consciousnesses connected with the lower centers are and remain unconscious as far as we, higher consciousnesses are concerned. Therefore, there is an unconscious will, an original source of action in every living organism. Acts of will exist not only, as we have seen, outside of brain-consciousness in living organisms; unconscious purposive actions may also be detected in the execution of a movement strictly willed. The decision, for instance, to move my little finger can be effected only through a number of intermediate stages of which I have no consciousness. For the movement requires that on the keyboard of the brain a

1872); *Erläuterungen zur Metaphysik des Unbewussten* (Berlin: Carl Dunker, 1873); *Kategorienlehre* (Leipzig: Hermann Haacke, 1896); *Grundriss der Naturphilosophie und Metaphysik*, in his *System der Philosophie* (Bad Sachsa: Hermann Haacke, 1907–09), vols. II and IV.

[1] *Philosophy of the Unconscious* (London: Routledge and Kegan Paul Ltd., 1950), vol. I, p. 60.

point "P" should be struck exactly fitted to call forth this result. No recourse to habit, practice, or to muscular feelings derived from similar cases, nor the influence of brain-vibrations will account for the phenomenon.

From the impossibility of a mechanical, material solution it follows that the intermediate link must be of a spiritual nature; from the decided absence of a sufficient conscious link it follows that the same must be unconscious. From the necessity of a voluntary impulse at the point "P" it follows that the conscious will to lift the finger produces an unconscious will to excite point "P," in order, by means of the excitation of "P," to attain the object, lifting the finger; and the content of the will to excite "P," again presupposes the unconscious idea of the point "P." The idea of the point "P" can, however, only consist in the idea of its position to the other points of the brain. ...[1]

The solution of the problem is at hand: every movement, however small, presupposes the unconscious idea of the appropriate central nerve-endings and the unconscious will to stimulate the same. There is even a much wider and deeper field in the phenomena of instinct for the activity of the unconscious mind. By defining instinct as a "purposive action without consciousness of the purpose,"[2] von Hartmann eliminates the materialistic explanation of instinct as being the mere consequence of corporeal organization, and also refutes Descartes' view whereby instinct is a cerebral or mental mechanism contrived by nature. He sets out to prove the presence of unconscious mental activity in instinct by many interesting illustrations. Horses that cross the bridle-path running past the cages of beasts of prey in the Berlin Zoological Garden become terrified and restless on scenting their wholly unknown enemies. In some countries where people live mainly on dog's flesh, animals from other regions become quite wild and uncontrollable in the presence of such people, as if they recognized in them their foes whom they were ready to attack.

This unconscious foresight is not confined merely to animals; it is quite often that a "Gretchen spies out a Mephistopheles." To this instinct of presentiment or unconscious clairvoyance (*Hellsehen*) is closely related the faculty of second-sight, commonly reported phenomenon among the northern nations, especially among the Scots and Danish, whereby certain persons, not in an ecstatic state but in the full possession of their senses, foresee future or distant events which have particular personal interest for them, such as deaths, battles, great conflagrations, etc. Although these latter phenomena, von Hartmann

[1] *Ibid.*, p. 77.
[2] *Ibid.*, p. 79.

admits, could not form alone the sole foundation of a scientific belief, nevertheless, they are worthy of mention and use as a complementary extension of the series of phenomena presented to our view in the clairvoyance of animal and human instinct. In conclusion, von Hartmann mentions another kind of instinct which in its nature is just as much social as it is individual; namely, the consentaneous cooperative instinct, which again shows how impossible it is to avoid the hypothesis of clairvoyance in instinct. The existence of this instinct can be best observed in the highly organized cooperative commonwealth of bees, where the activities of each individual bee and of different classes are performed in such a manner as to serve the best purpose of the one and the whole. Here again, it is obvious that the instinctive actions of the different classes are dependent upon concealed organic processes, which can manifestly have influence upon them only through an unconscious clairvoyance.

A brief summary of the above phenomena of nature as indicative of the existence of an unconscious cause can be given as follows: instinct is not the result of conscious reflection, nor a consequence of bodily organization, nor a mere result of mechanism founded in the organization of the brain. Neither is it the effect of an essentially foreign mechanism, externally adhering to the mind, but the individual's own activity, springing from his inmost nature and character. Thus von Hartmann is convinced that instinct, brute or human, cannot be understood any other way except by assuming the existence of the unconscious in instinct. In this instance its existence is manifested by one of its characteristic attributes, clairvoyant intuition.[1]

The next section provides a small metaphysical oasis in a monotonous desert of empirical data. Von Hartmann sets forth with the defi-

---

[1] There is an unusual and very interesting section in volume III of the 10th edition of the *Philosophie des Unbewussten*. As we have mentioned above, this volume contains the three Darwinian writings of von Hartmann, the first of which *Das Unbewusste vom Standpunkt der Physiologie und Descendenztheorie* was written with the purpose of confusing his critics. In this essay he takes apart with deceiving earnestness the explanation of the *Philosophy of the Unconscious* regarding the doctrine of the instinct, and assumes the Darwinian view, whereby the instincts can be fully explained on the basis of the hereditary brain and ganglia-predispositions. In the light of this scientific principle the assumption of a "clairvoyant unconscious intervention" of the unconscious is not only unwarranted, but absolutely superfluous. He reproaches himself because for the sake of scientific exactitude, the author of the *Philosophy of the Unconscious* should have investigated whether after the application of this natural-scientific principle anything has remained unexplained in the alleged phenomena, and only then would he have been justified in his recourse to the metaphysical. "The more urgent was this obligation, the more the purpose of this chapter is to support the truth of the hypothesis of the teleological view-point by the means of the unconscious (clairvoyant) intuition." Cf. *Philosophie des Unbewussten*, vol. III, p. 248. He adds, perhaps with more conviction than we suppose, that this is the weakest point of the *Philosophy of the Unconscious*.

nite intention of challenging the philosophy of Hegel and Schopenhauer by proving the necessity of the union of will and idea in any
philosophical first principle. The *a priori* argumentation employed here
is in obvious contradiction to his professed inductive method, and the
reader is more and more convinced after each line that this chapter has
served as the foundation to his later works on *Schellings positive Philosophie*, and the *Philosophisches Dreigestirn*.

Presently the unconscious becomes a more definite notion embracing
in itself as inseparable elements the creative force of will and its object
to be realized, the idea. The starting point of argumentation is the
"impregnable" position that volition cannot have the present state as
its *terminus ad quem* because we possess it, and it would be absurd still
to will it, for only a non-existing state can be willed, and this in the
form of existence. The object of volition, looked at from the present
moment, is still future, and as such cannot be present really (*realiter*) in
the instantaneous act of willing, and yet it must be in the will in order
to be possible; consequently, it must be contained in it ideally (*ideali-
ter*), i.e., as presentation. No one in reality can merely will without
willing something; only through a definite content does the will obtain
the possibility of existence, and this content is the idea. The words of
Aristotle hold absolutely true here, von Hartmann admits: ὀφεκτικὸν δὲ
οὐκ ἄνευ φαντασίας no volition without mental object.[1] The obvious
nature of this relation between will and idea and the impossibility of
finding any other substitute for the idea as the content of the will force
us to assume that the whole content of will is idea, regardless whether
the will and idea be conscious or unconscious. From the above reasoning
von Hartmann's contention should be clear: wherever we meet with
any kind of volition, a presentation must be united with it, at the very
least that which ideally represents the goal, object, or content of
volition. Accordingly, every unconscious volition also must be united
with ideas, for in our former observations and rational analysis nothing
turned up which would indicate the distinction between conscious and
unconscious will. The difference between the two consists simply in the
fact that in conscious volition the content of volition (idea) is conscious
to the cerebral consciousness, whereas in unconscious volition the content is unconscious to the cerebral consciousness, but conscious to the
subordinate, or peripheric centers of consciousness. In conclusion, we
may say that an unconscious will is a will with unconscious idea as con-

---

[1] *De Anima*, III. 10. b 27.

tent, for a will with conscious idea as content will always be conscious to us.

Examples of the existence of this unconscious will are numerous in reflex actions in which the impression made on the peripheric termination of a nerve is transmitted to a central organ, and thence, through the medium of a motor nerve, sets the muscles into motion. Examples are the simple sequence of a single contraction upon a single irritation, or the more complicated answers to an external stimulus, as we can see it in the adaptation of the eye to vision, or in the tendency to think aloud in a strong emotional disturbance. Such phenomena can be accounted for only as the instinctive actions of the subordinated nerve centers, or in other words, the absolutely unconscious presentations, which from the perception of the stimulus produce the reflex will, which is conscious for the center in question, but not to the brain itself. The presence of this unconscious will and idea in nerve-centers subordinated to the brain explains how complicated movements like riding, dancing, and performing gymnastic exercises are performed best unconsciously, while the very same actions become extremely slow, awkward, and coarse, if any step would call for reflection. All the examples von Hartmann has adduced in the case of instinct against its origination through conscious reflection, are utilized here in a higher degree.

The course of demonstration arrived at to this point can be summarized thus: reflex movements are instinctive actions of the subordinate nerve-centers, i.e., absolutely unconscious presentations which embody the will of the reflex action (conscious for the particular center, but unconscious for the brain), in consequence of the perception of the stimulus.

Up to now we have observed that there is an unconscious idea of purpose which united with the will, dictates the conscious willing of the means to attain it. We observe the same phenomenon, von Hartmann says, also when the sphere of influence is no longer external but the body itself. This new field of investigation takes us, to use a more familiar terminology, from the investigation of the mutual causality of the unconscious will and idea in the realm of extrinsic finality into that of the intrinsic. This new manifestation of the unconscious can be first observed in the reparative power of nature.

If we deprive the polyp of its tentacles or the worm of its head, the creatures must die for want of food; and if the animal replaces the tentacles or the head and continues to live, can anything but the unconscious idea of their indispensableness be the fundamental cause of restoration? [1]

[1] *Philosophy of the Unconscious*, vol. I, p. 143.

This restoration is effected through the *vis medicatrix* present in the organism which, however, is less and less perfect the higher the organism in question stands in degree of perfection in the totality of all organisms. Nevertheless, it appears even in the highest organisms through the increased flow of blood which helps to repair a local injury. It is the cure *per primam intentionem,* to use von Hartmann's expression, which so often assists the surgeon after an operation. We are further reminded that it should be obvious to every reflective mind that these effects of the *vis medicatrix* in the organism are not the results of conscious thinking and willing, since consciousness has little or no share in the healing of a wound or fracture. In fact, the most powerful curative effects take place at the time when consciousness is subdued as far as possible, as in deep sleep. Sufficient explanation for this wonderful harmony tending to a single goal can be attained only by the all-ruling monistic principle of the unconscious.

In the same chapter, after a lengthy argumentation supported by experiments, von Hartmann proves that diseases never arise spontaneously from the psychic basis of the organism, but they are imposed and thrust on it by disturbances from without. This statement allows him to establish another of the attributes of the unconscious, the property whereby it never falls sick or would produce sickness in its organism. In the line of subsequent investigations, von Hartmann examines the indirect influence of conscious psychic activity upon organic functions. The author holds that the influence of the conscious will upon muscular contraction is effected most efficiently and most naturally through the power-engine of the nervous system. He warns us that it would be a mistake to confine the exercise of will in organisms to the aid of nerves, since the intensity of volition in a certain direction and for a short time can occasionally be a substitute for an auxiliary mechanism. In the same manner, certain currents can be produced by conscious volition in the sensory nerves. Hypochondriacs, for instance, sometimes feel pains in every part of their body to which they direct their attention, and persons to be operated on are able to feel the touch of the scalpel even before the instrument has actually been in contact with them. Although the phenomena of mesmerism are also the indirect effects of the conscious will, yet for its satisfactory and final explanation, the hypothesis of the unconscious is required, since here also intervenes, as in all other descriptions of movement, an unconscious will which brings it about that a definite magnetic current and no other arises, and that this is concentrated in a certain definite part, and not in any other part of the body. Many people can blush and grow pale voluntarily, "especially coquettish women, who make a study of it." In his studies concerning the influence of the conscious will upon the body, von Hartmann tells us that he himself acquired:

> ... the power of instantaneously reducing the severest hiccough to silence by my mere will, while it formerly was a source of great inconvenience to me, and frequently would not yield to any of the ordinary means.[1]

From the evidence of such phenomena, he concludes that we possess a far greater voluntary power over our body than is generally supposed, but at the same time, it is also evident that the connection of the conscious and the unconscious will has been purposely made difficult in this department because the intervention of the conscious will would, as a rule, only be injurious to the smooth performance of the above mentioned faculties, and by such operation the conscious will would be needlessly diverted from its proper sphere of thought and external action.

The next step of investigation is the influence of conscious idea on the body. To illustrate this fact examples are taken from general, everyday gestures and looks, from mimic movements, and from the vegetative functions of the organism. The study of these actions will support von Hartmann's contention that the conscious idea of a definite effect can often excite the unconscious will to employ the requisite means without the conscious will, so that the realization of the conscious idea appears involuntary. The phenomena of pathology and miraculous cures can also be explained by applying the same principle. In all such cases we must recognize the presence of an unconscious will as medium between the conscious idea and the intended effect. For the successful realization of this conscious idea concerning the intended effect, the unconscious will holds the key; the more will, the greater the probability of the idea's execution. Instinct, reflex action, and the restorative powers of nature are but different aspects or stages of the materialization of the idea as such. The unconscious is the ruling principle in all organic structures and levels of existence. In this last chapter on the manifestations of the unconscious in the organic functions of the body, we still have to see how the functions of plastic energy shade imperceptibly into the previously considered operations of the unconscious.

The author starts his investigation from the assumption that the end or purpose of the animal kingdom is the preparation for and actual production of consciousness. It is this finality which explains the sepa-

---

[1] *Ibid.*, p. 178.

ration of nature into vegetable kingdom and animal kingdom. In addition, this supposition serves also as *raison d'être* for the necessity of the different systems in the organism: the system of movement, organs of sense, digestion, circulation of blood, respiration, the nervous system, and the reproductive system. The entire foregoing consideration is conducted by von Hartmann in order to prove the teleological organization of the animal kingdom with consciousness as its end. He further insists that the finality observed in the above examples proves that it extends even to the most minute details of this organization, and any objection brought up against it is based upon a misinterpretation of the notion. The presence, for example, of useless organs such as the eyes of the blind-mole, the caudal vertebrae in tailless animals, the swimming-bladder of fishes which always live at the bottom of the water, in no way militates against the assumption of a final cause in all existence. The *lex parsimoniae* is a law of nature, and nature finds it easier to leave here and there innocuous superfluities than to be making constantly new changes and executing new ideas: "She prefers to stop at the greatest possible unity of the IDEA, and makes only as many modifications as are indispensably necessary."[1]

In summing up briefly the results of the first part of the first volume of the *Philosophy of the Unconscious* as it investigates the different phenomena of nature, we can conclude that in the processes of bodily organisms it detects, above and beyond the individual's conscious will, other manifestations of wills correlated with different lower nerve-centers of an organism. The existence and activity of these unconscious wills point to the existence of a universal unconscious will, which can only be understood as the realizing force of the unconscious idea in nature, both being at the same time the functions of a kind of tutelary spirit or providence operating teleologically in corporeal organisms. This tutelary spirit is the unconscious, which is capable of correcting and supplementing the deficiencies of conscious will and intelligence and of originating, directing, and supervising a large number of actions and changes in the organism. It is limited only by certain material conditions that are not very clearly stated by von Hartmann. How the unconscious actually performs these functions attributed to it, and why it is necessary to assume its existence are never proved by him. We are left with the choice either to reject his explanations [2] or to trust blindly his clairvoyant intuition.

---

[1] *Ibid.*, p. 191.
[2] "There can hardly be another modern book in which the scientific material swept to-

The second part of the first volume of the *Philosophy of the Unconscious* illustrates the manifestations of the unconscious in the human mind as the next domain of its presence. The instincts in relation to our psychic needs are the first objects of investigation. At the beginning von Hartmann warns that just as it is impossible to draw a strict line of demarcation between body and mind, so it is in the case of instincts in regard to its relation to the organism and mind. Thus, a certain overlapping is inevitable.

Although consciousness is reached in the human organism, by this fact the operation of the unconscious does not cease, and the mental processes display the influence of the unconscious in no less a degree than did the strictly vegetable and animal kingdom. The different kinds of mental instincts rooted in the unconscious will be divided into the instincts of aversion, repulsion, and disgust. The most significant of the first class is the fear of death. This instinct makes us shudder at the thought of death, it makes our heart rush the blood through our veins by simply hearing the word. The cause of this instinct is not the fear of the last judgment nor some other metaphysical hypothesis, it is not even Hamlet's doubt of the hereafter, nor Egmont's childish delight in being and doing, which restrains the hand of the suicide, but the unmistakable manifestation of the almighty unconscious in our psychic life.

The instinct of repulsion is principally expressed by the instinct of shame, and it is almost exclusively related to the generative region of the human body. In von Hartmann's opinion shame and "the milder form of heat due to non-periodicity [1] are the two foundations which allow the elevation of the sexual relations of man into a higher sphere than that of the animals."[2] Shame is so deeply rooted in the unconscious that it is found among the most primitive and savage tribes.

The last of these instincts, disgust, with its two senses of taste and smell, guards us against improper food, and, added to the sense of sight, it is the safeguard of the cleanliness of skin. With an impressively keen observation of the life of the blind from birth, who were at the same time deaf and dumb, von Hartmann shows how deeply the instincts of purity, modesty, and beauty are embedded in the unconscious.

gether stands in such flagrant contrast to all the essential principles of scientific method."
Cf. Frederick A. Lange, *The History of Materialism*, trans. by Ernest C. H. Thomas (New York: The Humanities Press, 1950), bk. 2, p. 80.

[1] *Op. cit.*, p. 206, footnote. As a corroborative argument von Hartmann adduces Beaumarchais' cynical remark, "Boire sans soif, et faire l'amour en tout temps, c'est ce qui distingue l'homme de la bête."

[2] *Ibid.*, p. 206.

But the most wonderful instinct rooted in the unconscious is the instinct of maternal love, which increases in significance and range the higher we ascend on the animal scale, a scale graduated not zoologically but psychologically. This instinct does not stop short of the self-sacrificing love of the mother for her offspring, while the complete extinction of fondness, and often the hostility when the young of lower animals become independent, shows that not custom or conscious choice, but an unconscious necessity is the source of this impulse.

The next step discovers the role of the unconscious in sexual love. After reading this treatise, the phenomenal initial success of the work among the patrons of popular philosophy is much easier to understand. Von Hartmann should not have been surprised that most of his readers were mainly interested in this chapter and the one concerning pessimism. His indignation at being called a follower of Schopenhauer [1] is certainly far from being justified on the basis of this discussion. Von Hartmann follows Schopenhauer very closely not only in his mode of viewing the subject, but also in his style of presentation. The entire treatise is permeated by a coarse naturalism and cynicism, nourished by an early initiation into the art of *savoir-vivre*, and in parts borders on pornography. It took all the boldness and immaturity of a twenty-four year old man to deal with the problem in the manner he did. It is in his favor that he soon abandons this immature way of treating the question, as his later works show.[2]

The point of departure is the postulate that there is no essential difference between the love-life of animals and of men and that consequently we may begin our investigation with the observation of the former.

The male spiders take up the seminal fluid, which trickles from their sexual organs, with an extremely complicated apparatus contained in the last hollow joint of their tentacles, and by help of the same apply it to the aperture of the female. The male embraces the female frog and discharges its sperm, whilst the female simultaneously deposits the ova. The singing-bird applies the opening of its spermatic duct to the female anus, and animals possessed of a penis introduce the same into the female vagina. When fishes pour the spawn, which they feel impelled to discharge only on the eggs of their own kind, when species of animals in which male and female are of a very different form (as e.g., glow-worms) still find each other without fail to copulate, and when the male mammal, in obedience to an irresistible impulse, always introduces its penis into the female vagina of *its own* species, are we to suppose that there are really two different causes at

---

[1] *Schellings positive Philosophie* as Part D of the *Gesammelte Studien und Aufsätze* (Berlin: Carl Dunker, 1876), p. 725.

[2] *Mein Entwickelungsgang*, in the *Gesammelte Studien und Aufsätze; Zur Reform des höheren Schulwesens* (Berlin: Carl Dunker, 1875), p. 17.

work, or is it not rather the working of the same unconscious, which, on the one hand, *harmoniously fashions* the sexual parts, and, on the other, as instinct impels to their *right use*, the same unconscious clairvoyance which in creation, as in use, adapts the means to an end, which does not appear in consciousness? [1]

Would man, at whose command are so many means for satisfying the physical impulse, all equally efficacious with coitus, be likely to discharge the inconvenient, disgusting, shameless, reproductive function, did not an instinct always urge him anew, often as he has experienced that this mode of satisfaction yields him in fact no higher sensuous enjoyment than any other? But many do not attain even to this much insight, because, *in spite of experience*, they always measure future enjoyment according to the strength of *impulse*, or are so possessed by the impulse during the act, that they *never attain experience*. It might, perhaps, be replied, that man frequently desires intercourse although he is aware of the impossibility of procreation, e.g., with the notoriously infertile or the prostitutes, or when, as in illicit connections, he seeks to prevent procreation; but to such we reply that the knowledge or intention of consciousness has no direct influence on the instinct, since the design of procreation lies *outside* consciousness, and only the willing of the *means* to the conscious end (as in all instincts) appears in consciousness...the metaphysical (sexual) impulse is an instinct which wells up from the unconscious.[2]

Nor does marriage receive a more human and dignified treatment from von Hartmann. Its monogamous nature is no peculiar institution of human society, von Hartmann assures us, as there are many animals, for instance, eagles, storks, and the Mirikina apes, which remain as faithful to their mates as human beings. Why does this universal love concentrate itself upon this individual rather than on another? What, in fact, is the ground of sexual selection? The physical impulse as such is thoroughly incapable of explaining the concentration on one definite individual; neither does reciprocal esteem fully account for it. Such esteem may arouse friendship, but friendship and love are poles apart.

The one a beautiful mild autumn evening of full-toned color, the other an awful rapturous vernal tempest; the one the lightly-living gods of Olympus, the other the heaven-storming Titans; the one self-sure and self-satisfied, the other "hoping and fearing in passionate pain"; the one perceiving its limits with full consciousness, the other always striving after infinitude in longing, joy and sorrow, "now shouting in triumph, now sunk in despair"; the one a clear and pure harmony, the other the ghostly tinkling and rustling of the Eolian harp, the eternally incomprehensible, unutterable, ineffable, because never to be grasped by consciousness, the mysterious music sounding from a home far far away; the one a bright temple, the other an eternally veiled mystery.[3]

It should be clear from this that in love we are not dealing with mere romantic daydreaming, but with a formidable power, a real demon who forever demands his victims.

[1] *Philosophy of the Unconscious* (London: Routledge and Kegan Paul Ltd., 1950), vol. I, p. 221.
[2] *Ibid.*, p. 222.
[3] *Ibid.*, pp. 229–230.

The sexual behavior of humanity in all the easily pierced masquerading and mumming is so singular, so absurd, so comical and ridiculous, and yet for the most part so tragical, that there is only one way of failing to see the whole absurdity, that is by standing in the midst of it, when it appears to us, as to a drunkard in a company of drunkards; we find everything quite natural and in order. The only difference is that everyone can when sober have the instructive spectacle of a drunken revel, but not be sexless, or one must be far gone in years, or must (as I myself) have already observed and reflected on these doings *before* having taken part in them, and then have doubted (as I have) whether oneself or all the rest of the world was crazed. And all this is brought about by that demon, whom already the ancients feared.[1]

The goal of this demon is in reality nothing else but sexual satisfaction, and that with a particular individual. This end, however, remains completely unconscious, the highest love knows nothing of it and first-love abhors even the thought of it.[2] What is the significance of this unconscious purpose? The answer cannot be other than the one already given by Schopenhauer,[3] which was subsequently scientifically established as a general law of nature by Darwin, that the instinct of love through the law of natural selection intends the highest possible realization of the idea of the human race. In this process, in the case of man for instance, the dreamed-of bliss in the arms of the beloved is nothing else but the deceptive bait, whereby the unconscious deludes conscious egoism, and leads to the sacrifice of self-love in favor of the succeeding generation and the ennoblement of the species. The underlying principle in all three realms of our specific investigations is undoubtedly the same as it was before, i.e., the unconscious, applied here to procreation.

In the discussion which concerns the sensation of feeling, attention is called to the hitherto neglected distinction within the phenomenon of pain, wherein we must separate the sensuous perception from pain proper. This observation brings up the question whether the same distinction must be applied both to pleasure and pain, or does it exist merely in the producing and accompanying circumstances; namely, in perception? Corroborated by Wundt's experiments and findings,[4] von Hartmann draws his conclusion that pleasure and pain are perfectly homogeneous states and only quantitatively different. The fact that the two are commensurable, i.e., that which is compared to them is qualitatively identical, shows they differ not in kind but in degree. If we look now for the simple, homogeneous cause of these phenomena,

[1] *Ibid.*, p. 231.

[2] *Gesammelte philosophische Abhandlungen* (Berlin: Carl Dunker, 1872), pp. 86–87.

[3] *Die Welt als Wille und Vorstellung* (3rd ed.; Leipzig: J. Frauenstädt, 1859), vol. II, chap. 44, "Metaphysic of Sexual Love."

[4] *Vorlesungen über die Menschen- und Thierseele* (Leipzig: L. Voss, 1863).

we find that it is the will. Will exists prior to these phenomena; they can be resolved into will, but the will cannot be resolved into them. This psychic process is explained and supplemented by two propositions from the psychology of the unconscious:

1. Where one is conscious of no will in the satisfaction of which an existing pleasure or displeasure could exist, this will is an unconscious one; and
2. the obscure, ineffable, inexpressible in feeling lies in the unconsciousness of the accompanying ideas.[1]

The lack of notion of the unconscious will and idea forced psychology of the past to place the entire province of feeling into the domain of rational psychology.

The unconscious plays a vital role also in the formation of our character and morality. If the reaction of will were to depend solely upon the impelling motive in its operation, psychology and morality would be quite simple and the exact same for all individuals. This is not the case, as we all know it well from experience. The enigmatic and the unfathomable in the whole problem is the fact that while I derive great pleasure from the hearing of a magnificent symphony and the thrill of gambling cannot move me at all, the exact opposite may be the case with the next man. The reaction of different individuals to the same motive cannot be predicted, for the mechanism of volition is hidden in the unconscious; all we can see and analyze is the finished result. No one can penetrate into the unconscious depths of the soul where occurs the reaction of the will to motives and where its transition into definite volition is accomplished. Only from the repeated inferences of certain actions can we learn the core of the individual soul whose manifestation is the character. Morality, looked at as a responsible action from the part of the individual will upon the presentation of a motive, is rooted in the unconscious. But the distinction of moral and immoral, with the necessary implication of right and wrong, is a product of consciousness, and thus it has nothing to do with the unconscious. In this sense, we cannot speak of moral or immoral actions or persons in themselves, for these adjectives pronounce a judgment over them only from a point of view taken by consciousness. But to save morality, von Hartmann declares that since for this world of individuation consciousness surpasses the unconscious in importance, in the final analysis the moral stands higher than the natural.

The presence of the extraordinary in aesthetic judgments and artistic productions has been recognized in all history. The idealist, led by the

[1] *Philosophy of the Unconscious*, vol. I, p. 257.

theory of Plato, has recourse to an aprioristic explanation whereby the transcendental idea of the beautiful revealed in the soul serves as a criterion as to what is and what is not beautiful in nature. The view of the empiricists, which is in polar opposition to the idealistic view, places its explanation upon the psychogenesis of the aesthetic judgment and artistic production from given psychological and physiological conditions of the individual. There is a partial truth in each opinion, von Hartmann agrees, but the idealists are nearer to the truth when they infer that in the process of these creative phenomena there is something which lies beyond consciousness and is antecedent to the conscious aesthetic judgment and creation. The ordinary artist, whose work is a mere conscious combination and judicious selection, will never produce anything original, nor will he ever attain to anything great. The vivifying breath of the unconscious is wanting here, that unknowable and incomprehensible inspiration which the Greeks called μανία, and the Romans *furor poeticus*. The creation of the true genius is the result of that inflaming obsession by the unconscious which enraptures him into the state of ἔκστασις, where he becomes, in a manner inexplicable, partaker in the bliss of the gods. Or as Schelling says it: "... as the artist is urged to production involuntarily, and even with inner aversion (thus the expression of the ancients *pati deum*), so the objective is also added to his production as it were without his action, i.e., itself merely objectively."[1]

In summary, we may say that the positive perception and the discursive understanding of the beautiful are the work of consciousness, but the discovery of it and its creation are rooted in the innermost essence of the unconscious.

It is von Hartmann's opinion that in the original formation of language the role of the unconscious can hardly be emphasized sufficiently:

... the foundation of language could not have been consciously laid; ... the deeper we penetrate into it, the more clearly does it appear that its invention far surpasses in profundity those of the highest conscious products.[2]

He claims that any kind of conscious endeavor for the development of language is far behind the unconscious creative genius of humanity. This linguistic development goes on parallel with history and, eludes all efforts of consciousness. It follows its own set course, as if it were an independent creation, and the conscious mind serves only as a medium

[1] *Ibid.*, p. 279.
[2] *Ibid.*, p. 293.

in the development of its proper life. This practical observation can be substantiated by reflective reasoning, if we consider that the foundation of language is much too complicated and comprehensive to be the conscious work of one individual. It must, therefore, be the result of the labor of the masses, not in their conscious cooperation, but in their instinctive production. But as we have seen previously all instincts originate from the unconscious; so also the linguistic instinct. In support of his view, von Hartmann quotes the eminent philologists, Heyse and von Humboldt, when the latter writes: "Thinking of the natural instinct of animals, we may call language an intellectual instinct of reason."[1] In conclusion, von Hartmann appeals to the authority of Steinthal by quoting the final words of his book:

Language is not innate in man, not revealed by God – man has produced it; but not the mere organic nature of man, but his mind; and finally not the thinking conscious mind. What mind then in humanity, i.e., what form of action of the human mind has produced language? [2]

What else is it, is the interrogative answer of von Hartmann, than the unconscious mind?

Von Hartmann defines the essence of thinking in the proper coordination of ideas and time. This co-ordinative process can never be brought to full consciousness, and it rests on principles and ideas that neither an *a priori* nor an *a posteriori* approach can ever satisfactorily explain. Half of our mental activity consists of unconscious induction, which no laws of agreement or disagreement regulate; the other half is taken up by the processes of unconscious deductions, in which we form syllogisms with major premises suppressed. The highest phase of knowledge is intellectual intuition, because it teaches more at a glance than any other method does after a tedious demonstration. For instance, we can prove by demonstration that the angles at the base of an isosceles triangle must be equal; intuition sees that they actually are, and moreover, how they are equal. The fundamental categories of mind, such as equality, inequality, unity, plurality, totality, negation, disjunction, causality, etc., are themselves results of the unconscious. For example, the notion of equality as such cannot lie in the things themselves: A cannot, through the appearance of B, receive a property it did not have before. The notion of equality must be first created by the mind before it can be applied to things; but this creation is not arbitrary, for it is

---

[1] Christian W. L. Heyse, *System der Sprachwissenschaft* (Berlin: Steinthal, 1856); Wilhelm von Humboldt, *Über das vergleichende Sprachstudium* in his *Gesammelte Werke* (Stuttgart and Tübingen: Cotta, 1841–1872), sec. 13.

[2] H. Steinthal, *Der Ursprung der Sprache* (Berlin: Kümmler, 1858), 2nd ed.

effected by and in the unconscious through the medium of the abstractive faculty, and only the result comes into consciousness as concept of equality, or the judgment that A and B are alike.

With regard to the origin of sense-perception, von Hartmann sides with Kant in maintaining that the notion of space must be looked for in the mind, but he rejects Kant's treatment of the problem and the faulty proofs given for his assertion. The right foundation of the notion of space is the cardinal point of every philosophy, since it is the indispensable ground of sensile perception, with which consciousness takes its rise, and this, in turn, is the basis of all conscious thought. To support his theory with convincing proofs is of paramount importance for von Hartmann. The origin of the notion of space according to the school of empirical physiology is dependent upon the synthetic creative function of the mind, subsequent upon the received sense-impressions of touch and sight. Now, von Hartmann continues, we admit that both senses essentially cooperate for a more perfect elaboration of their original, separate tactile space-perceptions and visual space-perceptions but he goes a step further and contends that it is impossible for the combined perceptions to produce the idea of space unless it was previously contained in each singly. He supports his statement by experiments. Physiology reports that persons born blind can acquire and elaborate the space-perception of touch, even more perfectly than persons born with vision. In the event of obtaining their sight after an operation, before any conscious attempt to bring the new visual perceptions into relation with the tactile-perceptions familiar to them, they perceive at once the visual space of at least two dimensions. It is safe to declare that the tactile and visual space-perceptions do not create space, but that they merely relate these space-perceptions to the retina or tactile retina; the creative synthetic function, in this case, the formation of space-intuition, is the purely spiritual function of the unconscious. Only through this marvelous economy of the unconscious can the mind acquire a real basis for the cognition of an external world, whereas, without a space-intuition, it could never step out of itself.

Next von Hartmann leads us into the realm of mysticism. In order to clarify the content of this widely used and very little understood notion, von Hartmann uses a negative approach in his inquiry. Mysticism is not quietistic contemplation, nor is it a striving after mental and bodily annihilation. It does not consist of bodily fits, such as convulsions, epilepsy, ecstasies, imaginations, and fixed ideas of hysterical women and hypochondriacal men. It would be also a mistake to identify it with asceticism, because one can very well exist without the other. Is it then, perhaps, the wonders of prophets, saints, and magicians that occur in every age? The answer is negative, since all these phenomena can be comprehended either as simple therapeutics, conscious or unconscious magnetism, or sympathetic action, and thus belong to the domain of natural laws. Such phenomena are but the morbid outgrowths of mysticism. If we abstract from these impure elements in the mystical phenomenon, we realize that three things remain in it: feeling, thought and will. It is not surprising that these three also form the triadic component of our conscious life, for there is no difference in matter or essence between the mystical and conscious self-awareness. The difference lies in that special way in which the matter comes into consciousness and is in consciousness. This special way may be called a "divine inspiration," "inner light," "inner intuition,""contemplation," "rational faith," "intellectual intuition." At any rate, it is an immediate knowledge. Von Hartmann appeals here to the authority of Schelling to corroborate his own point of view, and the particular reference is made to the role of this intellectual intuition:

. . . as the indispensable orgin of our transcendental philosophizing, as the principle of all demonstration, and as the unprovable, self-evident ground of all evidence, in a word, as the absolute act of knowledge, as a kind of cognition which must always remain incomprehensible from the conscious empirical point of view, because it has not like it an object, because it cannot at all appear in consciousness, but falls outside of it.[1]

If these words were not taken as a kind of *apologia pro philosophia sua*, von Hartmann affords even more explicit proofs that this is exactly what he intends it to be. For him the history of philosophy is simply the conversion of a mystically-begotten content into that of the rational system, in order to make the mystically received vision, which is the private property of the philosophical mystic, the common treasure of thinking humanity. If the rational communication of this mystically acquired content is not successful, it may not necessarily be the fault of the philosopher, for the conviction and acceptance of this truth can only be mystically acquired also.

And thus it comes to pass that the different philosophical systems, however imposing they are to many, yet have only full probative force for the author and for some few who are able to reproduce mystically in themselves the underlying suppositions, e.g., Spinoza's substance, Fichte's Ego, Schelling's subject-object, Schopenhauer's will. . .[2]

---

[1] *Philosophy of the Unconscious*, vol. I, p. 257.
[2] *Ibid.*, p. 371.

This statement makes no explicit reference to the unconscious, but there can be no doubt that in von Hartmann's mind its discovery and comprehension is equally the result of this mystical experience.

A summary of the preceding discussion can be given as follows: the purpose of the mystical union is to provide consciousness with content: feeling, thought, and will, as it unconsciously and involuntarily emerges from the unconscious.

History or the development of the human race is the next field of study which, as von Hartmann states, reflects the fullest manifestations of the unconscious. It is the counterpart in the mind of the evolution of organic structure in nature, and it displays throughout the same finality and purpose. The possible doubts concerning the march of history arise simply from a too narrow point of view in regard to the development of man. A more universal survey, as it traces the gradual efforts of the unconscious in its self-realization, will recognize in different political institutions the necessary stages in the gradual development of the unconscious. This view is particularly opposed by the English rationalistic school, but von Hartmann finds the source of their error in the fact that:

... the English, even down to the present day, are essentially at that rationalistic standpoint which the Germans occupied in the last century; and that these historians of civilization, instead of trying to discover the unconsciously impelling ideas of history, fancy they can explain them as a product of conscious reflection.[1]

Such a standard as a sole measure of advance in culture is a partisan disregard for the harmonious cooperation of all mental forces and of values such as "sensibility, fancy and heart." It is Hegel's merit to have distinctly emphasized this view of history, and in particular to have shown how the philosophy of history exhibits a continuous evolution of the (unconscious) idea. But the true mirror of the spiritual development of mankind is the progress of philosophy. As the final convergence of all ideas which shape a certain period of civilization, philosophy is the genuine expression of the historical self-consciousness of the unconscious idea. That there is a real development in different philosophies was first shown by Hegel. Even if individual philosophers may not have been aware of their assigned role in the unfolding of the unconscious, and even if their first principles may have been merely instinctively welled up from the depths of the same, nevertheless, their contributions served as essential links in the concatenation of this purposeful, unconscious, development. In the light of this truth modern historiography of philosophy must endeavor to bring into consciousness

[2] *Ibid.*, vol. II, p. 6.

these unconscious relations existing between different philosophies to show the ever-existent presence of the unconsciously impelling ideas in the history of mankind. The providential care and the purposeful guidance of the unconscious extends not merely to the inner spiritual evolution of humanity, but the anthropological ennoblement of the race is just as much its concern as the other. The struggle for existence gradually and continually reduces and exterminates the less intellectual and industrial races of the earth. The laws of heredity are elevating step by step the mental refinement of the civilized, and a process of natural selection between races and nations is incessantly effecting the survival of the fittest. Nothing can stand in the way of this process, the unconscious moves on irresistibly to its final goal: to the most perfect realization of the idea of the race, and to the supreme hegemony of the conscious mind.

A brief comparison between the value of the conscious and unconscious for human life concludes this inductive preparation for a more profound insight into the nature of the unconscious.

It is necessary not to lose sight of the specific objectives of our investigation, i.e., to find the central idea, the moving, driving principle, the vivifying *pneuma* of the von Hartmannian *Weltanschauung*, and to acquire a more comprehensive knowledge of it. Hence it is well to recapitulate at this point the results of previous investigations.

Von Hartmann claims that a mysterious and hidden power guides to a definite end and goal all the phenomena of the objective-real world (nature) as well as that of the subjective-ideal (mind). At the same time, neither of them is self-sufficient and self-explanatory, and that each demands a cause outside of its sphere for a full elucidation of its being and understanding. In the first realm of the conducted investigations, the materializing (*materierende*) activity of nature, itself still immaterial, stands behind the objective-real phenomena of matter which is its first product, just as the organizing (organism-forming, *organisierende*) activity lies beyond the organisms, through which the organisms come into existence. In the same manner, as we have seen, the unconscious (pre-conscious) productive activity of the mind reaches out of the realm of the subjective-real sphere, because it is still unconscious and its first product, consciousness, takes its origin therefrom. The philosophy of nature and the philosophy of mind, viz., psychology and epistemology, unmistakably point to a sphere which lies beyond them. This third sphere is the realm of metaphysics.

The third part concerns itself with the metaphysical problems of the unconscious. The somewhat loose arrangement of these metaphysical problems in their first appearance in the second volume of the *Philosophy of the Unconscious* and in their last treatment in the *System der Philosophie im Grundriss*, volume four, can be summarized under the following three headings:

1. The genesis of consciousness, or the relation of the microcosm to the absolute.
2. The reduction of the twofold principle of reality into monism, or the relation of the macrocosm to the absolute.
3. The practical consequences of von Hartmann's concrete monism, or the Ego, the non-Ego, and the absolute in their unity or togetherness.

In accordance with the predominance of the physical sciences of his time, von Hartmann unreservedly accepts the conclusions of physiological research in regard to the origin of consciousness. The mere problematical tenets of the positive sciences concerning the necessary relation between brain and consciousness, between the material substratum and the psychic phenomenon are accepted by von Hartmann as incontestable facts. Instead of conceiving consciousness in its totality as the immediate intellectual awareness of existence, within which we find ourselves, as well as the object of our knowledge as given reality, he proceeds from one particular condition of consciousness, namely, from the kind of consciousness which in its present condition depends extrinsically on its material substrate, the brain, and sets forth with typical one-sidedness to show how the total phenomenon of consciousness has derived from this particular organ.

To prove this contention, von Hartmann's point of departure is the scientific hypothesis of a necessary connection between brain and consciousness, according to which where there is no material substratum there can be no consciousness. As a physiological entity, the brain is composed of cells and the cells of organic structure-units (plastidules).[1] Each of these organic units is composed of a number of molecules; these latter are complexes of a multitude of atoms, which in turn can be divided into groups of primordial-atoms (*Uratomen*). The brain is thus a physiological concatenation of structure-units of different kinds, and consciousness is but a dependent variable upon its cells and upon its final components, the primordial-atoms. Von Hartmann attempts to

[1] *Philosophie des Unbewussten* (Leipzig: Hermann Haacke, 1890), 10th ed. vol., III, p. 111, sqq. Cf. also Ernst Haeckel, *Die Perigenesis der Plastidule*, in his *Generelle Morphologie der Organismen*; 2 vols. (Berlin: G. Reimer, 1866); also von Hartmann's *Physiology of the Nerve Centers*, appendix to the 1st volume of the *Philosophy of the Unconscious*, 10th ed.

prove his hypothesis by the following consideration. As a complex result, dependent upon the sum-total of material primordial-units of the brain, consciousness can be called a "sumphenomenon" (*Summations-phaenomen*). But it can be such only if the singular component elements of the phenomenon independently possess that which is characteristic of the whole, in other words, if these component elements previously to their entering into the composition already possess consciousness. If the organ exhibits consciousness, then consciousness must already be contained in the component tissues; if in the tissues, also in the cells, in the plastidules, and so on down to the last primordial-atom. Otherwise it would be inconceivable how the phenomenon of the sum could contain something which was lacking in its constituents. The problem is simple: the origin of consciousness must be looked for in the primordial-atoms. If it can be found there, the truth of the rest of the inferences will necessarily follow.

What are these primordial-atoms? What is the process whereby consciousness arises in them so that they can become the carriers of consciousness? In this regard von Hartmann's doctrine of the primordial-atoms corresponds exactly to the basic principles of his genetic psychology.[1] This particular problem is also discussed at length in the *Kategorienlehre*.[2] His basic theory concerning the origin of consciousness holds that the primordial-atoms are in the last analysis the final structure-units of matter in the form of force-intensities or energies. This quality-less intensity of force-points or dynamic centers is the material element from which consciousness must be educed. The question can be formulated as follows: how can the psychic intensity of feeling, as the most primitive grade of consciousness, arise from the intensity of force as from the most elementary unit of matter? How can the conscious feeling-intensity originate from the material force-intensity? Von Hartmann's view is that the elements of consciousness are to be reduced to the intensive quantity of feeling.[3] This intensive quantity will serve as the middle term between the extensive quantity of the primordial-atoms and the perceptive quality of consciousness. For explanation of this transition from quantity to quality, from extension to intensity, from the material state of unconsciousness to the spiritual

[1] *System der Philosophie in Grundriss* (Bad Sachsa: Hermann Haacke, 1907–09), vol. III, p. 139.

[2] *Kategorienlehre* (Leipzig: Hermann Haacke, 1896), p. 28.

[3] *System der Philosophie im Grundriss*, vol. III, p. 156. "Aller ursprüngliche Bewusstseins-inhalt ist Gefühl der Lust und Unlust *ohne* hinzukommende Gefühlsqualität und Empfindungs-qualität'.' (All original content of consciousness is a feeling of pleasure and pain *without* their accompanying feeling- and perception-quality).

level of awareness or consciousness, he offers an ingenious theory fashioned according to the nature of the Leibnizian monads.[1]

As dynamically intensive centers of matter the primordial-atoms affect one another by a simultaneous influence, thus mutually limiting the spatial extension of their rectilineal "force-emanation." Each dynamically extensive monad undergoes this restricting and hindering influence of all the rest. It happens through this occurrence that the intensities of the energy-centers are thwarted in their tendency to expand in all directions of space. Consequently, since each monad is subjected to the same tendency of an infinitely expanding efficiency, each necessarily restricts the other in this endeavor, and they turn back, revert, so to speak, the intensity of one another. This mutual interception of the monads allows von Hartmann to distinguish between two different kinds of intensities: active or emanating, and passive or returned (backward bent). Thus, he concludes, the intensive quantity of feeling is nothing else than this returned, dammed up, accumulated intensity of the material central forces. The quality-less feeling, the intensive quantitative neutrality of consciousness is the accumulated and returned intensity of the dynamic structural-units, the primordial-atoms of matter. The accumulation itself results from the force-actions of the primordial-atoms, from a stratum of reality which is proper to matter. The product of the accumulation, or consciousness at the moment of its begetting does not belong any longer to this stratum, to this material sphere. It creates a new sphere of existence, which is related to the previous one as the psychic to the material, as ideal existence to real existence.[2]

Consciousness is thus explained as the result of this mysterious and mythical self-agitation of the ultimate particles of matter. The accumulated intensity as the first degree of conscious existence is neither dynamically-material, nor real in the sense of the force monads which are its carriers. Through the process of accumulation the intensity of the hitherto blind and unconscious primordial-atoms becomes inwardly intensified. During the reverting movement of the intensity into itself, an act of reflection arises, whereby the previously unconscious becomes inwardly opposite to itself, thus conscious.[3] Through the intrusion of

---

[1] *Kategorienlehre*, pp. 31–33.

[2] *Ibid.*, p. 35. This new world-stratum of consciousness stands to the sphere of reality, according to von Hartmann's expression, in a "perpendicular manner," and it is related to it somewhat like − 1 to the system of real numbers, i.e., as an imaginary great.

[3] In this passage there is a striking resemblance to Fichte's explanation of the origin of consciousness. The basic principle of Fichte's practical philosophy is: the Ego places the non-Ego as determined by the Ego. This becomes possible only when the primordial, infinite Ego

the conscious upon the original, self-contained peace and harmony of the will and idea in the absolute unconscious, the idea becomes emancipated from the will and it rises in opposition against its original basis, the will.

The great revolution has come to pass, the first step to the world's redemption taken; the idea has been rent from the will, to confront it in the future as an independent power, in order to bring under subjection to itself its former lord.[1]

This view also contains the teleological task and destination of consciousness in the world-process: it will serve as motive, or passive condition for the excitation of the will. Through consciousness such motives will be presented to the will which could not have been arrived at in any other way.

Only by means of consciousness can the will acquire that content to which it will arrive as the final result of the world-process, and without it the world-end cannot be reached.[2]

Only in consciousness will the goal of the world be grasped and understood. Through the above process the unconscious idea will be made conscious whereby alone can evolution attain its final end.

After it has been shown how the conscious psychic or the individual spirit is the product of a material, physiological unconscious, in concluding this section of our investigatory undertakings we have one further task to accomplish. This task takes us to the analysis of the relation of individual consciousness to the absolute unconscious.

The conscious individual spirit appears as the collective receptacle of all psychic activities of the individual. Despite its complex aspect it is a single unity due to the fact that all the partial activities of the comprehensive activity are related to a functional and final single organism. Furthermore, this organism relates all its partial activities to an ontological unity. The functional unity, therefore, guarantees individual consciousness or the soul's singular existence, whereas the ontological unity effects its strict connection with the absolute un-

performed an act of self-restriction and self-limitation, such as that which von Hartmann applies to the force-accumulation of the primordial-atoms. Perception was the boundary phenomenon of consciousness in the theoretical realm for Fichte, in von Hartmann's case it is the intensive quantity of feeling. Both agree also in the genetic history of their boundary concept when they define it as the product of the limited activity of a limitlessly willing entity. They differ only (quite an essential difference, however,) in the fact, that Fichte deduces the origin of consciousness from the concept of the Ego, whereas, von Hartmann, characteristically enough, from the structure-units of matter; consequently, in Fichte's case consciousness is the product of the interference of the non-Ego, whereas, with von Hartmann it is the intercepted activity of the material primordial-atoms.

[1] *Philosophy of the Unconscious*, vol. II, p. 84.

[2] "Die Allotrope Causalität," *Archiv für Systematische Philosophie* (Berlin: Georg Reimer, 1899), vol. I, pp. 1–24.

conscious. Thus the individual consciousness appears to be a partial function of the final ontological principle, the absolute unconscious.

The highest degree of this ascending consideration of the metaphysics of the unconscious consists in the reduction of the twofold principle of reality, will and idea, into the ontological monism of the unconscious.

The objective-real sphere, or the philosophy of nature and the subjective-ideal or the sphere of psychology, displayed throughout all our investigations a twofold activity that we characterized by the name of will and idea. This activity encompasses the production of both of these phenomenal spheres, and these in turn are the production of the metaphysical sphere. The multiplicity of the activities of the respective spheres is reduced to unity through the simple metaphysical principle, wherein the teleologico-dynamic and the logico-ideal aspects of all singular activities become one. The teleologico-dynamic force (*Vermögen*) and the logical possibility (*Möglichkeit*) are the two concepts in which the two sides of the absolute essence (*Wesenheit*) are presented to our minds.

> The immutability of the teleologico-dynamic force is the cause of the conservation of energy; the immutability of the logical formal principle is the cause for the continuation of the homogeneous adaptation of laws; the two-sided metaphysical essence is the cause or ground for the permanent duration of the twofold activity and their permanent product, the world.[1]

The metaphysical essence is, therefore, the unity of many. It is not necessary to assume more than two moments in it, i.e., that of will and idea. We have, therefore, a *biune essence* [2] as the source of the world of phenomenon. This is no dualism, von Hartmann contends, which places duality as something irreducible, but monism, which raises duality to the elevated moment of an original unity. In opposition to the previous philosophical systems of abstract monism (the Hegelian, for instance) which neglect the duality of the moments in the essence, von Hartmann insists that this monism must be called concrete monism. This is so also in relation to the individualizing process of separation. Only this latter is real in the proper sense of the word, whereas the unity enjoys a higher form of existence, super-existence. The world of individuation has a transcendent reality. Thus hopes von Hartmann to have fulfilled one of the tenets of his philosophical creed "... to allot the *individuum*

---

[1] *System*, vol. IV, p. 58.

[2] I realize that the adjective "biune" is an offensive term to linguists, but there is no other word in English to give back the meaning of the German "zweieinig" which was fashioned by von Hartmann after the adjective "Dreieinig," "triune," in reference to the divine essence.

a more worthy and relatively more independent position than it has in the abstract monistic and materialistic pantheism...."[1]

Will and idea find their unity in the fact that they are both attributes of the one and same substance. But the state of "in-each-other-being" (*das Ineinandersein*) of substance and attributes is called essence, von Hartmann continues. In so far as only the substance subsists in all activities, the essence of all phenomena is immanent. But it does not enter into the world in its totality nor is it consumed in it. For it is potentially infinite as unity of dynamic force and logical possibility, whereas activity is actually finite. Thus essence, as essence of the world is transcendent, although the same considered as entering into the activity of the world is immanent. The essence externalizes itself into plurality through space and time as through the principles of individuation, while in its noumenal reality it is space-less, time-less, immaterial, and unconscious. Positively, we can call it the absolute unconscious spirit.[2] Upon this unconscious spirit rests the whole world, and the world process originates from this unconscious essence and through nature it reaches the conscious spirit as its intermediate state until it returns again into the unconscious absolute spirit. His *Weltanschauung*, von Hartmann tells us, can be properly termed *pan-pneumatism*.[3] But why must this pneuma be unconscious? Von Hartmann gives eighteen reasons for it.[4] The most apodictic among them, in his opinion, is the problem just discussed. Consciousness is based upon material substratum; consciousness without matter belongs to the sphere of fairy tales. All higher operations of consciousness rest upon memory, and this in turn, upon the impression-capability of the matter of the brain, the plasm. Such a plasm-brain is utterly contrary to the nature of the unconscious spirit. Since it is lacking consciousness and memory it cannot be a self-conscious personality either. If it were conscious, then we find no answer to the problem of evil in the world process, for it is unthinkable for von Hartmann that in the case of a conscious absolute spirit so much suffering and pain could occur in the universe. Furthermore, if the absolute spirit had possessed eternal consciousness, the content of it obviously would be the eternal blueprint of the world. Whence, in turn, follows the eternity of the world, unless we separate thinking and

---

[1] See chapter V of this book. Also, *Geschichte der Metaphysik* (Leipzig: Hermann Haacke, 1899), vol. II, p. 99.

[2] The noun form "*Geist*" or "Spirit" is a later addition to the original hypostatised adjective "unconscious." This addition was made not without the constant fire of his critics.

[3] *System*, vol. IV, p. 79.

[4] *Ibid.*, vol. IV, pp. 119–130.

creating in God, which is an impossibility. But the eternity of the world is teleologically untenable, for in this case, the process would be without an end. Consequently, the absolute spirit is without consciousness.

Such is the monistic metaphysical creed of von Hartmann, wherein the panlogism of Hegel and the panthelism of Schopenhauer are united in one comprehensive principle; the two operative causes in the macrocosm, will and idea, are reduced to the status of attributes of an absolute unconscious substance. In the following chapters we shall learn more about the nature and properties of this unconscious. But first we intend to make a close analysis of the validity of the process whereby the principle was attained, and of the validity of the principle itself in the light of the criteria we accepted in our Introduction as criteria of true philosophy.

It is beyond the scope of this book to follow in all its details the errors committed by von Hartmann against formal logic in his attempt to establish the notion of the unconscious. It would be a useless task to try to count all instances, for example, of illicit illations of *a posse ad esse* reasoning in the afore conducted study of nature, the life of the soul, and the metaphysical realm. To quote one example, von Hartmann commits this fallacy when he denies the essential difference between human and brute consciousness on the mere basis of the possible likeness of behavior between the two under certain similar circumstances. To list the numerous instances of uncritical extension of analogy would be an equally impossible task. It is only one of such cases when von Hartmann, proving the presence of the unconscious in the organism, assumes the ganglia and the spinal cord to be independent centers of consciousness. He also seems to have a preference for "proofs" moving in a vicious circle, when, for instance, the willed lifting of the finger is explained through the causality of the motor nerves motivated by unconscious presentation, and this unconscious presentation in turn is motivated by the very willing to lift the finger. Furthermore, the unsubstantiated assumption of the clairvoyant intuition of the unconscious as the guiding light of the purposive action of the instinct would in itself be sufficient to discard the unconscious into the realm of fairy tales.

Likewise, it would be an aimless debate to enter into an unending controversy with von Hartmann regarding the violation of the fundamental principles of knowledge and reality in his endeavors to establish the metaphysical unconscious. We think, however, that three of these infringements are of paramount importance regarding the value of his metaphysical system; consequently, we deem it necessary to discuss them in particular.

The first such error that will entail the denial of the validity of von Hartmann's noumenal principle is the astounding statement, which is a complete reversal of all that von Hartmann stood for previously, that the truly convincing knowledge as to the existence and nature of the unconscious does not derive from experience, but from a mystically gained intuition.[1] This kind of intuition for von Hartmann is the knowledge that rises from the unconscious regions of the mind. The act whereby it attains its object of knowledge is outside of all norms of ordinary cognition, and the object's actual presence in the mind escapes all rational interpretation. The certainty such a knowledge conveys to the subject is of the greatest degree, but because it is incommunicable, its objective and demonstrative value is the absolute minimum possible.

In our view, intuition may be enigmatic in its psychological and metaphysical origins, but under no circumstances is there a logical justification to explain its direct origin from an absolute unconscious. It seems to us that this interpretation is another example of von Hartmann's disregard for the rules of formal logic, when the inference from the conscious mind to the absolute unconscious is given as a fact without any valid proof for the truth of this fact. How can we make an inference from the first to the second when there is no logical link between the two? Furthermore, if von Hartmann's statement were true, there would be no need for scientific induction as he claims it. In this intuitive vision, all that is to be known would be immediately intuited by the mind, and induction could arrive at no new truth at all, thus being wholly superfluous.

What is even more significant in this unequivocal claim for intuition is the fact that von Hartmann thereby implicitly admits that a pure inductive inquiry within the framework of an immanentistic view of the world will never succeed to the discovery of a truly metaphysical principle. If in spite of this von Hartmann demands the existence of a metaphysical realm, this can be done only in contradiction to his own original position of pure induction. Consequently, the inevitable inference is that it is not the real-objective world which will determine the subjective-ideal and the metaphysical worlds, but rather the subjective-ideal will shape the objective-real and the metaphysical realms. It is from this mystically intuited metaphysical principle of the absolute

---

[1] *Philosophy of the Unconscious*, vol. I, p. 362; p. 371. Cf. footnotes 1 and 2, p. 48.

unconscious that the entire universe of von Hartmann receives its origin. In final analysis, von Hartmann finds no results and studies no causes and effects, but merely discovers the manifestations of his mystically begotten absolute unconscious in the world of phenomena as well as that of the noumenon.

The second point that we intend to formally analyze is von Hartmann's explanation of the origin of consciousness. This also involves the violation of one of the basic principles of metaphysics, the principle of causality, and ultimately that of contradiction.

Von Hartmann, propounding his doctrine on the rise of consciousness, tells us that consciousness is a unified activity of force-intensities (matter) and quality-intensities (feeling).[1] It is the result of mutual interaction between spirit and the material organism. The two are so inseparably connected that where one or the other is missing, there cannot be consciousness. Consequently, in the absolute where all materiality is absent there can be no consciousness either. But, on the other hand, this same unconscious absolute substance is also the unitary substrate of all phenomena: logical and alogical, spiritual and material. It is also the principle of individuation, multiplicity, and substantiality of things. But how can the same reality simultaneously account for the identity and non-identity, for the unity and multiplicity of things, unless we deny the validity of the principle of rationality? Applying the same question to the problem at hand: how can consciousness derive from unconsciousness? If we admit this possibility with von Hartmann, then we simply state that the conscious and the unconscious are identical in content. A statement that is absurd and impossible of being proved. In order to become conscious in its phenomenal manifestations, the unconscious must have somehow contained the form of consciousness in itself, for consciousness is ultimately deduced exclusively from the absolute unconscious. In this case, the unconscious had to effect something which is not only above and beyond its own perfection, but which is diametrically opposed to its own nature. Unless contradictories are simultaneously possible in the same reality, this explanation of von Hartmann is absurd and unintelligible.

The third point is designed to take up the study of the final argument and justification of von Hartmann's metaphysical unconscious. This justification is based on von Hartmann's assumption that in the case of a conscious metaphysical ultimate reality, there can be no satisfactory explanation of evil in the world-process. For him it is unthink-

---

[1] *Kategorienlehre*, p. 28. Cf. footnotes 3, p. 52, and 1, p. 53.

able that in the case of a conscious absolute spirit so much suffering and pain could occur in the universe. Hence in the final analysis it is the problem of evil that forces von Hartmann to assume the existence of an absurd and self-contradictory metaphysical principle as the source of all existence. The importance of this central theme in his entire *Weltan-schauung* is so great that it is necessary to give a separate chapter to a discussion of the problem and mystery of evil.[1]

[1] See Chapter VI.

CHAPTER IV

DIVISION AND KINDS OF THE UNCONSCIOUS

Alle Tätigkeit, ihre Wesenheit und ihr Subject muss nicht viele, sondern Eine sein, und dieses Eine tätige Wesen ist das Unbewusste.[1]

In his anonymous self-criticism of the unconscious, *Das Unbewusste vom Standpunkt der Physiologie und Deszendenztheorie*, von Hartmann reproaches himself for undefined usage of the term unconscious, and believes that the lack of proper analysis of this notion is the cause for the shortcomings of the *Philosophy of the Unconscious* itself as well as for the carping criticism of its opponents. In its initial use, according to the intention of von Hartmann, the term unconscious encompasses the entire primordial foundation of all reality, which is a multitude of the most divergent things. Consequently, the diversity of these different elements in their comprehensive unity must be pointed out if the term is to have practical value. Thus von Hartmann proposes the following distinction in the notion of the unconscious:

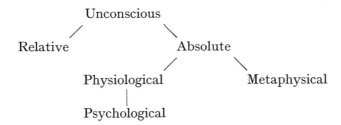

The *relative unconscious* is unconscious in relation to the total-con-

---

[1] The main sources for the present section are von Hartmann's *Philosophie des Unbewussten* (Leipzig: Hermann Haacke, 1890), 10th ed., vol. III, chapter XII; *System* (Bad Sachsa: Hermann Haacke, 1907–09), vol. IV, pp. 107–141, and his articles in the following philosophical magazines: "Zum Begriff der Unbewussten Vorstellung," *Philosophische Monatsheften*, ed. by Dr. P. Natorp (Berlin: Salinger, 1892), vol. XXVIII, pp. 1–25; "Zum Begriff des Unbewussten," *Archiv für Systematische Philosophie* (Berlin: Reimer, 1900), vol. VI, pp. 273–290. The present quotation is from the *System*, vol. IV, p. 109.

sciousness of the cerebrum (*Grosshirn*), but not to its subordinated nerve-centers.

The *absolute unconscious* is unconscious in every respect and sense.

The *physiological unconscious* denotes the molecular brain and ganglia predispositions of an individual. These predispositions are the causes of the characteristic distinctness of the physiological and psychological functions of an individual.

The *metaphysical unconscious* is the essence of all operations in the universe. These operations are understood according to the laws of nature in the atoms, wherein also the psychological inwardness (*Innerlichkeit*) is included.[1]

The *psychological unconscious* is a subdivision of the physiological, since it is included in the latter. Only after a thorough study of the physiological are we able to detect it in and distinguish it from the psychological unconscious.

This division of the unconscious is made in view of the objections of the natural scientists to the notion of the unconscious, and it bears the marks of a predominantly physiological outlook. In this regard, the obstacles von Hartmann has to overcome are the Darwinistic materialistic tenets of some of his contemporaries, such as, Lange, Schmidt and Maudsley, and their rejection of the unconscious as a sufficient principle for a teleological view of the universe. Realizing the inadequacy of the above division of the unconscious and intending to remedy it, von Hartmann proposes another division a few years before his death.[2] He blames the deficiency and incompleteness of the first task on the complexity and difficulty of the problem, and he promises to amend these shortcomings. The fact that he is so preoccupied with the theoretical aspect of the problem, combined with the obvious practical application of the notion of the unconscious in every sphere of existence (cf. *Kategorienlehre*), is another proof of his unjustified indignation at being called the "philosopher of the unconscious."[3]

While the first division bears the marks of a deductive approach to the problem, the second is inductive in character and can be summarized schematically as follows:

---

[1] The "inwardbent" or inner operation of a being, characteristic of its own nature.

[2] "Zum Begriff des Unbewussten," *Archiv für Systematische Philosophie* (Berlin: Reimer, 1900), vol. VI, pp. 273–290.

[3] *Philosophie des Unbewussten* (Leipzig: Hermann Haacke, 1904), 11th ed., Introductory, p. LXI. "It is always detestable to an author when his most successful work is not his best, and yet, public opinion, which is formed according to external results only, judges the author exclusively by this work and it can never be done away with."

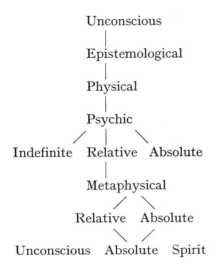

A.   THE EPISTEMOLOGICAL UNCONSCIOUS

1. *The unknown (Das Ungewusste)* – an object not yet actually known, as for instance, a star not yet discovered, the existence of which is not even supposed. Only the present content of consciousness is actually and directly known, that is, the sum-total of external and internal perceptions as that which it itself is. Everything else deduced from its inferences is actually and indirectly known and is here and now present in consciousness in the form of perceptions, presentations, concepts and thoughts according to what they mean, present, represent, or convey.

2. *The objective possibility of perception (Die objective Wahrnehmungs-möglichkeit)* an object not actually known at the present time; e.g., the table standing in front of me as a possible object of presentation while I close my eyes. Any one who hypostatizes this possibility of perception, as does John Stuart Mill, without reducing it to a physical, psychic, or metaphysical unconscious, may be inclined to call it "unconscious perception," as Hamilton does. This designation must be rejected, von Hartmann insists, since the object as long as it is unconscious is not in perception, and as soon as it is in perception, it is not unconscious any longer.

3. *The unknowable (Das Unwissbare, Unerkennbare).* For a pure empiricist whatever is above experience and cannot be known by experience is "unknowable." A transcendental idealist would call it the epistemologically transcendent; a phenomenalist, the metaphysically

transcendent; a rationalist, the alogical. Spencer's "unknowable" is frequently confused and interchanged with the psychic and metaphysical unconscious. The directly unknowable is all which cannot become the direct content of consciousness in the exact manner as it is; the indirectly unknowable is only that which cannot be the object of an indirect, representative, mediated cognition. All unconscious data must of necessity be directly unknowable, for by entering into consciousness it would cease to be unconscious; but were all unconscious data indirectly unknowable also, then it would be under no circumstances cognoscible and thus it could never be the object of a scientific debate. Hence the possibility of indirect cognition is the presupposition of any investigation into the field of the unconscious. As far as this investigation succeeds, the unconscious becomes an indirectly known object without ceasing, however, to be directly unknowable and unknown. As long as the possibility of a psychic and metaphysical unconscious is not thought of, it seems hasty and incorrect to say that the unknown and unknowable is unconscious; but as soon as these notions become the objects of debate, even if only for the sake of polemics, it will be necessary to apply to them the notion of the unconscious and to replace the previous expressions by the epistemological-unconscious.

B.   THE PHYSICAL UNCONSCIOUS

1. *The consciousness-less* (without being aware: *Das Bewusstlose*). It is the actual and momentary absence of that consciousness which someone under different circumstances may rightly expect from a certain degree of individuality; for instance, a man in a faint or in a dreamless sleep.

2. *The incapable of consciousness* (*Das Bewusstseinsunfähige*). A being which by its essence is without consciousness, a thing which according to its nature does not and cannot have consciousness; e.g., lifeless, insensitive matter, according to non-hylozoistic materialists, or inorganic matter, according to those who place the beginning of sensation in the organic matter.

3. *The stationary* (*or static*) *physiological unconscious* (*Das stationäre physiologische Unbewusste*). This unconscious connotes the relations of definite molecular positions to each other in organized matter (plasma); especially the molecular correlations of the central organs in complex (composed) organisms. Furthermore, it entails those hereditary or acquired cerebral and ganglionic predispositions which when excited pro-

duce definite sensations, presentations, or movements. It is the state of the material auxiliary mechanisms at rest (*in potentia*) prior to automatic motion, reflex movement, instincts, character, memory, feeling, talents, skill, connection of images, reduced connection of images, and motivations. These cerebral and ganglionic predispositions account also for the process of reconstruction whereby the originally conscious primary psychic actions become mechanized and carried into the highest central-consciousness. The explanation of memory-operations through molecular plasma-dispositions makes all hypotheses incorrect which seek to explain them through unconscious psychic activities or primitive potencies (Beneke). To interchange the psycho-physical parallelism of the primary psychic actions with the spatial arrangement of the material particles in the brain is incorrect and erroneous. There is no psychic correlative for the stationary physiological unconscious.

4. *The functional (or dynamic) physiological unconscious (Das funktionelle physiologische Unbewusste).* This is the state of the molecular conditions of vibrations beneath the threshold of excitation in matter capable of sensation which remain without parallel conscious psychic actions. It denotes those excitations of the plasma which are too weak to produce a sensation. They are wrongly described as "unconscious sensations," since an antecedent action, as long as it is unconscious, cannot as yet be called a sensation, and when it is sensed, it is no longer unconscious. It is irrelevant whether the origin of the sensation is peripheral or central, and whether it could appear in consciousness as a hallucinate sensation or desisted presentation through the increase of the functional excitation or not. The functional physiological unconscious without a parallel-action admits neither "unconscious presentations" nor "unconscious sensations." Its essence is nothing more than a mere physical antecedent change, a movement of the material particles, a mechanical functioning of the stationary physiological unconscious, whether with or without the modification of the quality of the exciting stimulation. It is a lack of consciousness of a particular kind, which will enter into a closer relation with the psychic phenomenon only by the fact that such a phenomenon, by the increase of an identical movement, appears as a secondary or concomitant phenomenon.

C.   THE PSYCHIC UNCONSCIOUS

a. That which is not definitely conscious (Das nicht auf bestimmte Weise Bewusste).

In other words, the indefinitely known. However, in the highest, clear, central consciousness of the individual it is somehow conscious. Its kinds are:

1. *The inferiorly conscious (das minder Bewusste)* that which is conscious to a lesser, lower degree. This notion presupposes that there are different grades of formal consciousness, apart from the quality of the content. If this presupposition is correct, then nothing stands in the way of assuming also a minimum grade of consciousness (consciousness-differentials), which upon addition to finite grades of consciousness can be neglected as zero-points of consciousness (*les petites perceptions* of Leibniz), although upon converging into an infinite multitude, they increase to finite grades of consciousness. When, conversely, the so-called grades of consciousness, are to be reduced to the different qualities of the content of consciousness, then these closer determinations of the content take their places and the notion of minimum consciousness loses its ground.

2. *The obscurely and indistinctly conscious (Das unklar und undeutlich Bewusste)*. An indefinite, dim, hazy, nebulous, vague, wan, dull content of consciousness which impedes the comprehension of the given concept and its demarcation and differentiation from others. The perception of the inner diversity and distinction of this consciousness is impossible.

3. *The unobserved in the content of consciousness (Das Unbeachtete im Bewusstseinsinhalt)*. It is that content in consciousness to which our attention is not directed, although it lies within the limits of the immaterial act of observation, but outside of the point of concentrated attention. In this sense, a very definite, clear, and distinct perception can remain unobserved, unnoticed, while the culmination of attention can be focused upon an entirely dull and indistinct impression.

4. *The unreflectedly conscious (Das nicht reflectiert-Bewusste)*, i.e., the merely immediately conscious. It is that state of consciousness of which some one is conscious, but not conscious of the fact of being conscious. In other words, when the mind possesses an object as the content of its consciousness without reflecting upon the fact that it is the content of its consciousness; or that which is perceived, but its being perceived is not apperceived. Whatever is unobserved is also unreflectedly conscious; but even the consciousness of the most acute attention can only be immediately conscious, if the reflection upon this "being-conscious" of the content of consciousness is wanting. For instance, this is the case when the act of intuition is fully and completely immersed in the intuited object. Many psychologists deny the possibility of a perception

without the simultaneous and connatural perception of the act of perceiving.

5. *The not to the Ego referred consciousness (Das nicht auf das Ich Bezogene)*. In the case of an unobserved and unreflected consciousness reference to the Ego is obviously absent, but this may also be the case in an observed and reflectedly conscious psychic act. In the first case, this lack of reference occurs when the attention is involuntary and reflex *(unwillkürliche und reflektorische)*, and in the second case, when there is a reflection upon the momentary form of consciousness of the given content but no reflection, either upon the temporal identity and continuity of self-consciousness, or upon the determining individual purpose.

b. The relative unconscious (Das relativ Unbewusste)

This unconscious is such in relation to the highest, central-consciousness of the individual, but not so for the other, peripheral consciousness of the same individual. Certain occurrences within the individual remain unrelated to the individual's central consciousness. In other words they remain unconscious, but only relatively so, for the peripheral centers of consciousness are fully aware of them. Von Hartmann retains the unqualified expression "unconscious" for those psychic acts only which, although appearing within the individual, are unable to become a direct content of consciousness whether central or peripheral.

1. *Relative unconscious which is conscious in lower consciousness (das in niederen Bewusstseinen bewusste relativ Unbewusste)*, the subconscious, subliminal conscious. In a descending grade of organization of beings which begins with man, we can nowhere recognize a firm and definite limit where the conscious-psychic phenomena cease. The observation of the order of gradation of the different individual beings shows that the higher organisms are composed of many degrees of lower individual things, such as various particles of the brain, sections of the medulla, ganglia-centers, groups of cells, and static and mobile singular-cells, which are partly connected with one another through imperfect connections. The history of evolution teaches that cells in the higher organisms come into existence only through the differentiation of the antecedent accumulation of individuals of single-cells, which have united in themselves all vital functions. Furthermore, evolution also shows that in various classes of animals, the highest central-consciousness is bound to different central organs, and finally, that the degree of centralization of the nervous system is considerably different in the composed organisms.

The theory of psycho-physical parallelism demands that not only each conscious psychic phenomenon correspond to a material movement, but also that each material movement have its correspondent conscious psychic phenomenon. Dreams, hypnosis, somnambulism, double consciousness, auto-suggestion and many other phenomena of the abnormal life of the mind point to a certain consciousness in the individual which is not directly subjected to the highest or central-consciousness, but only loosely connected with it. If the central-consciousness is repressed or incapacitated in any way, these lower consciousnesses can employ the organism itself.

2. *The relative unconscious conscious in higher, super-sensible, transcendental individual consciousness* (*Das in einem höheren, übersinnlichen, transcendentalen Individualbewusstsein bewusste relativ Unbewusste*), or the hyper-conscious. This hypothesis, advanced in modern times by Immanuel H. Fichte, Hellenbach, and du Prell,[1] corresponds essentially to the desire for the permanent duration of some kind of individual consciousness, even after normal, clear, central-consciousness has vanished in death with the dissolution of the organism. This theory assumes an immortal ethereal body which serves the transcendental individual consciousness as the carrier and receptacle of the material dispositions necessary for any consciousness, and it maintains that this consciousness is not some passive concomitant phenomenon arisen at the collision of the unconscious activities, but that it is an activity itself. This transcendental consciousness is not contained in the corporeal-spiritual individual as it actually exists. It is rather itself an individual, a spirit or demon, by whom the individual is possessed. The concept of the individual must first be subjected to a metaphysical expansion, in order to encompass in itself the transcendental consciousness. Without such expansion, its influences stand in relation to the empirical individual as "directly unknown," but by no means can they be called, in the proper sense of the word, unconscious.

c. Psychic absolute unconscious

1. *Absolute unconscious psychic individual-function* (*Die absolut unbewusste psychische Individualfunktion*), which is not conscious for any of the consciousnesses contained within the individual. The absolute unconscious is that psychic activity which brings forth the phenomenon of consciousness from the stratum of the physiological unconscious through a creative synthesis. This activity is essentially a categorical

[1] *Op. cit.*, p. 280.

function; if one accepts the intuited forms of space, time, and finality to be categories. It is the ideal anticipation of the content's real-becoming, i.e., the anticipative representation of a future occurrence, the logical determination of the not yet existent but capable of actual becoming through its inherent power of activity. It is the seat of relations whose final purpose is aimed at existence as well as at consciousness, an analytico-synthetic intellectual-function, and a teleologico-dynamic force of realization. It is presentation in co-existence and cooperation with willing for the materialization of the presented idea, according to Herbart and Hegel; or willing in connection with a definite, but still unrealized, ideal purpose, as Schopenhauer's voluntaristic psychology would have it; or a twofold function of the unconscious, which includes presentation and willing in an inseparable unity.

Absolute unconscious psychic activity must necessarily be conceived as heterogeneous and antithetic to the conscious psychic phenomena of all degrees of individual consciousness. In addition, whereas the consciousnesses are passive, receptive, representative, sensile, abstract, and discursive, the unconscious must be thought of only as active, productive, original (in the sense of prototype), super-sensile, concrete, and primordial-intuitive. Its notion can not be arrived at by a descent to lesser grades of consciousness or to consciousnesses of lower individuality-degrees, nor by the fact that some one, as if through a process of integration, would increase in himself the notion of consciousness to infinitude or to absolute greatness. It can be attained only by reaching beyond consciousness for its unconscious cause which, if it were a purely material occurrence, would be subconscious, but as psychic, intellectual function, it is supra-conscious. Just as the relation between cause and effect cannot be negative, so also the absolute unconscious psychic activity cannot be something negative in relation to the conscious psychic phenomena which are materialized by it. Although negative, unobserved psychic phenomena are possible, still, they may be called negative only in relation to what is known to us.

2. *The absolute unconscious individual-subject of the psychic individual function (das absolut unbewusste Individual Subject der psychischen Individual-function).* According to von Hartmann, these are Leibniz's monads, Herbart's "simple realities," Bahnsen's henads, and the created substantial souls of theism. If the activity producing the psychic phenomenon is already absolutely unconscious, then the subject, which exercises this activity, must also of necessity be absolutely unconscious, since it is a degree further removed from all consciousnesses possibly

present in the individual. Philosophers who accept activity as self-sufficient and self-explanatory reject this hypothesis as superfluous and unsubstantiated. Those who accept the reality of subject as an indispensable carrier of activity need not assume a plurality of subjects to support their theory. For the unconscious subject of the unconscious activities may not be interchanged with the phenomenal Ego of self-consciousness and, consequently, it may not be made a plurality. When each consciousness of each degree of individuality requires its own subject, then a composite individual must contain as many unconscious substantial subjects of unconscious activities as it encompasses consciousnesses of various degrees of individualities. Since this is the case, we cannot speak of a substantial individual soul, but only of a complexus of substantial individual souls in that higher composite we call the individual. Accordingly, the soul can be found first in the *substantial* subject of the particular psychic activity in question and not in the immediate organic subject of that particular psychic activity. Thus von Hartmann concludes that the soul resides in the substrate of the total unconscious psychic activities performed by the substantial subject. In the case when this substantial subject cannot be called a soul, it no longer belongs to the domain of the psychic unconscious. It has transcended these limits and it reaches into the realm of the metaphysical unconscious.

d. The metaphysical unconscious

1. *The metaphysical relative unconscious (das metaphysische relativ Unbewusste)*. This unconscious is absolutely such only from the psychological point of view in relation to individuals. In its metaphysical aspect, in relation to the absolute consciousness of the absolute, it is conscious. This is the opinion of von Hartmann concerning the positions of theism and pseudo-theism in explaining the consciousness of God. According to him, this hypothesis takes its origin essentially from theological motives. As far as it is related to a productive consciousness of the absolute, it is inherent in the original *a se esse* and in the activity of consciousness upon the conscious, whereas psychologically, we must maintain the dependence of the conscious upon the unconscious. As long as it is related to a receptive consciousness of the absolute, theism must assume the threshold of the consciousness to be an absolute minimum. But then this assumption contradicts the fact that the thresholds rise and become higher with the degrees of individuality. If absolute consciousness is contrasted as a separate substance to individuals, then

perhaps, these individuals can be affected by the energetic influences of the absolute consciousness which influences are "directly unknown" to them. In that case, these influences cannot be called unconscious at all. This is because for the individuals such influences are extrinsic and alien, and they cannot experience them any more than they can experience the content of the consciousness of another individual. On the contrary, if the individuals are considered as mere groups of partial activities of the absolute consciousness, then it is not clear how these conscious psychic activities can lose their consciousness in the individual, instead of entering into these individual consciousnesses and helping to construct them.

2. *The absolute unconscious universal-activity* (*die absolut unbewusste Universalthätigkeit*). If consciousness is accepted only as active, then there is a plurality of activities emanating from the plurality of concatenated consciousnesses. As soon as we recognize all activities as unconscious, causality and finality urge us to view the totality of all activities as a universal unity of intrinsic plurality and to look at the individual-activity merely as a partial activity, as an element within the absolute activity of functional monism. Metaphysical unconscious universal activity contains the materializing, i.e., the matter-building, matter-producing activities, as partial activities, the atom-forces, as well as the immaterial partial activities in the strict sense, and their groups, the souls. In each singular individual that aspect of the absolute activity can be first called unconscious which constructs in it its organic and psychic individuality. Absolute activity as homogeneous totality is to be called unconscious: first, in relation to the sum-total of individuals construed by it; and secondly, in relation to the absolute subject as opposed to the hypothesis of an absolute consciousness.

3. *The unconscious absolute spirit* (*der unbewusste absolut Geist*), or the unconscious absolute subject, or the substantial carrier of the unconscious absolute activity. If activity is acknowledged as homogeneous and universal, its subject must also be acknowledged as such. Thus we have displayed the ultimate metaphysical significance of the unconscious: that of substance, of which everything else is only an accident, attribute, or mode. This is the ultimate meaning of the unconscious for substantial or ontological monism. The "substantializing" of the adjective, the "subjectivization" of the predicate in the expression "the unconscious," here acquires more than a sheer grammatical significance, von Hartmann contends. The unconscious subject with the unconscious activity is that "identical third" for which the follow-

ers of the philosophy of identity are searching beyond the material and the conscious psychic phenomena in the field of psycho-physical parallelism, but they are unable to define it. It is clear that it can be an "identical third" only if it is distinguished from both of its phenomenal forms. That is when it is neither material nor conscious-psychic, but immaterial unconscious.

This is the sum of von Hartmann's doctrine concerning the meaning of his unconscious. Hereafter, when we refer to the unconscious in an unqualified and indistinctive manner, this absolute immaterial unconscious is to be understood as the universal substantial substratum of the unconscious absolute activity in the universe. In this sense von Hartmann gives the following attributes or properties of the unconscious.

1. The unconscious does not fall ill, like conscious mental operations, as a result of injury or other disturbances in material organs.

2. The unconscious does not grow weary and tired. This is obvious, for weariness results from material fatigue of the organs of consciousness and renders these organs temporarily ineffective in the performance of their duties. The closer we ascend to the domain of the unconscious, the less is fatigue observable, as, for instance, in the case of feelings. The less defined these feelings are in consciousness, the less is the possibility of their becoming fatigued, for with the proportion of their indefiniteness in consciousness grows the proportion of their relation to the essence of the unconscious.

3. Unconscious thought can be only of a non-sensory kind. Since every form of conscious thought is necessarily connected with sense impressions, this kind of cognition cannot be proper to the unconscious. All of our cognitions must be of the former kind; therefore, we cannot form a positive concept concerning the manner of thinking of the unconscious. The most we can say, in the form of a probable supposition, is that things are represented in the unconscious idea as they are in themselves, since it would be unintelligible why things should appear to the unconscious otherwise than they are. Or to put it more correctly: things are what they are because they are represented in the unconscious thusly and not otherwise.

4. The unconscious does not hesitate and doubt. It needs no time for reflection, but comprehends all results instantaneously. This means that the unconscious thinks the whole logical process which produces the result all at once and not successively. This is to say that the unconscious does not think at all but intuits the result immediately in an

intellectual vision with the infinite penetration of the purely logical. From this also follows that the intuition of the unconscious is not only timeless, but also non-temporal, i.e., out of all time.

5. The unconscious does not err. Apparent mistakes of the unconscious may be seen through erratic instincts, clairvoyant vision, unfulfilled dreams, faulty inspirations of mysticism, or delusive artistic conceptions. Thorough investigation reveals that these errors do not spring from the unconscious, but that consciousness has interfered somehow with unconscious operation, either in the form of excesses of the fancy, or as faulty education, false principles, judgments, and taste.

6. The unconscious lacks memory, and does not need it. It is absolutely immaterial, whereas memory is the sum of permanent sense impressions in the brain. It does not need memory since its manner of cognition is a non-temporal intellectual intuition wherein all is continually present.

7. In the unconscious, will and presentation are united in an inseparable unity. Nothing can be willed which is not presented, and nothing can be presented which is not willed. This is the true unity of will and idea in the absolute unconscious, wherein the will wills nothing but the realization of its own content, i.e., the presentation united with it.

8. The unconscious promotes life anywhere it can do so. Wherever there is a certain combination of organic matter wherein the possibility of life is given, the unconscious lays hold of this possibility to animate and vivify this organic nature.

9. The unconscious seeks to perform its work with the greatest possible preservation of energy. If it is at all possible, the unconscious intends to create a machinery of organization whereby the work can be done once and for all. Its intervention thereafter is restricted only to the reparative action in case of injury to the organism.

10. The unconscious is omnipotent and omnipresent. As we have already seen, all real existence owes its origin to the will, and the *raison d'être* of will is the absolute unconscious. Consequently, all operations of the will must be reduced to the nature of the unconscious. The ceaseless intervention of the unconscious at every moment and at all levels of conscious and unconscious existence proves its ever present essence in the universe.

11. The unconscious is omniscient. Each and every phenomenon observed either in the objective-real or the subjective-ideal realm of existence displays in the most striking and amazing manner this attribute of the unconscious. Its previously considered attributes that the

unconscious cannot err and that it cannot hesitate or doubt give a further corroboration of this statement. Its power of absolute clairvoyance together with the infallible and indubitable logical concatenation of the included data, and the most appropriate action at the most suitable moment, wherein omniscience is united with supreme wisdom, is the highest property of the unconscious. This attribute of the unconscious assures us that the world is contrived and guided "... as wisely and well as is possible; that if, among all possible ideas, that of a better world could have lain in the omniscient unconscious, certainly the better one would have come to pass instead of the present one."[1]

---

[1] *Philosophy of the Unconscious* (London: Routledge and Kegan Paul, Ltd., 1950), vol. I, p. 60.

CHAPTER V

HISTORICAL GENESIS OF THE NOTION OF THE UNCONSCIOUS

Es war nichts Zufälliges, dass die Philosophie des Unbewussten gerade dieses Stichwort wählte.[1]

Von Hartmann claims a long and distinguished line of ancestors for the notion of the unconscious.[2] In the third volume of the *Philosophy of the Unconscious* he writes:

... it (the unconscious) was in the air, and prepared from all sides; furthermore, it was also a requirement of progress in the direction of self-consciousness and self-understanding of mankind, and because it corresponded to the deep-seated desire of the human mind it found such a quick and favorable acceptance with the public. No wonder that even the sparrows chirp about it on the roofs.[3]

In the evolution of the unconscious, a long time had to elapse in consciousness before man realized the higher antithetic importance of the notion of the unconscious. This is why we do not find any explicit reference to it in either ancient or medieval philosophy. Von Hartmann complains that even in his day the notion is so much a *terra incognita* even in the mind of a cultured public that consciousness and being conscious of a thing are inseparable for them. It is no wonder, von Hartmann continues, that this naive view still prevails if we think of the influential philosophers who support it, like Descartes, Malebranche, and Locke.[4]

If we accept the findings of von Hartmann's historical research, Leibniz discovered and introduced first the notion of unconscious ideas into philosophy by refuting Locke. In Locke's opinion, the soul cannot

---

[1] *Philosophie des Unbewussten* (Leipzig: Hermann Haacke, 1890), 10th ed., vol. III, p. 298.
[2] The following works of von Hartmann are used as sources for this chapter: *Geschichte der Metaphysik* (Leipzig: Hermann Haacke, 1899), vol. II, Sachenregister: Unbewusste; *Die Moderne Psychologie* (Leipzig: Hermann Haacke, 1901), sect. III, Das Unbewusste; *Philosophy of the Unconscious* (London: Routledge and Kegan Paul, Ltd., 1950), vol. I, pp. 16–42, 434–438.
[3] *Op. cit.*, vol. III, p. 298.
[4] *Philosophy of the Unconscious*, vol. I, pp. 16–17.

consciously think if man is not conscious of it; according to Leibniz's doctrine of innate ideas and the ceaseless activity of the perceptive faculty, man must be always thinking. To solve the dilemma, no other possibility was left for Leibniz but to assume unconscious thinking. Consciousness results only through the consciousness-differentials, the *"petites perceptions,"* which are not consciousness in themselves but rather through their reciprocal cooperation rise to consciousness. They are *"perceptions insensibles"* or unconscious perceptions in opposition to *"perceptions sensibles"* or apperceptions, or simply consciousness.[1] Von Hartmann's only regret in regard to the theory of Leibniz is that he does not expound in its full importance all the implications of his discovery. This shortcoming in Leibniz's doctrine prompts von Hartmann to undertake his own study of the unconscious.

The notion of causality in Hume's philosophy also gave von Hartmann a powerful impetus to conduct this study. A careful analysis of Hume's treatment of this metaphysical problem will show that it is much more closely related to Leibniz's doctrine than it is commonly believed. Hume asserts that in our thoughts and inferences according to causal relations there is an unconscious manifestation of an instinctive power.[2] This unconscious mental instinct is far removed from discursive thought and must be looked upon as an original gift of nature. Von Hartmann accepts the conclusion of Hume's inquiries in regard "to the hypothetical restitution of the critically purified causal instinct" as the only path to objective reality, and he himself follows it in his epistemology.[3]

Kant's opinion concerning unconscious ideas is laid down in his *Anthropology,* where he says:

> To have ideas, and yet not be conscious of them – this seems to be a contradiction; for how can we know that we have them, if we are not conscious of them? ... We can, however, indirectly be conscious of the fact that we have an idea, and yet, directly unconscious of the same.[4]

He calls these ideas "dark," or "obscure ideas" (*dunkle Vorstellungen*), and simultaneously asserts that the field of their activity is great.[5] The terms "obscure" and "unconscious" ideas are far from being equivocal

---

[1] *Ibid.,* p. 17.

[2] *Ibid.,* p. 20.

[3] *Kritische Grundlegungen des Transcendentalen Realismus: System* (Bad Sachsa: Hermann Haacke, 1907–09), vol. I.

[4] *Sämmtliche Werke,* ed. by Rosenkranz and Schubert (Leipzig: Baumann, 1838–1842), in 12 vols. The present reference is made to vol. II, p. 793.

[5] *Ibid.,* ftn. 5.

for Kant, and in his theory of knowledge, the unconscious ideas yield in importance to those of the conscious. Von Hartmann cannot include Kant in the line of his predecessors regarding the origin of the unconscious, except by calling him non-committal concerning the existence of obscure ideas in man's intellective life. As to whether they are to be explained by the interference of the original intellectual intuition of the noumenal being or not, Kant takes no decisive stand. When the problem is stated this way, Kant's position is irrelevant to von Hartmann on two grounds. First, for Kant the obscure ideas are not unconscious ideas; secondly, the intellectual intuition of the absolute is not unconscious as von Hartmann holds it to be. Therefore, the measure of its interference would prove nothing for the case of the unconscious.

Nor does Fichte's subjective idealism bring the theory of the unconscious much further, except in the interpretation of von Hartmann. When Fichte declares that "god's existence" is "merely knowledge itself,"[1] von Hartmann rejects consciousness of this knowledge on the basis of his own principle, whereby consciousness can never be ascribed to an infinite substantial knowledge.

From the Fichtean idealism, Schelling develops his own principle of the eternally unconscious. Von Hartmann objects that this aprioristically established principle was to Schelling's disadvantage, since the spirit of the times demanded an empirical derivation of the notion in order to perceive its necessity and accept its importance. Schelling not only failed to do this, but he restricted the simultaneous cooperation of the conscious and unconscious exclusively to the realm of aesthetics: "The aesthetic alone is such (simultaneously conscious and unconscious) activity."[2] Moreover, in direct proportion with his emancipation from the Fichtean system of thought the notion of the unconscious lost ground in Schelling's philosophy. While in the philosophy of identity or in his negative philosophy, the eternally unconscious plays a role of absolute importance, in his latter or positive philosophy it is completely neglected and discarded. None of his numerous disciples were concerned with the examination or further development of this Schellingian first principle.

To support his contentions, after these unsuccessful and disappointing endeavors, von Hartmann quotes the "divining poet-mind" of Friedrich Richter, a somewhat obscure "theologian" of myths, who

---

[1] *Philosophy of the Unconscious*, vol. I, p. 23.
[2] *Ibid.*, p. 25.

places his faith and anchors his hopes in the unconscious. This is expressed in Richter's last work, the unfinished "Selina":

Our measurements of the rich territory of the Ego are far too small or narrow when we omit the immense realm of the unconscious, this real interior Africa in every sense... Nothing is left for the receptacle and throne of the vital energies but the great kingdom of the unconscious in the soul itself... May we not hope that we perhaps unconsciously love God more heartily than we know, and that a calm instinct for the second world works in us, while we yet consciously give ourselves up so entirely to the external one?[1]

Von Hartmann admits that the notion of the unconscious appears nowhere explicitly in the philosophy of Hegel. Nevertheless, by his exoteric interpretation he declares that Hegel's absolute idea in its pure *in se esse*, before its externalization into nature and return into itself as spirit, fully corresponds to Schelling's eternally unconscious, and Fichte's substantial knowledge. The Hegelian idea in its primordial status of "being-in-self" is unconscious and only through the process of "being-for-self" does it become conscious in the synthesis of "returning-to-itself." Not only Hegelian idealism, but every objective or absolute idealism must of necessity, at least tacitly, presume the theory of the unconscious.[2] At this point von Hartmann goes as far as to call the *Philosophy of the Unconscious* "the elevation of Hegel's unconscious philosophy of the unconscious to a conscious one," thus making it a consciously unconscious philosophy.[3]

For Schopenhauer thought or idea is merely a phenomenon of the metaphysical principle, the will, and as such, an idea may or may not be unconscious. The "unconscious rumination" of which Schopenhauer speaks [4] has reference only to the obscure and confused ideas of Leibniz and Kant, which differ from conscious ideas only specifically and not generically. Schopenhauer's philosophy in no instance comes near to the true conception of the absolutely unconscious idea. Hence von Hartmann thinks that it needs the same supplementary expansion as Hegel's panlogism.[5] The few "hints and intimations," which von Hartmann finds in Schopenhauer's philosophy reach full completion in his own theory of the unconscious.

There is no need to pursue further the line of von Hartmann's prede-

---

[1] *Ibid.*, p. 26.

[2] *Über die Nothwendige Umbildung der Hegelschen Philosophie ihrem Grundprinzip heraus*, in the *Gesammelte Philosophische Abhandlungen zur Philosophie des Unbewussten* (Berlin: Carl Dunker, 1872), Nr. 2, p. 25.

[3] *Philosophy of the Unconscious*, vol. I, p. 28.

[4] *Ibid.*, p. 29.

[5] *Über die Nothwendige Umbildung der Schopenhauer'schen Philosophie ihrem Grundprinzip heraus*, in the *Gesammelte Philosophische Abhandlungen* ..., Nr. 3, p. 57.

cessors in regard to the notion of the unconscious. The term is henceforth employed merely in some secondary meaning, as for example, in the case of the "non-conscious" ideas of Herbart, or the "threshold of stimulation" of Fechner. In these instances, there is no danger that von Hartmann's unconscious is confused with these partial and remote indications of the term unconscious. The same may be said with regard to natural scientists who were von Hartmann's predecessors, for instance, Carus, Perty, Wundt, Helmholtz, Zöllner, Bastian, and others.[1] In the field of history, Freitag and Lazarus are mentioned by von Hartmann as the protagonists of the idea of the "unconscious national soul," whereas in the field of aesthetics, Carierre and Rötscher made considerable contributions to the notion of the unconscious.[2] Von Hartmann names a great number of prominent and less prominent men in history as his forerunners in regard to the central concept and principle of his philosophy.

Curiously enough, he omits to mention one who advanced in his philosophy a notion that bears a deceivingly close resemblance to his unconscious, Ralph Cudworth, one of the best known philosophers of seventeenth-century England.

In his *True Intellectual System of the Universe* the English thinker advances a principle which could easily take the place of von Hartmann's unconscious, but with the all important difference that Cudworth has never made his "plastic nature" the final and ultimate unreason of all existence.[3] Cudworth was also preoccupied by the task of unifying science, philosophy, and religion, and the concept and principle of "plastic nature" seemed for him to fulfill the requirements of this

---

[1] Prof. Oskar Schmidt in his brief (86 pp.) criticism, *Die naturwissenschaftlichen Grundlagen der "Philosophie des Unbewussten"* (Leipzig: Brockmans, 1877) reproaches von Hartmann for making Carus' work *Psyche und Physis* his main source in regard to the biologico-psychic part of the *Philosophy of the Unconscious*. In Schmidt's opinion "the physiology and psychology of Carus are absolutely incompatible with that of a Dubois-Reymond, Virchov, Goltz and Wundt, who accepts these authorities cannot have anything to do with Carus." Von Hartmann emphatically denied that Carus was an authority for him, or that he followed anyone else, for that matter, and calls the whole polemics of Schmidt a "nonsensical and insipid bungling, a sad *testimonium paupertatis*, unworthy of being even noticed." *Philosophie des Unbewussten* (Leipzig: Hermann Haacke, 1890), vol. III, pp. 495, 516. Father Victor White in his work *God and the Unconscious* (Chicago: H. Regnery Co., 1953), p. 31, seems to place Carus' and von Hartmann's unconscious in the same category, thus making the latter indirectly dependent upon the former, whereas they are worlds apart. Von Hartmann left it up to the judgment of the reader to decide it for himself how much he actually borrowed from Carus; cf. *Philosophy of the Unconscious*, vol. I, p. 38. In my opinion Carus' unconscious is much more akin to the plastic nature of Cudworth than to the unconscious of von Hartmann.

[2] *Philosophy of the Unconscious*, vol. I, p. 42.

[3] *The True Intellectual System of the Universe*, indexed by J. Harrison (London: R. Royston, 1845), 3 vols.

endeavor.[1] Such a plastic nature would avoid the dangers of atheism, on the one hand, and the necessity of a continued creation and divine interference, on the other. In Cudworth's opinion, without such a plastic nature, things must either happen with sheer fortuitousness or "God himself doth all immediately, and, as it were, with his own hands, form the body of every gnat and fly."[2] He assumed, therefore, a plastic nature, alogical and without consciousness, but promoting the final good and ultimate end of all created existence. The description of this plastic nature closely resembles von Hartmann's phraseology. It "doth never consult nor deliberate"; it "goes on in one, constant, unrepenting tenor from generation"; it "acts artificially and for the sake of ends," but itself "understands not the ends which it acts for"; it "resembles habits, which do in like manner gradually evolve themselves in long train or series of regular and artificial notions, readily prompting the doing of them without comprehending that art and reason by which they are directed"; it corresponds to those "natural instincts that are in animals, which, without knowledge, direct them to act regularly, in order, both to their own good and the good of the universe... Wherefore the plastic nature, acting neither by knowledge nor by animal fancy, neither electively nor hormetically,[3] must be concluded to act fatally, magically, and sympathetically."[4]

For Cudworth this plastic nature is not independently self-subsistent, but it is conceived as the subordinate instrument of a higher power.

Perfect knowledge and understanding without consciousness is nonsense and impossibility. If there be φύσις there must be νοῦς; if there be a plastic nature, that acts regularly and artificially in order to ends, and according to the best wisdom, though itself not comprehending the reason of it, not being clearly conscious of what it doth then there must of necessity be a perfect mind or deity, upon which it depends. Wherefore Aristotle does like a philosopher in joining φύσις καὶ νοῦς, a nature and mind both together; but these atheists do very absurdly and unphilosophically that would make a senseless and unconscious plastic nature, and therefore without mind or intellect, to be the first original of all things.[5]

It seems that Cudworth reveals the true meaning of von Hartmann's unconscious even before it appears in philosophy.

It is with mixed feelings that we undertake the criticism of von Hart-

---

[1] *Ibid.*, I, chap. 3, no. 2, p. 218, ftn. 37.
[2] *Ibid.*, I, chap. 3, no. 3, p. 220.
[3] Horme (ὁρμή-impulse). Psychologically it is employed to denote the vital energy as an urge to purposive activity. Its present usage, therefore, means acting with an intrinsically purposive activity, teleologically.
[4] Cudworth, *op. cit.*, I, chap. 3, no. 18, p. 249.
[5] *Ibid.*, I, chap. 3, no. 21, p. 255.

mann's basic philosophical principle. The reason is that it is impossible to say anything in its favor on the basis of a rationally founded philosophical outlook. The difficulty of evaluation still increases if we reflect that the unconscious represents for von Hartmann the sum-total of a life-time dedicated to philosophical studies. It can be stated without reservations that it would be very difficult to find a philosopher who worked with more earnest self-dedication to find less at the end of his endeavors than von Hartmann. What is the unconscious? [1] What does the unconscious explain? What is the difference between giving the unconscious as an ultimate explanation and saying that we do not know whence the phenomena of the world at large have come. The unconscious as explanation explains nothing.

Once more, we cannot pursue the unconscious in all its aspects and ramifications as the metaphysical noumenon of all phenomena in von Hartmann's philosophical system. We propose rather to examine here only one of its attributes thoroughly, the attribute of omniscience. In doing so, our intention is to show that once this attribute is reasonably predicated of the unconscious, it either destroys the very nature of the unconscious, or it must necessarily deny the foundation of all being and intelligibility.

As a beginning of this analysis, we propose to follow a dialogue between Socrates and his disciple Protarchos as recorded by Plato in his *Philebus*.[2] When instructing his pupil concerning the ruler and orderer of the universe, Socrates tells him that it was the common opinion of all the sages of the past "that intellect is the king of heaven and earth" νοῦς ἔστι βασιλεὺς τοῦ οὐρανοῦ τε καὶ γῆς. Examining further this opinion, Socrates asks his pupil: "Or should we say, Protarchos, that this universe is ruled by some irrational, alogical temerarious and fortuitous power: ... τὴν τοῦ ἀλόγου καὶ εἰκῆ δύναμιν καὶ τὸ ὅπῃ ἐτύχεν, or contrary-wise, just as our forefathers thought, it is governed by the order of some intellect and admirable wisdom?" ... νοῦν καὶ φρόνησίς τινα θαυμαστὴν συντάττουσαν διακυβερνᾶν. The conviction of the master was also expressed by the answer of the pupil, when Protarchos said that he must acknowledge the governance of all these by

---

[1] The term "unconscious" is used here in its revised meaning as "absolute spirit," wherein at least an illusion of substantiality is included. As we have already noted, in its original adjective form it was lacking even the possibility of the perfection of *esse in se*, and, since, being the absolute ultimate principle, it could not have had an *esse in alio*, it destroyed the very metaphysical basis of its *posse esse*.

[2] Renatus Arnou, *Textus et Documenta*, Series Philosophica, No. 4 (Rome: Gregorian University, 1949), p. 20.

intellect, ... τὸ δὲ νοῦν πάντα διακοσμεῖν, "the face of the earth, the sun and the moon, all the other stars and the entire universe."[1]

The same line of thought is taken over by St. Thomas and expounded in a more profound manner.[2] In five different ways he passes from the empirical, potency-mixed existence of things of nature, to the potency-less existence of the uncreated creator, the omniscient, all-intelligent ruler of the universe. He has created everything through his infinite wisdom with the intention of an end, consequently, all that happens, has happened or will happen, happens for the sake of an intended end, aim, purpose. Metaphysically, i.e., in regard to the conscious purposive-ness of the first being, each occurrence and happening, each transition from potency to act, each becoming, insofar as it is operation, tendency or striving, really happens for the sake of a consciously intended end. This first cause and ultimate agent is all reason and absolute wisdom.

There are other data of our experiences, potency-mixed perfections of existence, which could have been employed to establish the existence of an all-wise absolute cause. There are some other, more or less exact and coercive ways to lead us to the existence of God which, however, St. Thomas has not exposed and treated systematically or at least not explicitly. Such are the notion of spirituality, the fact of self-consciousness, thinking, willing, the ability of reflection in man, the immutability of the logical, moral, and aesthetic principles, the desire for existence, unity, and happiness in all creatures according to their own manner of existence, the perfection of living and personal beings; these all could be "ways" for the proof of the existence of God. They all find in God's essence their absolutely necessary, actual, most perfect reality, and fulfillment. Why does St. Thomas treat the divine wisdom with a certain preference? The answer is simple, for through the analogy of human wisdom, which is inherent in human operations, he can ascend to the absolute necessity of subsistent wisdom in the ultimate cause of all purposive operations. Upon this subsistent wisdom in the act of creation is based the universality of the principle of finality, and upon this, the universality of the principle of order, wherefrom the entire philosophical system of St. Thomas is organically developed as a mighty oak from an acorn.

---

[1] *Ibid.*, p. 20.

[2] The following passages synopsize St. Thomas' proofs for the existence of God, particularly the one called the fifth way, or the argument taken from finality and order as observable in the universe. The main source of reference is *Summa Theologica*, I, qu. 2, a. 3. Related passages: *S. Th.* I, qu. 24, a. 2; I. II. qu. 1, a. 2. *Summa Contra Gent.* lib. I, cap. 44–45; li.b III, cap. 2.

The principle of finality asserts two things: first, all operations of God owe their existence to a divine purposive action; wherefrom follows the second, that all created existences, without any exception, always operate with a view of the end. Von Hartmann would readily agree with the second assertion. Thus, the question may be put in the following way: What is the manner of purposive operation of an irrational creature? Von Hartmann once more would agree that the irrational creature does not manifest in its operation its own, i.e., understood and elicited ends, but the end of a higher principle operative in its nature.

But the expressions "operation" and "action" in metaphysical usage mean much more than a metaphor according to human analogy. They reveal the essential property of the created being: purposive-being, purposively being. The efficacy of final causality in the order of reality works just as actually and really as that of the efficient causality. There is, however, one important difference. While the principle of efficient causality has its ontological validity before its reference to the first cause, the principle of finality receives its real ontological value only in the light of the existence of a rational, intelligent first being. We can speak of finality, purposiveness, purposively executed operations in a philosophical meaning and sense only if there is a real goal, a genuine purposiveness of being, which is really and actually an end, i.e., which is set knowingly by an operative, intelligent, conscious being. Because of the given empirical facts, and by force of the principle of sufficient reason, we must conclude that finality permeates with essential necessity each and every creature exactly as far as this created being is real, as it actually participates in the perfection of its creative cause.

Were it different, were there, *per absurdum*, any created thing which is not actualised through this process of actual-becoming, which would, therefore, exist and operate without being aware of it, subjectively or objectively, then, drawing these consequences to their final conclusions, either divine finality has been denied in its efficiency toward that creature, or God has created without his essence, without his wisdom, and consequently without finality. Both are, however, ontologically contradictory, and therefore impossible. God cannot fail his creatures; moreover, he cannot be active without his essence. Furthermore, God could never will that a creature act for the sake of another end than himself. Otherwise he would cease to be the subsistent end, to be the highest value in the order of existence: the absolute Good. The ultimate rational explanation, therefore, of finality cannot be anything but the absolute intelligent, consciously purposive being, God.

Von Hartmann pays an immense and disproportionately high price for the appeasement of the materialistic physiological scientists of his time. On the one hand, he denied himself any possible rational explanation of the universe and its phenomena; and on the other, he banished himself from the circles of genuine scientists as well. His unconscious was described with the most unflattering epithets by the great majority of those scientists whose approval he sought so eagerly. Lange [1] goes so far as to compare it with the "devil-devil" of the Australian aborigines. "The Australian savage ... and the philosopher of the unconscious halt where their power of natural explanation ceases, and attribute all the rest to a new principle, by which a single word very satisfactorily explains everything."[2]

We repeat the same objection for its metaphysical value as well. At the end of our investigation we must confess that we do not belong to those "few who are able to reproduce mystically in themselves the underlying suppositions," as von Hartmann requires, and, as a consequence, the unconscious remains without any probative force for us whatsoever. One thing has become perfectly clear and obvious in the course of this investigation of the unconscious: whether it is sub-rational or meta-rational, it is not rational. Whatever would be von Hartmann's final choice of the alternatives neither has any place in philosophy, in the pursuit of wisdom.

Von Hartmann is truly a child of his time. It is no wonder, therefore, that in the turbulent period of the middle and late nineteenth century, when in the struggle concerning the supremacy of sciences, each and every scientific advancement and discovery was intended to be the final and absolute word concerning the truth, von Hartmann also sought to do his utmost. The last, and we may add, most daring and venturesome "storming of heaven" which came out from Germany as a result of that period was von Hartmann's theory of the unconscious. By a bold *coup de grâce* it intended to conquer the entire universe, unaware of the fact that in doing so, it pronounced its own death-sentence. Von Hartmann's life was spent in an era which was about to witness a climactic scene in the intellectual bankruptcy of godless

---

[1] *The History of Materialism*, trans. by E. Ch. Thomas (New York: The Humanities Press, 1950), 3rd ed., 3 vols. "The aborigines of Australia refer everything which they cannot explain to the devil-devil, manifestly only a name, derived from the English devil, for a deity of whom they have not preserved any distinct conception." (Schmidt, Doctrine of Descent and Darwinism). Devil-devil is to the Australian black probably omniscient, omnipotent, and so on, without therefore being a person; exactly like the "unconscious." Footnote, vol. 2, ch. 4, p. 72.

[2] *Ibid.*, p. 72.

reason. After Kant, Schelling, Fichte, Hegel, and Schopenhauer something strikingly extraordinary and unheard of had to emerge if it hoped to excite a public for which phantastic philosophical systems became commonplace. Logically it was inevitable that after the metaphysical ultimate of Schopenhauer's *Wille zum Leben*, Bahnsen's *Wille zum Tode*, philosophical irrationalism would find its final culmination in von Hartmann's *Das Unbewusste*.

CHAPTER VI

PESSIMISM AND AXIOLOGY

Pessimisme: C'est une sorte de maladie intellectuelle, mais une maladie privilé-
giée, concentrée jusqu'à ce jour dans les sphères de la haute culture, dont elle
paraît être une sorte de raffinement malsain et d'élégante corruption.

Caro [1]

The problem and mystery of evil takes us to the very heart of von Hartmann's philosophy. Only in the light of his attitude concerning the
presence of evil in the universe can his views and evaluation of all the
other problems of life and existence, and his proposed solution of them
be fully understood.

The study of the problem at this point is not accidental. The preceding analysis of von Hartmann's philosophy emphasized the fact
that all phenomena of life are interpreted in the exclusive light of the
unconscious. This interpretation cannot be understood unless we realize
that his purpose is to conclude to a preconceived aim, namely, a negative evaluation of existence. Similarly, the remaining part of this work
could not be clearly comprehended without an awareness of von Hartmann's conviction that the basic aspects of man's ethical and religious
life can be explained only by a negative judgment concerning the value
of life.

For von Hartmann the problem of evil is the metaphysical problem.
In order to justify his *a priori* postulate, according to which the victorious presence of evil in the universe is incompatible with the existence of an all-good and intelligent creator, he devises for his practically accepted and professed pessimism the metaphysical substructure of
the unconscious.[2] The allegedly inductive acquisition and deductive

---

[1] E. Caro, *Le Pessimisme au XIXe Siècle* (Paris: Hachette et Cie, 1880), 2nd ed., preface,
p. III.

[2] The origin of the term "pessimism" is obscure and it is difficult to pinpoint its actual
appearance in philosophical literature. The most probable explanation is that it came into
existence and usage as antonym of the term "optimism." Its earliest historically established

application of the notion of unconscious serve merely as a means to find an acceptable solution for the presence of evil in the world. For von Hartmann the study of the problem of evil is the culminating point of his philosophy. The summary evaluation of the problem will conjoin the phenomenal world with the noumenon, and in this total, transcendental resolution of evil his philosophical system is brought to a synthetic unity in the monism of the unconscious absolute spirit.

If essence is spirit, then nature, or the objective-real sphere is also a product of the spirit, obviously not of the conscious, individually limited, but of the unconscious absolute spirit. Then the process leads from the unconscious spirit through nature to conscious spirit as its next aim, and from here back to the unconscious absolute spirit.[1]

The commencement of this process is bizarre in von Hartmann's metaphysics and the return is complex. But ultimately it is the empirical or actual observation and evaluation of the process of return which necessitates his pessimistic explanation of all existence. It is logical therefore to study first his pessimistic evaluation of phenomenal existence, and then to follow him as he constructs a metaphysics to justify his empirical findings.

In one of his works dealing with the history and nature of pessimism, von Hartmann distinguishes between philosophical and non-philosophical pessimism.[2] Of the second he recognizes three kinds: first, *Entrüstungspessimismus*, wrathful or despondent pessimism, which manifests itself in outbursts of indignation against the hardships of life that make men discontented with their lot and blinds them to the rational aspects of life. The second is *quietistischer Pessimismus*, quietistic pessi-

use occurs in 1776 in the writings of George Ch. Lichtenberg, who is quoted by Ludwig Marcuse as referring to different philosophers interpreting philosophy "one with his optimism, the other with his pessimism." Cf. Ludwig Marcuse, *Pessimismus* (Hamburg: Rowohlt, 1953), p. 13. Soon afterwards it appears in different adaptations and in various countries. Jacques Mallet du Pan uses it in 1793, in 1794 it shows up repeatedly in the letters of Samuel Taylor Coleridge and also in the dramatic works of Friedrich M. von Klinger about 1801. Kant never uses the expression. In the first edition of Schopenhauer's *The World as Will and Idea*, published in 1819, "pessimism" can not be found at all. None of his critics apply the term to the work either. The Académie Française approved the literary right to existence of "pessimiste" in 1835, and in 1878 "pessimisme" was added, 116 years after approval of "optimisme." In 1844, in the second edition of *The World as Will and Idea*, "pessimism" is used by Schopenhauer at the first time, but only three times in the entire work.

[1] *System*, vol. IV, p. 79.

[2] *Zur Geschichte und Begründung des Pessimismus* (Berlin: Carl Dunker, 1880), pp. 1–2. Further references concerning von Hartmann's pessimism are his: *System*, vol. IV, and sections A and B of vol. V. *Philosophy of the Unconscious*, vol. 3. chap. XIII and XIV. *Philosophische Fragen der Gegenwart* (Leipzig: W. Friedrich, 1885). The following articles in the *Zeitschrift für Philosophie und Philosophische Kritik*, "Das Kompensations-Äquivalent von Lust und Böse," vol. 90, pp. 50–63, 1886. "Der Weltbegriff und der Lustwert," vol. 106, pp. 20 ff. 1895.

mism. This second sort of pessimism is worse than the other, for it destroys the root of activity, i.e., faith in the ability of mankind for progress and improvement. Such an outlook on life robs man of the satisfaction that results from his actions and endeavors, thereby annihilating the hope of a progressive evolution, which is the necessary condition for the deliverance of the absolute from its torment. The third kind, *Miserabilismus*, or miserabilism, is the most dangerous of all, for it combines in itself the failures and defects of the other two kinds. It is wrathful pessimism in so far as it is pure *Situations-Schmerz*, or pain resulting from avoidable subjective or objective conditions; it is quietistic pessimism in so far as it believes in the impossibility of improving the individual's lot as well as that of mankind's.[1]

It is a common belief even in academic circles that von Hartmann's doctrine is a mere imitation or a slightly modified revision of the pessimism of Schopenhauer. In so far as von Hartmann is concerned nothing can be further from the truth. First, von Hartmann emphatically denies that there is any significant resemblance between his pessimistic theory and that of Schopenhauer. Secondly, in his opinion, Schopenhauer's is not a philosophical pessimism at all.[2] It lacks the sober objectivity, order, and clarity that are indispensable conditions of any philosophical theory. Instead it is a display of subjective feelings, emotions, and moods, and a pathetic extreme of "abnormal personal dispositions," an "unscientific subjective effusion of the heart."[3] Although in principle it is raised to the level of a scientific conviction and assumed as an integral part of Schopenhauer's philosophical system, in its origin and foundation it cannot deny its psychological ancestry from individual moods and temperament-disposition. Taken in its totality, it is a transitory form of pessimism from poetic *Weltschmerz* to scientific pessimism. Von Hartmann holds that feeling and phantasy play a much more important part in Schopenhauer's philosophy than reason and logic. Schopenhauer's lack of genuine scientific objectivity becomes most obvious in his pessimism and in those parts of his metaphysics which are directly connected with his pessimism. Although von Hartmann agrees that a unique combination of subjective fancy and objective observations lends to Schopenhauer's works a special charm, and project the image

---

[1] *Zur Geschichte und Begründung des Pessimismus*, pp. 86–87.
[2] While von Hartmann is not consistent in defining Schopenhauer's pessimism, whether as wrathful pessimism, as on page 24 of *Zur Geschichte...*, or quietistic pessimism, as on page 87, he is adamant in calling his pessimism "diametrically opposed" to Schopenhauer's. Cf. *ibid.*, p. 87.
[3] *Ibid.*, p. 68.

of a forceful and original literary personality, he believes at the same time that they also impair the true value of his scientific investigations. Von Hartmann finds it deplorable and unpardonable to create arguments for the truth of philosophical pessimism out of purely personal, wrathful pessimism and to insert such an argument as an essential constituent of a philosophical pessimism in order to weld together the two heterogeneous elements. Von Hartmann does not hesitate to single out this fact as the most vulnerable point of Schopenhauer's pessimism.[1] The common but mistaken belief that pessimism is a mixture of personal temperament-disposition supported by objective observations is due mainly to Schopenhauer's writings, and it is characteristic of his pessimism alone. But, as we have seen, von Hartmann is most intent to make it clear that Schopenhauer's pessimism is a mere transitory phase in the development of the history of pessimism from an unphilosophical form to the philosophical.

True philosophical pessimism, von Hartmann holds, begins with Kant. This opinion is merely a restatement and application of his axiom: "Philosophy ends and begins with Kant."[2] Consequently, philosophical pessimism must also begin with Kant, and Kant is the first philosopher who justly deserves the title of the "father of pessimism."[3]

Von Hartmann spares neither time nor effort to prove his point. As an introduction to Kant's position concerning the problem of life's worth, he refers to Kant's description of the four possible views of life.[4] The first of these looks at life as a tavern where patrons quickly change and no one is a permanent guest. The second treats life as a prison or a sort of penal institution for the correction and purification of fallen spirits. According to the third view, life is a madhouse or lunatic asylum, where each inmate not only destroys his own happiness and works against his own good, but also finds his greatest pleasure in afflicting his fellows with all imaginable pain and suffering. Lastly, life is a cesspool, where all rubbish and rejects, thrown out from other worlds, are collected and abandoned to bear their sorry lot.[5]

If we look for Kant's scientific treatment of the value of life, we find that he answers it first positively or in an optimistic sense. This is the period in Kant's life when he was still under the influence of the Leib-

---

[1] *Ibid.*, p. 28.
[2] *Gesammelte Studien und Aufsätze* (Berlin: Carl Dunker, 1876), Part A, p. 14.
[3] *Op. cit.*, p. 19.
[4] *Ibid.*, p. 20.
[5] *Immanuel Kants Sämmtliche Werke*, ed. by Rosenkranz and Schubert (Leipzig: Baumann, 1838–1842), vol. VII, p. 416.

nitz-Wolffian philosophy. The witness to his "optimistic slumber" of the time, if we may paraphrase his own time-worn expression, and positive evaluation of existence is his *Versuch einer Betrachtung über den Optimismus*, published in 1759.[1] Soon afterwards there is a gradual change of heart in Kant, which steers him from complacent optimism towards philosophical pessimism. His *Versuch den Begriff der negativen Grössen in die Weltweisheit Einzuführen*, published only four years after the defense of a positive value-judgement on life's worth, unmistakably bears the marks of a mind at odds with the world around it.[2] Although in it he still reproaches Maupertuis for arriving at negative results in his search for world-wisdom and on the value of human existence,[3] but, this is not, as von Hartmann points out, "from optimistic prejudice any more but rather because Kant deemed the solution of the problem impossible on technical grounds."[4] Kant agrees with Maupertuis that pleasure and pain are related to one another as $+ a$ and $- a$, thus being capable of some exoteric comparison, but he denies Maupertuis' postulate according to which they are commensurable. Not only are pain and pleasure heterogeneous but even the different kinds of pleasure are irreducible to one common denominator. This opinion notwithstanding, Kant arrives at the conclusion that the balance of good and evil is zero, in other words, that in life pain and pleasure are equal in quantity. But this opinion does not remain the Kantian position for long. In his *Beobachtungen über das Gefühl des Schönen und Erhabenen* Kant agrees with Maupertuis' theory and accepts his axiom that life's worth measured positively or in terms of happiness is intrinsically false.[5] Life's balance of good and evil is not only zero but irrefutably negative. This gradual revision of Kant's opinion concerning life's worth, this successive transition from a positive to a negative value-judgment regarding the amount of good and evil in existence, is the main reason why von Hartmann calls Kant the "father of pessimism."[6]

There is a slight inaccuracy in this title and von Hartmann is fully aware of it. Kant never calls himself a pessimist, and the term can nowhere be found in his works. Although this is a matter of concern

---

[1] *Versuch einer Betrachtung über den Optimismus* (Königsberg: Hartung, 1759).

[2] *Versuch den Begriff der Negativen Grössen in die Weltweisheit Einzuführen* (Königsberg: Hartung, 1763).

[3] *Oeuvres* (Lyon: Bruiset, 1756), 3 vols. Reference is made to vol. I, *Essai de Philosophie Morale*, pp. 193–252.

[4] *Op. cit.*, p. 21.

[5] *Beobachtungen über das Gefühl des Schönen und Erhabenen.* (Königsberg: Hartung, 1765).

[6] *Op. cit.*, p. 19. For further references on Kant's pessimism cf. *Immanuel Kants Sämmtliche Werke*, vol. IV, p. 332; vol. VII, pp. 128–267, 360–361, 382; vol. XI, pp. 240–339.

for von Hartmann, he minimizes its importance and resolves and dismisses the problem with the following words:

... the notion and content which is denoted by this word today is in Kant's writings in its readiness, and his treatment of different philosophers, who professed a pessimistic *Weltanschauung*, shows that the question concerning the worth of life was quite well known to him and often discussed.[1] .... (Even if in his works) a coherent treatment of the subject is missing, and thus, in spite of a definite pessimistic conviction he does not give it as a pillar of his own philosophy.[2]

As we shall see presently, this "definite pessimistic conviction" of Kant will not be so apodictically maintained throughout von Hartmann's analysis of Kant's pessimism, and von Hartmann realizes the parting of the ways between his and Kant's total evaluation of existence at the most decisive and crucial point of the theory. Von Hartmann's zeal may have succeeded in making Kant a pessimist in the phenomenal order of things, but any attempt to extend this negative evaluation of existence beyond the limits of the world of phenomena is a futile task and cannot but result in a dismal failure.

Thus von Hartmann does his utmost to make a case for philosophical pessimism from Kant's views of the things men generally consider to be the sources of happiness in this life. Kant admittedly has harsh criticism for the value of happiness men expect from the pleasurable goods of life and declares that the expectation itself is based on an optimistic self-deception.[3] All our attachments to temporal things rest upon illusions. It is a sort of slavery that is not based on force, rather on the fact that we depend too much on the fleeting opinion and estimation of other men. But it is foolish to expect true happiness from these things, for they are today and cease to be tomorrow.[4] Likewise, it is deceptive to expect satisfaction from leisure, from the *"dolce far niente,"* envied by so many, because leisure without work can never refresh and satisfy, can only bore and stupefy.[5] Nor can the possession of wealth and riches provide lasting enjoyment since actual possession deprives us from the excitement of striving after something more valuable. This holds true for the possession of immaterial objects as well, like the love of another person, for love is unlimited only in the intellect and not in the senses.[6] Kant has a somber and disillusioning

---

1 *Ibid.*, p. 20.
2 *Ibid.*, p. 68.
3 *Ibid.*, p. 37. Cf. Kant, *op. cit.*, vol. VII, p. 128.
4 *Ibid.*, p. 37. Cf. *op. cit.*, vol. XI, p. 244.
5 *Ibid.*, p. 37. Cf. *op. cit.* vol. XI, pp. 256–257.
6 *Ibid.*, p. 37. Cf. *op. cit.*, vol. XI, pp. 337–338.

warning also for those who would look to the cultivation of sciences in the hope of gaining happiness. Science, in Kant's opinion, is not a matter of necessity but a comfort of life, and as such it belongs in an eudemonological sense to over-indulgence. Furthermore, the pleasure we claim to have found in the pursuance of sciences can well be feigned for others, or even for ourselves. The advantage of science lies partly in the restraint of evil which science itself brought about, partly in the promotion of morality by teaching man to fulfill his obligation assigned to him by creation. From an eudemonological standpoint whatever science can offer to man is negative and what is positive in it does not further happiness but morality.[1]

The careful analysis of the above objects as possible sources of personal happiness yields only negative results. It is illusory to expect that anything could gratify our egoistical hopes for individual happiness. Yet, our drive and desire for happiness are not easily shattered. If the search for individual happiness proves to be in vain and futile, toiling for the improvement of the race, promoting the well-being of future generations may be more rewarding. This is the next step von Hartmann intends to extricate from Kant's thoughts in his attempt to make him the first theoretician of philosophical pessimism.

The task is not an easy one, for Kant accepts divine providence as the original designer of the universe and its ruling power. His unshakable conviction in the teleological view of the world necessitates the existence of such a power. Without it, teleology is simply unthinkable and impossible for him.[2] This teleological view extends to the sphere of history as well as to that of nature. Creative providence has endowed every creature with certain natural dispositions which serve the purpose of the complete development of the individual in the vegetative and animal kingdoms. In the case of man these natural dispositions serve not only for the enfolding of individual capacities, but also for the potencies of the race as such. This is for Kant the guiding *a priori* principle which holds him fast in his faith in the teleological development of the universe. To further this development and to cooperate for the evolution of the race is the duty and obligation of each individual, which will become obvious to them in their consciousness. In the psychological process of becoming conscious of this obligation, another fact will simultaneously be realized, namely, that every fulfillment of obli-

---

[1] *Ibid.*, p. 37. Cf. *op. cit.*, vol. XI, p. 339.
[2] *Ibid.*, p. 29. Cf. *op. cit.*, vol. VII, pp. 257–258.

gation is also "a contributing action for the betterment of the world."[1]

At this juncture Kant links evolution with morality. For there is a reciprocal interaction between the actual promotion of the objective aims of the human race and the moral development of the individual. By adding his toils to the common endeavors of all men, the individual not only contributes to the realization of the objective end of the race, but also promotes his own moral perfection. Kant meanwhile is aware of the fact that if the enfolding of this conscious and purposive evolution were entrusted to man alone, there would be little hope of ever attaining the end, but providence chose its means so that all things serve its purpose, and man, willy-nilly, consciously or unconsciously, must cooperate with it.[2] In this regard all human propensities, even the rudest and most antisocial, have their teleological values, including the evils of war itself.[3]

Von Hartmann draws the conclusion from these premises that Kant clearly shows that there is an opposition between evolution and happiness, and having chosen the teleological view of the world, happiness cannot be considered the end of evolution, nor is evolution a vehicle for the realization of the well-being of humanity. It is rather the sublimation of its morality and culture, the gradual enfolding of its natural potencies. These considerations prompt von Hartmann to call Kant's evolutionism "teleological" and not "eudemonological." The task of humanity is not a passive life of pleasure, but a determined struggle against the obstacles of the teleological development. Not happiness but perfection, a fulfilled enfolding of its disposition, is humanity's final aim and purpose. In continuing his arbitrary exoteric exegesis of Kant, von Hartmann declares that no matter how strong or optimistic such a faith may be in achieving its aim, it cannot be called anything but pessimistic in view of the immensity of the hardships in this struggle. Kant's standpoint, von Hartmann concludes, is an evolutionistic optimism which does not exclude but rather subsumes eudemonological pessimism. The necessity of their reciprocal relation is explained by the fact that eudemonological pessimism without evolutionistic optimism would represent such a bleak and dreadful view of life that no man would be able to face it. Without faith in a secretly working wisdom in the universe men would be in constant fear that the human race, due to its natural proclivities, would finally end up in an inferno of evil and suffer-

---

[1] *Ibid.*, p. 31. Cf. *op. cit.*, vol. X, p. 209.
[2] *Ibid.*, p. 33. Cf. *op. cit.*, vol. VII, p. 263.
[3] *Ibid.*, *loc. cit.* Cf. *op. cit.*, vol. VIII, pp. 261–262; 265; 327 and passim.

ing. Actually faith in providence supports the hope that mankind in the present critical phase of its evolution is undergoing the hardest period of the evil awaiting it. Only the conviction refrains us from total despair, that just as the individual is allowed a certain minimum of well-being in order to fulfill its positive aim in life, the same way humanity may also be allowed a certain minimum of welfare to help it in fulfilling its goal. Von Hartmann is quick to add that from this by no means follows that by admitting a minimum well-being in the life of the individual and in the history of the race Kant meant to alter the sum-total of the algebraic formula of happiness. In other words, the theory of evolutionistic optimism does not require that the balance of happiness be positive, or even that it strike an equilibrium between good and evil. The balance remains overwhelmingly on the side of eudemonological pessimism which merely refrains evolutionistic optimism from turning into total desperation on the one hand, or passive quietism on the other. Thus, in the final evaluation eudemonological pessimism safeguards evolutionistic optimism from pathological degenerations and guarantees its conceptual purity together with its practical utility.[1]

It is an easy temptation, and it is, perhaps, possible for a confirmed pessimist, like von Hartmann, to take Kant's words describing the value of life in the order of phenomena in a pessimistic sense, but to expand it any further and make Kant a pessimist, in von Hartmann's sense of the term, would be to falsify completely Kant's position regarding the presence of evil in our lives. Kant may have lamented the hardships of existence and may have ridiculed the uncritical views of eudemonological optimists, but for him earthly existence is not worthless. His evaluation of life is not that it is an irrational pining and self-tormenting of the blind will, as for Schopenhauer, nor is it the desperate fury and mad carnival of men on their way to the unconscious, as for von Hartmann. Regardless how much von Hartmann wishes to ignore the fact, ultimately he is bound to acknowledge that "there is an ample room in Kant's philosophy to overcome phenomenal pessimism by his transcendental optimism."[2] No student of Kant can be oblivious to his metaphysical axiom that *the whole and perfect good* is that "toward which all finite rational creatures must drive according to their nature and which encompasses happiness together with the sense of reward."[3]

---

[1] *Ibid.*, p. 36.
[2] *Ibid.*, p. 51.
[3] *Ibid.*, p. 51. Kant, *op. cit.*, vol. VII, pp. 246–247.

Kant's thoughts are based on the consideration that since the antinomy between reality and happiness is insoluble in the phenomenal world, its solution can be expected only in the transcendental world of the noumenon. We must consequently assume the continuation of conscious existence of the finite rational individual in a life hereafter, as well as the existence of God for the sufficient rational explanation of this transcendental harmony. From this Kant also infers the necessity of an infinite duration of the soul, for only an infinite progress will allow the asymptotic approximation of a final rational being to the necessary end of perfect sanctity and beatitude.[1] This end of united reward and perfect happiness is the highest good as well as the absolute end of all creation, the rationality of which justifies not merely the choice of this world as the best of all possible worlds, but the existence of any world at all.[2] In this manner Kant explains the final victory of transcendental optimism over against all forms and aspects of phenomenal pessimism.

Von Hartmann follows up the twofold aspect of Kant's phenomenal pessimism with his first and third "stages of optimistic illusions" in his *Philosophy of the Unconscious*.[3] The "second stage" and a later work *Zur Geschichte und Begründung des Pessimismus* are compiled with the intent to disprove not only Kant's claim to the necessity of a transcendental optimism, but of any philosophical system that would justify evil in this life with a reference to an eternal, transcendental remuneration.[4]

In the first stage of illusion, von Hartmann takes up the problem of proving the negative value of life. The line of reasoning is a simple appeal to personal experience and historical events. The representative historical period of the vanity of eudemonistic expectation of happiness here on earth is the ancient Jewish-Greek-Roman world. He approaches the analysis of the possible objects of happiness of this first stage of illusion with the principle of Maupertuis and Kant, which declares that the amount of pain in this life far outweighs the amount of pleasure. Appeal to facts and individual psychic moments is intended merely to support this *a priori* statement. Thus, the goods of life, health, youth, freedom, are of no positive value; they are merely privations; the absence of poverty, sickness, old age, and slavery. Work, which hardly anyone can avoid in this life, is itself an evil. No one would work on his

---

[1] *Ibid., loc. cit.* Kant, *op. cit.*, vol. VIII, pp. 261–262.
[2] *Ibid., loc. cit.* Cf. *op. cit.*, vol. X, p. 6.
[3] Vol. III, pp. 12–79.
[4] Cf. footnote 4, p. 75.

own free will. There are also the deceptive pleasures of love, but can they compensate in any degree for the sufferings of childbirth, asks von Hartmann. All the glittering images of love are sheer illusions, and the sacrifices love demands are anything but equivalent to the ephemeral moments of self-deceptive bliss. An unbiased view must accept that love brings more suffering than pleasure to the individual. Its unavoidable paradox lies in the fact that one must love by the impulse of an unconscious instinct, and when experience discovers the illusion, the individual is already the victim of what von Hartmann calls the "moloch of love."

Compassion, friendship, marital happiness are similarly placed in the same category of evil. Sympathy is evil, reasons von Hartmann, for it always brings more pain than pleasure to the one who wants to share in the misfortune of others. Friendship is nothing else than the alleviation of the pain of a lonely life. "Domestic happiness" is but an empty phrase, since in most marriages there is so much "discord and aggravation, that when we look at it objectively and are capable of sifting the facts from appearances, we can hardly find one in a hundred that is to be envied."[1] Thus, the truth of the adage "separation is best for union" has its full force in married life.[2] Children cannot possibly bring happiness into the lives of their parents, since the care they demand far outweighs the joy they may occasion.

Ambition, in all its forms, is equally a delusion. What can other people's opinion possibly add to or detract from my well-being? Men also talk of the pleasures that ensue from the cultivation of the sciences and arts, but this is hardly the case. The sciences and arts are pursued for the most part from ambition and vanity, and seldom go beyond the "accomplishments" of pretentious amateurs, and if they do, it is at the price of hard perseverance and bitter sacrifice, in other words, through pain, toil, and disappointment. Similarly, it is vain to expect relief from the miseries of daily life in our sleep or dreams, they are simply the repetition of the troubles of the day. But the greatest folly of them all is to look for happiness in the possession of wealth, for it can do nothing more than to secure those pleasures of life which have already been discovered to be vanity. Hope, indeed, could be thought of as a harbinger of pleasure, but again, nine-tenths of all our hopes are doomed to disappointments, and the bitterness of unfullfilment is far greater than the sweetness of expectation. Thus, the only thing worth hoping for in

---

[1] *Op. cit.*, p. 46.
[2] *Ibid.*, p. 47.

this life is not the greatest possible happiness, but the least possible unhappiness, as was clearly seen by Aristotle.[1] The first stage of illusion concludes with the statement that pain not only preponderates in this world in general to a high degree, "but also in each individual, even in the one who finds himself in the most favorable circumstances."[2] The intellectual refinement and development of the individual not only does not alleviate, but, on the contrary, it intensifies the pain of existence. There is ample proof that individuals of lower and poorer social standing and of more primitive nations lead happier lives than those of wealthier classes and more civilized nations. In fact:

... the brutes are happier (i.e. less miserable) than man, because the excess of pain which an animal has to bear is less than that which a man has to suffer. Just think how comfortably an ox or a pig lives, almost as if it had learned from Aristotle to seek freedom from care and sorrow, instead of like man searching feverishly for happiness.[3]

The individual must make his the sober warning of the Preacher in the Old Testament, "All is vanity," illusory, worthless.[4]

After man has realized the deceptive nature of all egoistical hopes of individual happiness, his mind is susceptible to the thought of working for the betterment of this earthly existence for the sake of future generations. Von Hartmann develops this idea in his "third stage of illusion," which runs parallel with Kant's theory of evolutionistic optimism.[5] This stage sets its happiness in the future evolution of mankind. The individual no longer works for his own interest because he realizes the redeeming truth that the "ego is a mere phenomenon of a *being* which for all individuals is one and the same."[6] The individual has now acquired an attitude of self-denial and renunciation that will not manifest itself externally either by suicide or by egoistical mortification, but rather by active production, untiring action, and participation in the common economic and intellectual promotion of civilization. But if man has any hope in a future positive happiness as a result of the development of the race, von Hartmann stands ready to shatter it and call it as futile as all our previous hopes.

However great the progress of mankind, it will never get rid of, or even diminish the greatest of sufferings: sickness, age, dependence on the will and power of

---

[1] Von Hartmann's reference is made to *Eth. Nic.*, bk. VII, ch. 12.
[2] *Op. cit.*, p. 76.
[3] *Ibid., loc. cit.*
[4] *Ibid.*, p. 78.
[5] *Ibid.*, pp. 94–119.
[6] *Ibid.*, p. 98.

others, want and discontent. Regardless of how many new remedies are found against diseases they will always increase in a quicker pace, especially the tormenting slighter chronic ills, than medical science.[1]

Hunger and starvation will become commonplace with the increase of population. Discontent will grow in direct proportion with the civilization of nations. Immorality will not lessen, only the form of its criminal character will become changed. Crime can never be totally eliminated from the life of society, merely confined by the dikes of law and order. The course of science will also alter its direction in the future. While the basic character of scientific work was intensive in the past, it will be expansive in the centuries to come. There will be an ever diminishing number of men of genius and, as a result there will ensue a certain tendency toward respectable mediocrity. The arts will also grow less and less original, and they will end their purpose by being a mere opiate for ennui. Thus, the future promises only an ever increasing expansion of sheer superficiality in every field of human endeavor, a future which produces no longer excellence of any kind merely poor imitations of past greatness.

Were the ancient Greeks to come alive today they would declare *with complete truth* our works of art in all departments to be thoroughly *barbarous*. (It is enough to think of our literary productions and stage-plays, statues and exhibitions, the products of architecture and especially the maddening beat of music).[2]

In view of these facts where is the progress of the world? Who could point to any acceptable evidence of it? Which one of the above considerations could give us any hope for happiness? The very thought of happiness is futility, self-delusion and nightmarish folly. The future of the race is the same as that of the individual. The world is growing old, and we may hope that some day it will see how barren are all its past attempts and realize that it will never attain the balance-quotient between good and evil but always remain below it, pain being forever in excess. What remains there to be done? Nothing but to renounce the folly of striving after positive happiness, and to long for absolute painlessness, nothingness, the Nirvana. This must be the aim not only of the individual alone as before, but of the whole human race. There must be a cosmic-universal negation of will, and once this has been accomplished, there shall be no more volition, striving, and consequently suffering. Consciousness will hurl back actual volition into the unconscious absolute.

[1] *Ibid.*, p. 118.
[2] *Zur Geschichte und Begründung des Pessimismus*, p. 50.

The climax of von Hartmann's total, metaphysical pessimism is reached in his "second stage of illusion" which runs counter to Kant's transcendental optimism.[1] The goal von Hartmann aims at is shattering the individual's hope of attaining happiness in a life hereafter. This hope is represented historically by Christianity.

There is a contrast between Judaism and Christianity, according to von Hartmann, in that Judaism tended to find happiness in an earthly satisfaction, "that it may be well with thee, and thou mayest live long on the earth,"[2] while the religion of Christ regards this earth merely as "a preparation and trial for the life hereafter."[3] Its essence lies in looking forward with cheerful hope to the blessedness of a future eternal life. Von Hartmann believes that this expectation of happiness in a life beyond the grave is as great an illusion as the earlier expectations. Apart from the difficulties such a faith involves, like the subjection of the flesh and the doubts and fears which inevitably ensue regarding the possibility of the attainment of this happiness, it is based on principles the philosophy of the unconscious cannot grant. Singularity, in this philosophy, whether of the organic body or of the conscious-self is simply a phenomenon, an appearance vanishing with death, what remains is the all-one unconscious which produced the individual phenomenon. No monistic system, whether naturalism, pantheism, panpsychism, or panpneumatism, can allow individual immortality without the greatest inconsistency. Thus, von Hartmann's panpneumatism grants the endurance of the noumenal will alone, and even this only until the termination of the phenomenal world-process, because only this will is simple. This he intends to prove in the following manner: the stream of will-acts of the unconscious, which is directed upon a particular individual organism, cannot possibly have a longer conscious duration than the object onto which it is directed.

If the organism has entered into dissolution and the organic individual has lost its existence, if, in consequence, the consciousness has ceased that was bound to this organism and has stored up its ideal treasures, and possessed the determining ground of its individual character in the molecular arrangement of the cerebral molecules of the same, then the summary root of action of the unconscious, which afforded to this individual mind its metaphysical foundation, is without an object, and thereby becomes impossible as continued action. The power to will is not thereby altered, but this is no longer individual, but resides in the universal and unique unconscious essence.[4]

---

[1] *Op. cit.*, pp. 79–94.
[2] *Ibid.*, p. 80.
[3] *Ibid.*, *loc. cit.*
[4] *Ibid.*, p. 83.

Thus, von Hartmann warns, it is futile to try to wrap up the bitter but beneficial pill of pessimism in the future hope of immortality, as Christianity endeavors to do. The hope in a life hereafter has lost its comforting power as a result of critical attacks upon it. Humanity has become immune and indifferent to the prospect of eternal life in face of the present formidable evils of existence, which are thrust upon it with inevitable necessity.

In order to complete the argument against the expectation of happiness after this life von Hartmann attacks it also from the viewpoint of morality. The hope of a future felicity is a eudemonistic contamination of morality, von Hartmann maintains, therefore, it should be rejected. Thus, his final conclusion is that the effort to mitigate phenomenal pessimism with the future promise of transcendental optimism is not only impossible on metaphysical grounds but immoral as well.

Von Hartmann's final, comprehensive metaphysical foundation of pessimism is given in the fourth volume of his *System der Philosophie im Grundriss*.[1] It is intended to be a summary exposition of his metaphysical creed wherein the necessity of phenomenal as well as noumenal or transcendental pessimism is intended to be proved as the only logically tenable outlook on existence.[2] The immediate genesis of the problem begins with a reflective analysis of the most common phenomenon: motion, change, becoming.

Experience reports change everywhere. But what is change or becoming? Phenomenally, answers von Hartmann, it is the coming into being or cessation in existence of something qualitative or quantitative; metaphysically it is the transition of essence into activity.[3] As soon as we discover this, the mind is faced with a new problem: how can the eternal, the absolute and unchangeable unconscious essence change itself into a state which, as temporary und mutable, is the exact opposite of its metaphysical nature? Just as an eternal truth cannot of itself suddenly change into its opposite, so also, we would think, the eternal essence cannot of itself change into a temporal act, or pass from the eternal state of being-identical-with-itself into that of being-non-identical-with-itself. Yet this must be the case, since it is an actual occur-

---

[1] *System*, vol. IV, pp. 80–106.

[2] The importance and comprehensive value of this exposition is further emphasized by the frequent references to his other works, especially the *Kategorienlehre*, "Zeitschrift für Philosophie und Philosophische Kritik," vols. 99 and 108, *Kritische Grundlegungen des Transzendentalen Realismus, Religionsphilosophie*, vols. I, II, *Neukantianismus, Schopenhauerianismus und Hegelianismus, Gesammelte Studien und Aufsätze, Kants Erkenntnisstheorie und Metaphysik, Ethische Studien, Philosophie des Unbewussten*.

[3] *Op. cit.*, pp. 80–81.

rence. Moreover, this paradoxical position of the essence must be called contradictory or antilogical. The contradiction that underlies every single change must be sublimated into the primordial contradiction of every primordial change, and as such, it must be considered as the absolute alogical origin of all alogical in the process of becoming.[1]

The passing from rest into activity, of pure eternity into a combination with temporality, is called beginning. This beginning, this commencement of world-evolution is uncaused and without a motivating idea, for if it were preceded by a cause or motive then the process must have had been in existence prior to its beginning, which is absurd. Thus, the primordial beginning of the process is absolutely undetermined, it is the absolute original chance (*Urzufall*). This consideration forces the mind to assume that such a beginning could not have originated from the logical, consequently, it must have taken its origin from the alogical, and as such it is contradictory in nature. To state the case positively, for the explanation of the beginning of the world-process nothing else remains but the will or power alone. The will becomes primordial movement when its potency in rest sublimates itself to decisive willing. Movement or beginning at this stage is merely potency in the state of stimulation, a drive, urge, desire for action. On the other hand, it is activity not yet real or fulfilled, but activity before the actual moment of beginning. Von Hartmann calls it willing-willing (*Wollenwollen*), or empty willing.[2] This state of the will affects or shocks the logical instantaneously, *in statu nascente*, into the unfolding of the idea. In this moment the empty will immediately becomes willing with idea-content, or a twofold activity.

Thus, the logical cannot completely withdraw its participation in the actualization of the essence, for it stands in substantial unity with the will. The logical is drawn involuntarily (*willenlos*) into the process of actualization of the essence, involuntarily and not contrary to its willing, since it has no will for itself, consequently it does not possess any capacity to oppose its own participation in the process. The logical discovers this state of "being-posited" against itself, which occasions its participation in the process. Its contribution to the process of actualization is, therefore, not goodness, love, or any such anthropomorphic property, but will-less logical compulsion (*willenloser logischer Zwang*).

The primordial origin of the world-process must be looked for in the essential opposition between the logical essence and the state of activity forcefully im-

---

[1] *Ibid.*, p. 81; *Kategorienlehre*, pp. 326–327.
[2] *Ibid.*, p. 83.

posed upon it, by means of which a logical opposition will arise between the attributes.[1]

The effective origin of the world stems from a logical opposition,[2] from the conflict of the metaphysical alogical (will) and its counterpart, the logical (idea). This is the supreme axiom of von Hartmann's exposition of the phenomenon of becoming from the unchangeable unconscious essence.[3]

Since this occurrence is the result of chance, i.e., it is not logically planned or intended, it should not continue in existence but must be suppressed. In the instant of its solicitation for action the logical could not repress the will into its primordial rest or inertia, for, as we have seen, the logical does not possess any force or power. Thus, this repression and final annihilation of the process must be achieved through a lengthier course of the world evolution.

The first condition for the successful completion of this negative evolution is the self-division of the will, one part with a positive, the other with a negative content, in order ultimately to annihilate each other. This dichotomy of the will can occur only if there is a consciousness for which the idea or presentation of the "cessation of volition" (Nichtmehrwollens) becomes a content to pursue, in other words, the world-evolution logically necessitates the origin of consciousness. Only in consciousness can it be understood that the existence of the world and with it the will is to be suppressed. Until this state comes to pass, the idea must undertake many tasks and undergo many experiences. It must seek out all possibilities for the appeasement and pacification of the will, until the will realizes that its instinctive aims have all failed, and the only satisfactory aim is to be found in the gratifying peace of not-willing.

The world-process must be retrogressively finite. This is inferred from the impossibility of its contrary, i.e., from the notion of a completed infinity. Progressively, it must also be finite, otherwise it could not have an end, and consequently would be an aimless drive tending nowhere. The fact that the world has a goal and a final end in von Hart-

---

[1] Ibid., p. 84.

[2] How this opposition can be called "logical" is difficult to see, since the primary motor of the entire process is the alogical will. To be sure this explanation is only a later development in the philosophy of von Hartmann and it is adopted for two reasons: 1. to avoid Schopenhauer's insurmountable difficulties concerning the content-less operation of the will; 2. to restore the Hegelian principle, the "Idea" to its rightful metaphysical domain.

[3] In his earlier works von Hartmann assumes a certain eudemonistic drive in the absolute essence, with the intention of overcoming through it the absolute unhappiness in God as the result of the world-evolution. In his later works he postulates only a pure logical opposition in the absolute as the IVth volume of the System shows.

mann's system is merely one of his unsubstantiated assumptions; he could never prove it logically from his point of departure, i.e., from the alogical primordial chance.[1]

The progress in the world, therefore, has an end or purpose, but it is a negative one: the cessation of the process through the return of the essence from its contradictory state of activity to its proper and original state of rest. Since this will be achieved by the means of individual human consciousnesses, their end is also negative: to bring about as soon as possible the end of this alogical, irrational, painful, and worthless progress of the world. At this juncture von Hartmann's metaphysics and axiology meet in the negative evaluation of all conscious existence.

Thus, from the finality of the process not only its finitude becomes obvious but also the negativity of the end, which is confirmed by the logical deduction of the aim from the relation existing between the logical and the alogical in the unconscious absolute essence.[2]

To sum up von Hartmann's combined metaphysico-axiological position concerning the total value of all existence let us quote once more his own words:

Metaphysical pessimism stands in opposition to the empirical. The latter states that the eudemonistic balance of the world is -a, the former declares that the eudemonological balance in the absolute is -A. Thus, absolute pessimism can deduce the final conclusion that the eudemonological balance of existence in its totality (meaning the combined eudemonistic amount of the world and the absolute) is $-a -A = -(a + A)$. The truth of absolute pessimism is independent from the quantitative proportion between -a and -A; for even if -A were smaller than -a, $-(a + A)$ would, nevertheless, be greater than -a. In the hypothesis that A were equal to zero $(A = O)$, absolute pessimism would still remain correct, for the eudemonological total-balance of God and the world would equal -a, i.e., negative.[3]

This is von Hartmann's final judgment and according to it all existence is inescapably marked with the sign of doom. The irrationality of existence itself condemns everything irrevocably to suffering, pain, and unhappiness. There is no ray of hope in this all-embracing darkness, for not men alone are doomed forever, but so is God together with us. To

---

[1] The authority von Hartmann can appeal to in his ascribing sense to the world-process is some kind of inner experience, spiritual necessity, the common sense of mankind. This is his dilemma: the world *must* have a purpose, otherwise, all the endless toils and pains of humanity are in vain and meaningless. But this "purpose" is not and cannot be inferred from the metaphysical origin of the world-process. Teleology cannot be logically justified in his system, it is merely a gratuitously assumed postulate.

[2] *Op. cit.*, pp. 91–92.

[3] "Das Kompensations-Äquivalent von Lust und Böse," in *Zeitschrift für Philosophie und Philosophische Kritik*, vol. 90, pp. 50–63, 1888.

expect and hope for deliverance from a self-tormenting and tormented God is obviously sheer folly. This is the concluding position of the philosophy of the unconscious.

The attempt to describe von Hartmann's metaphysico-axiological position demands a strange combination of terms. The paradox warranting this combination, however, is not in the critic, rather in the system itself. Von Hartmann's endeavors to resolve the failings and inadequacies of those philosophical systems which appeared in the immediate past before him, put him in a rather precarious predicament. The task is no less than to reconcile and amalgamate such antagonistic views as Kantian dualism, Hegelian idealism, Schopenhauer's voluntarism, and Schelling's idealistic mystical monism. The outcome is no less surprising than the undertaking itself. It can be best labelled as a sort of irrational and dynamic pessimistic panpneumatism.

It is inconceivable to call anything else a metaphysical system but irrational in which the origin of all things is attributed to an absolute primordial chance. Having neither cause nor purpose the existence of things simply happens, occurs without any explanation at all, as we have seen it above. If von Hartmann expects anyone to accept chance as the final, metaphysical answer for the actual existence of things, he demands more than sane reason can grant. For chance, as explanation in the metaphysical order, explains nothing. This is the mind of Aristotle when he writes:

Chance is an accidental cause of teleological events involving purpose. Hence chance and thought are concerned with the same objects; for purpose implies thought. The causes of chance events are inderterminate, and therefore chance is difficult for us to predict; it is an accidental cause, but in the unqualified sense a cause of nothing... Since nothing accidental is prior to the essential, accidental causes are never prior. If, then, chance or spontaneity is a cause of the material universe, reason and nature are prior causes.[1]

And again:

Now nothing is moved at random; there must be some *moving cause*. Thus, a thing moves in such and such a way *by nature*, in another way *under compulsion*, in another way *under the influence of reason*.[2]

These references mirror the mind of Aristotle as it is expressed in various places of his works in all of which the final conclusion is the same: chance cannot, by its very nature, ever be the ultimate expla-

---

[1] *Met.* bk. XI, 1. 8.
[2] *Ibid.*, bk. XII, 1. 6.

nation of anything it is itself always explainable by causes in which there is no chance.[1]

St. Thomas allies himself with the view of Aristotle and finds the notion of primordial chance as the explanation of the origin of things just as incomprehensible as Aristotle:

A thing can escape the order of a particular cause; but not the order of a universal cause. For nothing escapes the order of a particular cause, except through the intervention and hindrance of some other particular cause; as, for instance, wood may be prevented from burning, by the action of water. Since then, all particular causes are included under the universal cause, it could not be that any effect should take place outside the range of that universal cause. So far then as an effect escapes the order of a particular cause, it is said to be by chance or fortuitous in respect to that cause; but if we regard the universal cause, outside whose range no effect can happen, it is said to be foreseen.[2]

There is another important element required for the understanding of chance according to St. Thomas. In the *Summa Theologica*, I, q. 116, a. 1, utilizing the conclusion of the sixth article of the preceding question, he says:

... that what is accidental, is properly speaking neither a being nor a unity. But every action of nature terminates in some one thing. Wherefore it is impossible for that which is accidental to be the proper effect of an active natural principle. No natural cause can therefore have for its proper effect that a man intending to dig a grave finds a treasure... We must therefore say that what happens by accident, both in natural things and human affairs, is reduced to a pre-ordaining cause, which is the Divine intellect. For nothing hinders that which happens by accident being considered as one by an intellect... And just as an intellect can apprehend this so can it effect it... Consequently, nothing hinders what happens by accident, by luck or by chance, being reduced to some ordering cause which acts by the intellect, especially the Divine intellect.[3]

From these words of Aristotle and Thomas Aquinas it is obvious that the basic conditions for the intelligibility of chance are missing in von Hartmann's theory. First, as we have seen, the possibility of chance occurrence presupposes the mutual interference of two or more independent lines of causation. Chance involves an irreducible pluralism, and it is the clash at a given moment of these multiple causal series which constitutes chance. Where there is no plurality, or at least duality, the possibility of chance is excluded. This condition of the possibility of chance is lacking in von Hartmann's explanation. Apart from the fact that spontaneity as metaphysical reason for the beginning of a

---

[1] *Phys.*, bk. II, 1. 5 and 6; *Perihermeneias*, bk. I. 1. 14; *Meteorologica*, bk. I, 1. 1; *De Coelo*, bk. II, 1. 7 and 11.

[2] *S. Th.* I. q. 22. a. 2 ad 1; also, *ibid.*, q. 103. a. 5 ad 1; q. 115. a. 6.

[3] *Ibid.*, q. 116. a. 1 c; also II. II. q. 64. a. 8 c; *C. G.* II. ch. 2, ch. 40, ch. 83; III. ch. 3, ch. 6, 74; *Comp. Theol.* I. ch. 137.

movement is contradictory, in his view it is the spontaneous movement of the *monistic* will which brings about a chance event, the beginning of the world. In this case the very basic notion of chance is lacking: the fortuitous encounter of two or more independent and unrelated orders of accidental causes. Since only one line of causation has no possibility of intercepting itself, as in the theory of von Hartmann, his explanation as to the chance becoming of the universe is unintelligible.

The second aspect we want to point out is the accidental, secondary, caused nature of the elements involved in the constitution of chance. But accidentals, as Aristotle says, are preceded by essentials; they cannot be first and prior to the essentials. Yet it is the exact denial of this von Hartmann asks us to accept. In this theory it is the essential element, the will, that is responsible for the primordial chance. But we cannot have it both ways: if it is chance, it has to be accidental, if it is accidental it cannot be the essential constituent of the metaphysical essence.

Thirdly, since chance is a clash of accidentals, it is not a genuine being because it is not truly one, as St. Thomas shows. This is not to say that chance is not real, but merely that it does not have a real being, a real essence of its own, because it does not have a real unity of its own. It is a sheer coincidence of contingent facts, the multiplicity of which can be unified only in thought. This being the case, chance is not an ontological entity but merely being of the mind, and as such it does not demand a cause from which it would necessarily follow, nor can it necessarily cause anything in the ontological order of things. Yet the clash of the accidental causal series involved in the constitution of chance presupposes not only the existence of a being prior to them by virtue of which they are, since of themselves they are only secondary and accidental, but also of an intelligent being who sets these causes on the course of their action and foresees the line of their direct as well as interrupted operations. The multiple factors involved in an interrupted operation necessarily demand a mind to bring this multiplicity to unity and thereby to give it being which it lacks of its own. This series of reasoning inevitably leads to that mind which is the cause of all nature, which sets all accidental causes on their proper course, disposes all their operations in accordance with his providence, unifies all manifold in the indivisibility of his essence, to whom nothing is unknown, nothing chance-like.

In the light of these considerations, it appears obvious that the notion of primordial chance as the metaphysical foundation and justification

of transcendental pessimism is unintelligible and untenable, and because it is such it is metaphysically impossible.

Another equally incomprehensible and consequently inadmissible
aspect of von Hartmann's metaphysics is the teleological development
of the world which ultimately issues from an unconscious absolute
spirit. It is impossible to maintain reasonably and logically that a
world where teleology is found and intelligent and conscious beings
exist, has its ultimate reason in an unconscious absolute. As Aristotle
states:

... the common characteristic of all beginnings is their being the original sources
whence things either exist, or are produced, or are known.[1]

St. Thomas commenting upon Metaphysics, bk. X, 1. 5, observes:

... the end is that which is the last in the thing and which contains the thing, so
that nothing whatever can exist outside of the end.[2]

These statements demand, as an unchangeable condition of human
cognition, that whatever perfections are found in the world, the ultimate
metaphysical principle must contain them in an eminent manner. The
ultimate principle cannot be less than that of which it is the principle.
If the world is truly the mirror of the unconscious, which *ex hypothesi* it
is in von Hartmann's explanation, wherein purpose, design, intellect,
and consciousness are patently present and operative, then, the noumenal principle of the phenomenal world must be pre-eminently purposive,
intelligent, and self-conscious. Von Hartmann's logical alternatives are
either to deny teleology in the world, which he admittedly does not do,
or to explain how phenomenal conscious and purposive tendency issues
from that which itself is unconscious, which he possibly cannot do.

It is possible, of course, to write sentences and utter words like "irrational nature's rational ordination of all things to a universal negation," or "an unconsciously and unknowingly designing designer,"
but it does not follow that such statements can convey the idea of a
supposedly or even possibly existent reality. It is also possible that von
Hartmann demands that we liberate ourselves from the fetters of human reason which thinks according to the inchoatively innate laws of
our nature, in order to be able to comprehend the meaning of the above
statements, but to ask this is to ask that we free ourselves from the
ordinary forms of human cognition. And since no other cognition is
available to us, his demand is tantamount of renouncing all reason and

---

[1] *Met.* bk. V, 1. 1.
[2] *In Metaphysicam*, bk. X, 1. 5.

logic, after which the romantic fancy of a pseudo-scientific imagination can take over. But then he should not claim the role of a philosopher, rather that of a sooth-sayer, or a clairvoyant oracle. Thus our difficulty in understanding how the unconscious absolute could be the final cause of teleology in the world does not lie in the subtlety of the proposition, rather in the fact that it is contrary to the laws of human thinking. It is itself an absurdity, nonsense, or in von Hartmann's own language, an *"Unding."*

If we proceed now to examine the main reason von Hartmann gives for the truth of empirical or phenomenal pessimism we find it equally incorrect and unacceptable. Apart from his own observations and interpretations he bases his conclusive argument as to the negative value of our temporal existence upon the quantum-theory of unhappiness of Maupertuis. This principle resolves that the sum-total of happiness in this world is overwhelmingly on the negative side of the scale. On closer examination this whole idea appears to be a chimera. It presupposes that an objective and mathematical comparison of the duration of pleasureable and painful moments is possible and a universally applicable criterion is attainable. This assumption is obviously unsound. For the duration of the eudemonistic units, as the components of a pleasureable individual psychological state is by its nature subjective. From this it follows that the *time* which enters into the composition of these eudemonistic units is also subjective. This subjective estimate is not only of varying quantity, but a quantity varying within a very wide range. The same individual estimates the same amount of objective time according to the incalculable psychological motives which actually determine for the individual the greatness or smallness of the chronological unit. To measure this objectively and attempt to construct an universally valid mathematical standard of comparison is an impossibility. But the difficulties rise to insuperable heights when intensity, the other component element of the eudemonistic units is to be determined. Who can determine with any degree of certainty the intensity of pain stemming from a toothache in one individual and in another, and what kind of mathematical formula could tell how much pleasure is needed in either case to offset the amount of pain? Obviously it is not the quantitative difference of the same kind of pleasurable object, since hypothetically we deal with a quantitatively identical pain, for what is the source of pleasure for one individual may be totally undesirable and repugnant for another. Thus, the "easiness of comparison" of which the proponents of the quantum-theory of unhappiness speak becomes

a mere chimera when they pretend to determine the eudemonistic e-
quivalent of pleasures which differ not only in degree but also in kind.
Perhaps Pascal could help them to sense the absurdity of the mere
thought which attempts to stabilize this pleasure-quotient when he
writes that the sufferings of Christians:

> ... are not without pleasure and are overcome only by pleasure... piety does
> not consist only of bitterness without consolation: and who could measure the
> joy contained in the jubilant realization of the victorious delectation of grace.[1]

Neither Maupertuis, nor von Hartmann nor any one of the hopeless
prophets of darkness could fathom, much less compress into a mathematical formula, the delights and joy of those who draw near, even in
the midst of pain, suffering, and trials of life, to the source of happiness
and life with an open heart.

Yet, these considerations are far from suggesting that man's life on
earth is unbroken happiness. This would be as untrue and unrealistic
as to maintain with the pessimists that it is in its core an interminable
line of pain and suffering. Nor do we disagree with von Hartmann's
contention that evil in this life is something real. As St. Thomas observes: "... something is said to be evil because it hurts."[2] To be hurt,
harmed, and injured is as real a fact in man's consciousness as the fact
of his existence. A theistic metaphysics is in no need to explain away
the obvious presence of evil and misery in man's temporal existence. In
refusing to turn his back to this problem von Hartmann comes closer
to the true spirit of Christianity than those Christians for whom technical advancement and material improvement of the conditions of the
masses are the panacea for the ills of the world. We also believe it with
von Hartmann that education alone, as a mere intellectual development of the individual, will not necessarily bring with it the increase of
happiness in men's life. The present state of atheistic scienticism is
ample proof for our statement.

It is not strange to say, therefore, that to the extent to which von
Hartmann refuses to be deceived by an unwarranted and illusory optimism we share his views. It is true that within the framework of a
theistic metaphysics the value of life is in the ultimate analysis positive,
whereas for von Hartmann it remains negative, yet, despite this fundamental difference theism and the pessimism of von Hartmann are one
in refusing to disregard and ignore the darkness in life's picture. What

---

1 François Mauriac, *Men I Hold Great*, trans. by E. Pell (New York: Philosophical Library,
1951), p. 9.
2 *S. Th.* I. II. q. 49. a. 4 ad 3.

is more, this refusal is based not on a *de facto* observation alone, but also on a *de iure* conviction. This is clearly expressed in the words of St. Thomas:

> ... the perfection of the universe requires that there should be inequality in things, so that every grade of goodness may be realized. Now, one grade of goodness is that of the good which cannot fail. Another grade of goodness is that of which can fail in goodness, and this grade is to be found in existence itself; for some things there are which cannot lose their existence as incorruptible things, while some there are which can lose it, as things corruptible.
>
> As, therefore, the perfection of the universe requires that there should be not only beings incorruptible, but also corruptible beings; so the perfection of the universe requires that there should be some which can fail in goodness, and thence it follows that sometimes they do fail. Now it is in this that evil consists, namely, in the fact that a thing fails in goodness. Hence it is clear that evil is found in things, as corruption also is found; for corruption is itself an evil.[1]

Whether we take what St. Thomas says as relating to the material universe or to the order of morality, we are justified, for there are failings in the order of nature as well as in the order of free choice of the individual. Thus, regardless of the nature of the answer given to the anxiously searching mind as to the fact of evil either in nature or in the free actions of the individual, the answer necessarily remains inadequate and circuitous. For whether we point to the greater good achieved in the universe by permitting evil in it, or to the safeguarding of our freedom, in either case the insistence cannot be avoided: could not God have created a material world without corruption and death in it and a world of freedom without sin; and if not, why not?

If our question is restricted to the purely possible and conceivable we must obviously say that God might have created a world without evil. But as soon as we leave the realm of what is purely possible and deal with the concretely given, we must say that God has actually willed a world in which evil is inevitable, and permits it to have its proper role and purpose in the universe. Whence the inference logically follows that an exclusively rational, philosophical evaluation of our earthly existence in its actual circumstances cannot be unreservedly and without qualification viewed as optimistic. In as much as the universe is a work of creative art, and man is part of this universe, it is in the order of things that he be fallible together with all the other parts of this universe. It is so designed that man be involved in sorrow, suffering, and death, because by his very essence he is involved in nature which is corporeal, subjected to universal laws of generation and corruption.

---

[1] *Ibid.*, I. q. 48. a. 2 c. for further reference concerning St. Thomas's doctrine on evil see: *S. Th.* I. q. 19. a. 9; q. 48. a. 1, 2, 6; q. 49. a. 1; *De Malo*, q. 1. 3; *C. G.* III, ch. 7, 8, 9; *Comp. Theol.* I, ch. 115; *De Potentia*, 1. 6.

Moreover, as long as man is capable of asserting his freedom against God, as long as he can be an adversary of God, and in so doing he can bring destruction and death upon himself as well as on other human beings, evil remains a constant companion of everyone in this life. In view of these facts the question is wholly legitimate: do we have to conclude with von Hartmann and with the pessimists at large that the existence of this world is worse than its nonexistence?

This is not necessarily so, for the conclusion is a *non sequitur* from von Hartmann's metaphysical premises. This must be concluded to only within the framework of an essentially irrational philosophy, on the assumption that the origin of this world is due to an inexplicable original chance and that the underlying noumenon of all reality is an unconscious, irrational absolute. On the basis of such metaphysical principles there is no possibility of a rational explanation of anything, whether life, pain, suffering, or death. But once von Hartmann admits teleology, purpose, and design in the progressive development of the universe, then he is no longer in the position of denying them logically in the ultimate source of this development. Once design and purpose in the universe have been admitted, it is illogical to maintain that they are the manifestations of an unconscious absolute spirit. On the contrary, the ultimate principles of human thought, the principles of sufficient reason and contradiction, demand the existence of a rational designer who *"attingit a fine usque ad finem fortiter, et disponit omnia suaviter."*[1]

This quotation entails an admission by Thomistic philosophy that there is no satisfactory answer to the problem of evil by merely metaphysical considerations. The answer to the anguished heart of man in the face of evils about him will not be found in the efforts of the mind alone, but in a living faith and enduring hope of the individual. The problem of evil is not only a problem but a mystery. Like all other mysteries, it too has its light to bestow, a light not of the order of rational explanations, but no less humanly reassuring to the heart and also to the mind. To lift the veil from the purely intellectually inscrutable mystery man must employ all his faculties; in a word, he must assess his existential situation. This assessment cannot be a purely intellectual undertaking, that of a spectator of the world merely seeking explanations of the phenomena passing before his eyes. It must be a total evaluation of our creaturely position which first and above all reveals our existential dependence upon an uncreated and self-sufficient

[1] *Sap.*, 8 : I.

Creator. It is in this total assessment that man must take his decisive choice either of the scandal of evil that causes us to trip and fall or of submissive reverence to the inscrutable ways of God. The parting of the ways between revolt and worship lies in the secret depths of the heart, where we make the choice either for ourselves, as autonomous arbiters in all matters of life, or for God, as the infinitely transcendent source of all creation. What it ultimately comes to is a frank acceptance of our condition as creatures which must be more than intellectual, it must be all-comprehensively human. As the Creator's partners by virtue of our freedom we have to realize our condition as unequal partners of the living God and so voluntarily submit to be led where he wills.

The path of his divine guidance includes in its total design the ever remaining mystery of evil. A creation without evil would certainly manifest God's goodness and wisdom, but it would not be complete manifestation of his love and pity, of that love and God-imparted goodness over all creation which in its final culmination expresses itself in the redemptive death of his only begotten Son.[1] Evil is, therefore, ultimately present in creation so that God's loving pity could be shown for us who, of ourselves, have neither beauty nor goodness. In this gratuitous loving is shown most clearly the mystery of God's goodness towards us in its sovereign character.[2] This is our answer to von Hartmann's transcendental pessimism and his theory of the annihilating return of the phenomenal individual to the absolute unconscious: that through the purifying love of Christ the individual is transformed by the submission of his will into a partaker of the everlasting happiness of God.

Sin therefore, taken as a disaster of that whole which we call the person, and as an offense against God – sin and the suffering and sorrow which form its retinue are not permitted for the greater perfection of the machine of the world; they are themselves connected to the manifestation of divine goodness as transcending the very universe of creation and expressing itself in the universe of grace or of the transfiguration of love of created persons become God through participation. The creature's liability to sin is thus the price paid for the outpouring of creative Goodness, which in order to *give itself personally* to the extent that it transforms into itself something other than itself, must be *freely loved with friendship's love and communion*, and which to be freely loved with friendship's love and communion must create *free* creatures, and which in order to create them free must create them *fallibly* free. Without fallible freedom there can be no created freedom there can be no love in mutual friendship between God and creature, there can be no super-natural transformation of the creature into God, no entering of the creature into the joy of his Lord. Sin, evil, is the price of glory.[3]

---

[1] *S. Th.* III. q. 1. a. 1.

[2] *Ibid.*, II, II. q. 30. a. 2 4; q. 67. a. 4; III. q. 46. a. 2 ad 3.

[3] Jacques Maritain, *St. Thomas and the Problem of Evil* (Milwaukee: Marquette University Press, 1942), pp. 18–19. The Aquinas Lecture 1942.

CHAPTER VII

PHILOSOPHY OF MORALS

Nur der absolute metaphysische Pessimismus kann als Motiv zu sittlichen Betätigungen mitwirken, insofern die universelle Erlösung als Ziel der religiösen Heilsordnung gedacht wird, aber auch nur für diejenigen, denen die Erlösung von Übel und Schuld für wichtiger gilt, als die Gewinnung positiver Seligkeit.[1]

Absolute metaphysical pessimism finds its first application in the order of moral behavior. It is the motivating force of all of man's moral actions performed in view of his ultimate end: the universal deliverance of all existence from evil and guilt. "Moral" and "immoral" for von Hartmann are mere descriptive terms for the moral agent's relationship to a definite stratum of higher consciousness. Morality has meaning only in the sphere of consciousness; there is no morality for the unconscious. The problem of morality appears only at a certain stage in the phenomenal unfolding of the unconscious. Prior to the realization of individual consciousness there is no morality, because there is no conscious presentation or motivation. Whether an intended act will materialize according to this conscious motive or not, in other words, whether an act will be morally performed or not, depends on our character which, in turn, is completely unknown to us and it can be known only through our actions. But if morality depends on our character, that is, on something unknown to us, then in its final analysis it depends on the unconscious, which forms the character as one of its means for self-expression, as its functional channel for self-realization. Thus morality is rooted ultimately in the unconscious.[2] This interdependence of von Hartmann's ethical doctrine and the theory of the unconscious becomes most obvious in his critical unfolding and developing of the

---

[1] *System*, vol. VI, p. 12. "Only absolute metaphysical pessimism can contribute as motive to man's moral behavior, insofar as the universal salvation is assumed as the aim of the order of salvation, but only for those whom the salvation from evil and guilt has a greater value than the attainment of positive happiness."

[2] *Philosophy of the Unconscious*, vol. I, p. 260.

different principles of morality. In two of his works, the *Phänomenologie des Sittlichen Bewusstseins,* and the sixth volume of the *System* he examines all major moral theories and lists their advantages as well as their shortcomings in order to clear the way for the formation of his own principles. In his critical search through the various ethical systems he adopts the Hegelian dialectic as the value-criterion of these systems, with the modification that the characteristic thesis-antithesis-synthesis structure is minimized in the detailed analysis of the principles. The unfolding of the idea is not based upon the thesis-antithesis antinomy, but upon the relative deficiency and necessarily limited nature of each level of morality. Since this scrutiny of moral phenomena is allegedly conducted in an inductive manner, the historical development of morality from its primitive to its highest stage will be employed as proof for the objectivity and truth of his own ethical system. Each moral level, with the exception of the highest, has a relative value only; consequently it demands a higher development of morality. The highest and the ultimate moral level has a universal value, but he holds that this universality can be explained only from the standpoint of a concrete monistic system.

The first and hence the lowest, degree of moral consciousness is individual eudemonism, that is, hedonism.[1] Pleasure, which is a mere effect

---

[1] It may be of help and interest at this point to acquaint ourselves with the more important terms of von Hartmann's ethical terminology. The terms *Sittenlehre,* study of custom or behavior, and *Moral,* morality, have their origin from the Latin *mos: Sitte,* custom, habit, practice, and they refer to an involuntary action of our nature or to an unconscious act of man as indicative of the evolving species. The word *Ethik,* ethics, derives from the Greek ἔθος rite, usage, which denotes the core, the essence of a conscious spirit's activity, describes its opinion or conviction, i.e., a human act (*Gesinnung*). The term *Sittenlehre,* therefore, refers predominantly to the socio-ethical order as it is established at any given moment of the process of evolution of human customs and behavior, while *Moral* denotes principally the subjective casuistry of individual morality. *Ethik* encompasses both, the common opinion of socio-ethical groups as well as the subjective conviction of the individual. Of all these expressions von Hartmann prefers the usage of the term *Ethik,* and at times he uses its adjective form *ethisch,* ethical interchangeably with *sittlich,* moral. He has retained the conventional compound term *Moralprinzip,* moral principle, for such a term could not very well be composed from the noun *Ethik.* The same way he employs the term *Pseudo-moral* in order to avoid the hyphen in *Pseudo-Ethik.* By the term "Pseudo-morality," verbally deceitful or illusory morality, von Hartmann designates a doctrine which presents itself as morality without being truly one, and in opposition to it he sets the term *echte Moral,* genuine morality. The often used *Eudämonik* is a literal translation of Kant and von Hartmann of the Greek εὐδαιμονία and is employed in a generic sense including satisfaction, pleasure, blessedness, felicity, beatitude, happiness, etc. *Eudämonologie,* eudemonology, doctrine or theory of happiness; *eudämonologisch,* eudemonological, with reference to the doctrine of happiness or treated from the viewpoint of the doctrine of happiness; *Eudämonismus,* eudemonism, the ideological concept of the world wherein happiness is the normative and highest principle; *eudämonistisch,* eudemonistic, belonging to or following from such a view of the world. Von Hartmann remarks that in this light his pessimism is eudemonological but not a eudemonistic pessimism; for it is pessimism only with regard to the value of existence according to the norm of happi-

of the will's activity, is erroneously considered in this theory as the cause and aim of moral motivation; it should not be treated as a moral principle.[1] Such a moral outlook is mere egoistic pseudo-morality. Individual eudemonism that seeks its positive fulfillment here on earth is a coarse naturalism, a sort of moral indifferentism that hinders the ethical refinement and uplift of man. If it looks for its full realization in a life hereafter then it assumes a false metaphysics of transcendence, which, von Hartmann declares, cannot serve as moral motivation for a discriminating and thinking person. "Eternal punishment in a future life for temporal sins is highly unjust because of its disproportion, and in the light of a just judge of the dead it is unworthy of belief."[2] On

ness. His pessimism is opposed to any system which accepts happiness as the highest principle of the view of the world and its task is to show the absurdity of such an outlook on the world. Individual-eudemonism, social-eudemonism, absolute-eudemonism are systematical standpoints, in which the happiness of individuals, society, or the absolute respectively, is the highest practical principle, and the correspondent adjectives formed from the nouns, for instance, individual-eudemonistic, are self-explanatory. The term, individual-eudemonism is equivalent to egoism; social-eudemonism to utilitarianism or to the principle of the common well-being, i.e., more exactly to the highest possible happiness of the greatest possible number of individuals. Eudemonism which regards happiness as something positive, and consequently attainable, is called *positiver Eudämonismus*, positive eudemonism. On the other hand, the view which considers the highest possibly attainable state of happiness not in something positive, but only in the negative, or in the annihilation of the common and actually attained condition of happiness and goods, is called *negativer Eudämonismus*, negative eudemonism, for it remains eudemonism as long as a "relative" (proportionate) or "privative" (brought about by self-denial, or education) or "negative" (antithetical to the positive condition of happiness) eudemonism, attainable through negation, remains its determining principle. *Irdisch*, earthly or present is that eudemonism which hopes that *Eudämonie*, be it positive or negative, can be realized here on earth; *transzendent* or *überfliegend*, transcendental, is that which believes that its aims can be attained through the sublimation of the earthly conditions of existence into an existence of hereafter.

The contrary of eudemonism is *Evolutionismus*, evolutionism, a view of the world which accepts evolution as highest practical principle of development, *Entwicklung*. Evolutionism as a practical outlook on the world is simultaneously a "teleological" evolutionism, i.e. such a theory of development which views this process teleologically. *Teleologie*, teleology, is the doctrine of aim or goal, i.e., of the objective aim which rules over the world and which enfolds itself in an immanent system of aims in the world or as a teleological order of the world, *teleologische Weltordnung*. In its teleological view evolutionism is at the same time an *evolutionistischer Optimismus*, evolutionistic optimism, i.e., confidence in the highest possible rationality or in the best possibility of the purposive development. The "evolutionistical optimism" and the "eudemonological pessimism" are not contradictory because their *point de départ* in viewing the world, although commences from a different standpoint, the teleological and the eudemonological, nevertheless, only their unity can give us a complete and true picture of the world. *Heteronomie*, heteronomy, and *Autonomie*, autonomy, in their nominal definition mean "legality from without" (*Fremdgesätzlichkeit*) and "legality from within" (*Selbstgesätzlichkeit*), i.e., the condition of the decisions of the human will under external or under self-imposed laws. In so far as the will subjects itself to the law, heteronomy and autonomy gain the additional secondary meaning of "determination from without" (*Fremdbestimmung*) and "self-determination" (*Selbstbestimmung*); in the former case the determination of the will depends upon the will of a law-giving third one, whereas in the latter, upon the will of the person himself who is performing the action. Cf. Ed. von Hartmann, *Das Sittliche Bewusstsein* (Leipzig: Hermann Haacke, 1899), 2nd ed., Vorwort, pp. 7-11.

[1] *System*, vol. VI, p. 15 ff.
[2] *Ibid.*, p. 22.

the other hand, if the only ethical aim of a system is the avoidance of pain in the form of a negative eudemonism, then its progress is merely an ill-hidden egoism manifested in some sort of pseudo-asceticism which entails the denial of the will. Despite these shortcomings of the egoistic ethical system, positive eudemonism has value in insisting upon the importance of autonomy, while negative eudemonism has value in its principle of self-denial.[1]

Having concluded to the illusory character of all yearning after individual happiness here or hereafter, man, in von Hartmann's historical survey is driven to search for a new moral aim and in doing so he submits to heteronomy. He soon realizes once more that in any kind of heteronomy he is not confronted with true morality but merely with legality, for in all forms of external morality what is apparent is the law itself and not its content.

The first manifestation of this heteronomous morality is the family. The initial encounter of the child with obedience is paternal authority; he must obey because his father so commands. After he has learned to subject his own will to an imposed supra-individual aim, the content of the given command can and must be explained to him according to the measure of his developing understanding. Thus parental education prepares in the child's mind through patriarchal heteronomy the basis for the acceptance of a heteronomous morality which will be replaced later on by another exoteric authority.[2]

This authority is the state and von Hartmann analyzes its laws insofar as they reflect moral ideals. After examination of various possible political systems (tyranny, aristocracy, democracy), the search for genuine moral principle among the principles of civil law ends in the negative. As he criticizes these different political theories, his greatest disdain is reserved for socialistic democracy and its social-eudemonistic moral outlook. Von Hartmann is convinced that all social-eudemonistic morality leads only to one end: man's relapse into his primitive animal condition (*Wiederverthierung*). In social democracy the pursuit of intellectual ideals as conducive to happiness is not only neglected but eventually even forgotten. The highest moral obligation is to become dumb (*Verdummung*) and return to the state of mere brutes (*Verthierung*) as necessary conditions for happiness. That in such a state there is no longer any purpose (*Ziel*) but only an end (*Ende*) is obvious.[3] The

[1] *Ibid.*, p. 21.
[2] *Ibid.*, pp. 29–30.
[3] *Op. cit.*, p. 443.

national customs of different peoples are as inept as principles of morality as are those already examined.

The authority of the Church,[1] the divine will, and moral autonomy are studied next as possible moral principles of genuine morality. The Church's authority looks upon the prescribed and distinctive rites of religious worship as the expressed will of God, and as a consequence it underestimates or even fails to recognize the significance of a purely human ethics. The will of God can be further discovered in the free, individual interpretation of the Bible or in one's own soul. Both ultimately lead to moral autonomy. Only the recognition of a free, autonomous conscience can render possible an unbiased investigation of the individual moral principles.

The primary and most obvious manifestation of genuine, autonomous moral consciousness is the morality of taste or liking (*Geschmacksmoral*). The morality of taste is the moral qualification of an action on the basis of an evident and immediate judgment of value stemming from the unconscious. The unconscious value-judgement externalizes itself as a moral taste, as the principle of right behavior for the individual. Moral taste is the highest expression of morality, since it derives directly from the unconscious. But it fails in the fact that it is merely a formal principle, inasmuch as its content will be manifested only in singular, concrete cases. The next task of morality is to discover ways whereby this unique character of moral taste can be expanded. This von Hartmann hopes to find in the moral principle of the golden mean or right measure, but he has barely discovered it when he is compelled to amend it. This principle is also insufficient inasmuch as of itself and in itself it is a mere apotheosis of mediocrity. Furthermore, it varies with different cultures and even with different men in an identical culture-cycle; consequently, it cannot be accepted as a definite objective norm of morality. The next norm to be examined is harmony as a moral principle. Viewed from the standpoint of the individual, it denotes balance among the powers of the soul. In this respect it is undefinable, and more of an obstacle than promoter of moral progress. Viewed from the standpoint of universality, as an artistic vision of all things, it cannot be proved, and it thus fails in face of facts. Consequently, the search must go on for more universal expression of the moral principle. Von Hartmann believes that it is found in the princi-

---

[1] "Church" is understood as the "infallible interpreter of the divine will and the dispenser of grace" and not merely a free gathering of similarly inclined proselytes. Cf. *System*, vol. VI, p. 32.

ple of perfection of ethical ideals and artistic form. But perfection of itself is undetermined; it has need of ethical ideals to provide it with
positive content. Again, ideals as products of human imagination have
only a relative value. Although in their absolute aspect they are inex-
haustible, but as such they cannot be expropriated by any one theory,
whereas morality needs concrete ideals. In a disillusioned realization of
the complete insufficiency of the *Geschmacksmoral* to provide the
necessary principles of morality he turns next to the field of the moral
sentiment, i.e. *Gefühlsmoral*.[1]

Feeling is considered as moral first under the aspect of moral sentiment, consciousness, and concomitant emotion. The principle of moral
sentiment is understood by von Hartmann as the sum total of all
functional moral principles. It is not one single homogeneous principle,
but a collective view of all feelings and emotions of which every one
corresponds to a singular moral principle. The principle of moral self-
feeling (*Selbstgefühl*) is the reflection of morality in the inner sensation
of self-awareness or in consciousness. This awareness of our moral
personality can easily engender moral pride, and thus lead to coolness,
narrowmindedness, and lack of sympathy toward others. Moreover,
self-feeling is subject to fluctuation in direct proportion to the moral
value of a performed action. There will be an increase of our moral self-
feeling following upon a good deed, decrease of the same if our action
is felt to be immoral. There is a special sentiment consequent upon an
immoral deed called remorse (*Reue als Nachgefühl*); and because it plays
a significant role in morality it must be considered as a particular principle of practical morality.

Remorse is sadness over the fact that man has fallen into immorality.
It is of a twofold nature: intellectual and characterological or natural.
The former is a subsequent evaluation of the effects of our moral action,
wherein we realize the errors of our antecendent moral judgment with
regard to the goodness of the effects of our action. The latter is a mere
change in our emotional disposition with regard to the value of the act
after we have performed it. Remorse in either of its aspects is very far
from genuine morality. It is still the unmistakable expression of a
eudemonistic and egoistic moral outlook. In the measure that the individual and society will outgrow the narrow confines of heteronomous
morality, remorse will also disappear and give place to genuine moral
consciousness.

Stronger and more accurate expressions of the moral sentiment as

[1] *Ibid.*, p. 50.

the ones considered hitherto are found in the sentiments or natural drives for mutual remuneration (*Vergeltungstriebe*), such as reward, companionship, and sympathy.[1] The first is manifested in the feelings of revenge and gratitude. Revenge as such is immoral. Gratitude can incite men to noble deeds as well as to injustice and corruption. The instinct for companionship shows considerable progress toward true morality inasmuch as it is an undeniable sign of victory of the social instinct over individual interest. In this sense it is closely related to sympathy, which is displayed in the sentiments of sharing in the sorrow and joy of others. These sentiments are rarely disinterested, and most of the time they are only natural reactions without any direct or indirect reference to morality.

There is a further manifestation of the moral sentiment in the virtues of piety, fidelity, love, and sense of duty.[2] Again, piety cannot be considered a moral principle since it presupposes the distinction between morality and immorality prior to the performance of an act. Fidelity is understood as trustworthiness, but as such it is one-sided and needs further completion to become a universal principle. Love is desire for togetherness. As an individual emotion it is egoistic and unjust toward others; as a universal emotion it seldom exists, and when it does, it is too undetermined to be able of supplying sufficient force for the performance of singular acts. The sense of duty presupposes the existence of duty and obligation. Duty becomes known only by means of reason, and insofar as sense agrees with it it is already unconsciously rational.

Thus the moral principles based on individual taste (*Geschmacksmoral*) and feelings (*Gefühlsmoral*) prove to be ineffective, insufficient, and consequently demand and find their fulfillment in the morality of reason (*Vernunftmoral*).[3] *Vernunftmoral* may manifest itself under different forms, the first of which is the moral principle of the practical reason. In its ultimate analysis everything must be reasonable in one way or another, and reason must be embedded in nature. But reason attains the stratum of self-consciousness only gradually and under certain specific aspects that appear to it as imperatives. These imperative forms are commands manifested to consciousness by the unconscious reason. The practical reason is not merely a law-giver, it also

---

[1] *Ibid.*, p. 57.
[2] *Ibid.*, p. 68.
[3] *Ibid.*, p. 86 ff.

assumes the role of judging whether the universal laws are sufficient or not in particular instances.

But, as has been pointed out, the morality of reason achieves consciousness only gradually and more or less from a particular point of view because of its abstract, discursive nature. Thus it becomes mandatory to treat those particular aspects in their singularity under which the moral principle of practical reason attains its maturity in consciousness. One important note must be kept in mind here, i.e., the carriers of the moral principle of reason are just as imperative in themselves as is the principle itself. These carriers or more simply, the secondary aspects of reason are, we are told by von Hartmann, the moral principles of truth, the diverse aspects of freedom, equality, order, and justice.[1]

Truth demands the harmony of the moral law between theoretical knowledge and sincerity in its execution. Von Hartmann accepts truth as a powerful foundation of morality, but denies that it could be identified with it. Freedom is considered to be too negative, abstract, and devoid of content in-itself and for-itself to be an all-encompassing moral principle. Equality is brushed aside with an even more disparaging remark that "the greatest equality with the gradual development of culture would become the greatest inequality."[2]

The principle of moral freedom can be viewed theoretically or practically, and the former again either rationally or aesthetically. Theoretical reasoning establishes the basic laws for moral action, and the aesthetic judgment furnishes the fitting manner of its execution. In this regard theoretical moral freedom is merely the preparatory stage for morality. Practical freedom, on the other hand, is mere license, and hence it is unrelated to genuine moral freedom. This latter is individual self-activity, spontaneity, subjective responsibility, conscious activity of our creative intellectual faculties, self-control, self-denial, triumph over egoism, autonomy of the will, and control over the other powers of the will. All these must be present in true moral freedom. However, such aspects of moral freedom present only formal, and thus empty, definitions, and leave a need for more exact and accurate definitions.

The following expression of the morality of reason is the moral principle of *liberum arbitrium indifferentiae*. It is understood by von Hartmann as the "freedom of the will from legal determinations through its character-dispositions and motivations."[3] Psychological determin-

---

[1] *Ibid.*, p. 91 ff.
[2] *Ibid.*, p. 100.
[3] *Ibid.*, p. 112.

ism rigidly upholds the predetermination of the will's every choice, whereas indeterminism admits the freedom of some acts of the will. Moreover, it makes little or no difference insofar as the truth of the principle is concerned whether the *liberum arbitrium* constantly functions or remains habitually latent, whether it manifests itself in its genuine purity or that in its initial stages it is connected with deterministic factors. For these factors are overcome in the developing stages of a decision and the final determining impulse is the act of the principle itself. But once more, we cannot accept moral indeterminism as the true moral principle for it is merely a prerequisite of moral responsibility, but not morality itself.

The principle of transcendental freedom is described as the independence of the individual's characteristic essence or distinctive quiddity, free from all external influences. It is the "freedom-to-will" in a formal but not in a realistic sense.

Transcendental freedom... has no *real* value for ethics; it has nothing to do with undetermined freedom either in the world of phenomena or in the world beyond it. Within the world of phenomena undetermined freedom accounts for responsibility in every sense; but when it is projected back into the transcendent-metaphysical sphere as transcendental freedom, it will reflect responsibility merely as something belonging to the order of morality, whereas this sphere *transcends* the order of morality (Übersittliche).[1]

Von Hartmann's next step takes up the consideration of the principles of order, legal order, right, and justice. Order correlates the diverse powers for the performance of a common task, in order to be effective, it requires more concrete determinations by positive rules and laws, thereby becoming the legal order. Parallel with the objective order of law runs the order of subjective rights. This latter demands justice as a complement to the order of objective legality, otherwise, *summum jus summa injuria*. But justice, in von Hartmann's opinion, is a mere instinctive, unconscious manifestation of the immanent reason in man, unaware of its rational sources. Therefore its criteria are to be valued only negatively, and the task remains to search for its genetic principle. If found, it could finally become the source and fountain of rational moral principles, partly because of its immanent nature and partly because of its transcendence. Only the immediate "practicalization" of the intellect could correspond to such a demand, but the intellect becomes practical only when it is necessitated by its very own nature to turn toward something else than itself. The first form of this

[1] *Ibid.*, pp. 118–9.

externalization of reason, i.e., the application of the logical to the illogical expresses itself in a concrete purpose or aim.

It is the function of the logical, or reason, to set these aims, and the possibility of a genuine ethics and ethical action depend upon the existence of objective goals. In view of the existence of this objective series of aims man must realize that his self is not an ultimate aim, merely a relative one in the universal teleological organism of the world. Von Hartmann pays tribute to Hegel by calling attention to his idea of objective aims against the Kantian ethics of a subjectivistic rationalism. It is Hegel's lasting service to morality:

... that he destroyed the vagueness of the morality of feeling and eliminated the sentimental coddling of the individual by pointing to the order of objective universal aims.[1]

Only through reason can we obtain a realm of objective aims, and the realization of these aims is the moral obligation. The subjective set of aims appears after this knowledge as the conscious reproduction of objective aims.

The moral principle of aims or finality is merely a partial sector of the principle of aim in general which, as universal finality, extends throughout and pervades the entire universe. Only with the aid of the principle of purpose can man solve the conflict of his different obligations, which result from the fact that no man can ever fully know the total series of objective aims. If man possessed such a knowledge, he would be no human any longer, but a purely logical and heartless being. Therefore, taste and feeling must retain their role in morality alongside with reason, otherwise, we would be engulfed by a kind of "Jesuitism."[2] Notwithstanding his dislike for the Jesuits, von Hartmann accepts the so-called Jesuitical principle that "the end justifies the means." For him it assumes a universal importance and value. Each action becomes moral, i.e., justified, only through the fact that it stems from a definite conviction which is directed to a higher, objective aim. Consequently, each action will be moral only insofar as it is a means to a moral aim. It is needless to point out the absurdity of such a moral interpretation whereby each means could be justified by the end. For we must bear in mind that each action has its secondary aspects which may well destroy the morality of the primary purpose.

This analysis of teleology is too formal, and the question arises almost

---

[1] *Op. cit.*, p. 443.
[2] *System*, vol. VI, pp. 138–139. Cf. also *Ethische Studien* (Leipzig: Hermann Haacke, 1898), p. 2; *Philosophy of the Unconscious*, vol. I, p. 267.

automatically: what is the content of moral aims, what are the positive moral aims? Von Hartmann answers his own question by saying that there are three positive aims or objective moral principles. The first is the moral principle of social-eudemonism, or the moral principle of the common good. This school of thought examines the existing conditions of the State and accepts the common good as the highest moral aim of the individual. Von Hartmann labels this ethical outlook social-eudemonism and banishes it into the camp of social democracy. He loathes and abhors social democracy with its social-eudemonistic principle of morality, claiming that it drives humanity back to its primitive, animal condition. In this state of matters of forever levelling down and never attempting the upward climb, the highest moral obligation is a gradual retrogression into obtuseness and stupidity (*Verdummung*), "a relapse into our former bestial condition" (*Wiederverthierung*) through which happiness will be realized.[1] This levelling-down is extended equally to material goods and to the sciences and arts. Therefore, that man will best serve the welfare of humanity who can render the race less subject to refined desires and more carefree, more frivolous, and more shallow, in other words, the one who can bestow on it once more the hallmark of a universal animalism (*allgemeine Verthierung*). Thus, von Hartmann reaches the conclusion that the cultural development of the race is a mere illusion if understood in a eudemonistic sense. Consequently social-eudemonistic moral principle cannot be a purpose (*Ziel*), but a mere end (*Ende*), cleverly employed by the demagogues of social democracy for the exploitation and subjugation of the masses.

The cultural progress of the race is a correct principle as long as it is not interpreted in a eudemonistic sense. This misinterpretation will be avoided by the new evolutionist principle of culture-development, the progressive self-realization of the idea. In imitation of Darwin, von Hartmann claims that upon natural evolution there immediately follows economic, material, and technical, and finally cultural development. As soon as the organic form of the human type was reached in the evolutionary series no further progress in the improvement of the external, material element of man was possible. Thus, if the law of evolution is to be further verified, we must look for it within the individual. From the viewpoint of the subject, this is found in refinement of intellect, aesthetic taste and feeling, and also in the will, to the extent that it is motivated by the idea. In the objective sense, it is materialized in the development of socio-ethical views. But here the self-perfecting of

[1] *Ibid.*, p. 155.

the individual is no longer a self-aim or an independent moral principle; it is a mere means in the service of the all-encompassing development of culture. Whether this aim as an ideal to be pursued is present in consciousness or not does not matter. If it is present and we are aware of it, this subjective ideal itself is a means in the service of the objective idea's self-realization.

Amelioration of the socio-ethical conditions on the one hand, and refinement of the spirit, taste, feeling, character, and the technique of the moral self-discipline on the other, work together to raise morality, and this may well be achieved without the actual increase of the essence of moral sentiment itself. This latter, properly called the will-to-good, or in theology grace, can in similar manner endure and even expand in depth. First, because it operates under more favorable circumstances inwardly as well as outwardly; secondly, because it is more clearly present in consciousness, thereby exerting a greater influence upon the technique of moral self-discipline. This will explain how the development, increase, and refinement of morality can take place in the course of the culture-process without being necessarily connected with the increase of the essence of the moral sentiment itself.

Another significant point, von Hartmann warns, is the illusory nature of the commonly assumed harmony between the social-eudemonistic and the evolutionistic moral principles. Instead of an agreement, there is a sharp antagonism between them in every field of their application. There is an acute antinomy between the principle of the "greatest possible happiness for the greatest possible number" and the principle of culture-development. Every step forward in the development of civilization must be purchased with a disproportionately great sacrifice for the common good. This is easily seen in the disappointment and discontent issuing from each completed culture-cycle. But for other, yet to be completed cycles there remains in man an ineradicable illusion that they will bring about an increase of happiness, and this belief spurs him on to work for its realization regardless of the sufferings it entails. The existing antagonism between the social-eudemonistic and evolutionistic moral principles is the strongest argument for eudemonological pessimism, for it proves that the balance of happiness must always be in disproportion to the progress of civilization. In this antagonism lies also the independence of evolutionistic optimism from eudemonological pessimism as well as the superiority of the evolutionistic norm of values over against the eudemonological ones. Yet this opposition between the two objective moral principles in the moral consciousness of humanity, and the mere suppression of the first by the second cannot be the final aim of morality. At this juncture the problem is to find in moral consciousness a principle higher and more comprehensive than either eudemonism or evolutionism, which will resolve this antagonism and incorporate both as its integral parts. Von Hartmann believes to have found it in the principle of the moral world-order.[1]

This principle is looked upon as the sublimation of a one-sided eudemonism and evolutionism as well as the correction of their shortcomings. In this positive aspect it may be viewed as the teleological organization of the universe. It was the radical error of the adherents of the social-eudemonistic principle to ignore this teleological subordination of ends, and to leave out of consideration the new individual end which arises on each successive stage of individuation. They have vainly imagined that this new end could be identified with the sum of the individual ends of the constituent units. This was a fatal blunder. The end of the State may be, and frequently is, antagonistic to the end of most of the individuals who compose it. Again, the end of the family is by no means the sum of the ends of the members of the family, but points beyond this sum to the furtherance of the end of the community. The end of the community is in turn directed to the end of the province, which to that of the State, race, peoples, tribes, and finally, humanity in general. When we understand it clearly that at each stage of individuation a new self-dependent end springs into being, an end which is not in the least to be identified with the sum-total of the ends of the individuals of the preceding order, we have found the correct point of view whence we can now rightly estimate and judge between the conflicting claims of eudemonism and evolutionism. We have discovered the principle of the moral world-order:

... which is not only the highest but also the all-encompassing, exhaustive objective moral principle, of which the social-eudemonistic and evolutional ⸢moral principles are but one-sided reflections.[2]

This objective moral world-order becomes gradually realized in consciousness as an organic complex of ideas, and it strives to establish itself as a universal and necessary law, or code of laws. Since it is a consciously realized precept, to infringe upon it is culpable. The principle of the moral world-order becomes in this sense the presupposition of the possibility of evil, which consists in the pursuance of the lower

[1] *Ibid.*, p. 173.
[2] *Ibid.*, p. 176.

individual ends over against the aims of higher individual spheres. Essentially it is the inordinate drive of the relative illogical, the assertion of the egoistical self-will in opposition to the aims of higher individual stages, the lack of subordination of egoism to moral aims. In order to eliminate this conflict in the individual, two things must be understood. First, it is mandatory for man to realize the irrationality of his volitional drives, and secondly, he has to recognize with equal importance the illusions of his self-sufficiency and independence by referring his individual nature to its metaphysical origin. This essential identification of the individual with the metaphysical absolute will convince him also of the positive dependence of morality upon metaphysics, in other words, it will show the prerequisites of the binding force of the moral law.[1]

Once this twofold obligation is recognized we are ready to abandon the objective phenomenal world as well as to transcend the sphere of individuality, admit the illusion of the ego, and seek the foundations of morality in the metaphysical sphere, in the absolute. This ultimately basic stratum of morality is called the sphere of the absolute moral principles, and the first of these is the monistic moral principle of the essence-identity of the individuals.

Two possible objections could be raised against his position regarding the ultimate source of morality, according to von Hartmann. The first is by pluralism, the second by abstract monism. But he claims from his previous considerations he can show that these objections are of no real importance, since in either of these systems "genuine morality" is impossible.

In pluralism the unity of the universe is reduced to an external aggregate of completely independent substances, wherein the self-sufficient, hypostatized ego is considered as absolutely sovereign; whether we regard this substantiality as metaphysically simple, or as consisting of an aggregation of atoms. In this system there are only egoistic, self-seeking considerations, which may impose some restraint on the arbitrary choice of this sovereign being, but the only morality possible within pluralism is an outmoded egoistical pseudo-morality.

In abstract monism, on the other hand, all plurality of individuals is a mere subjective illusion. All changes, therefore, taking place in this illusory show, such as life and death, individual action and suffering, are devoid of reality and truth, consequently the only possible ethical outlook is indifferentism. All types of materialism, naturalism,

[1] *Ibid.*, p. 189.

and mechanism, as well as transcendental idealism and monism, Spinozism, and gnoseological idealism can arrive at an ethical system only by means of obvious inconsistency.

For von Hartmann it is clear that if we are to have any genuine morality, it must be found in some metaphysical system which can mediate between these opposite extremes of pluralism and abstract monism. There are two possible theories effecting this mediation, a false one: theism, and the true one: concrete monism.

In the system of theism the gap between the "one and many" is fixed and cannot be abridged. The Creator is the one, creation is the many. The proponents of this theory have correctly grasped the truth that the metaphysical foundations of plurality must be laid in the sphere of "unity," but in doing so they have committed the unforgivable mistake of ascribing substantiality to the created as well, entailing thereby a substantial dualism wherein God and men are set in opposition to one another as separate personal substances.

The historical origin of theistic metaphysics is traced by von Hartmann to the desire of supplementing the primitive and bleak order of things in this world with a future state of more righteous and permanent retribution. For this purpose immortality and freedom of the will are essential conditions. But immortality involves substantiality and freedom entails absoluteness. The substantiality of the creature, again, involves likeness to the creator, which in turn results in the concept of divine personality. Thus, in so far as theism maintains a substantial pluralism with regard to creatures, it concludes to an individual-eudemonistic pseudo-morality, and inasmuch as it teaches the existence of a personal creator as the source of morality, it terminates in a heteronomous-authoritative pseudo-morality. The union of these two aspects of pseudo-morality in theism is contrived, however, simply as a bait to make us content with our hard lot here below, to bless and praise our creator for the heavy burden with which all creation is laden, and this in the hope of a future reward. The sufferings of this life are bearable only on the moral grounds of a just reward in the life to come. But as soon as this subtle deceit is realized the myth of transcendental theism crumbles.

There is no cause for alarm, von Hartmann assures us, for even if the hope of a just reward in a future life is done away with, Schopenhauer, the new Messiah, will show us the way in the discovery of true morality. It is his undying merit to bring about the turning point in the development of Christian morality inasmuch as he taught that the noumenal "one" alone is immortal, and its manifold will-manifestations or real objectivations in the sphere of phenomenal individuality are alone personal. In holding fast to his conviction, Schopenhauer eliminates "moral personality" from the one, and "substantiality" and "immortality" from the many. To be sure, this doctrine must be interpreted in the sense of transcendental realism, of which Schopenhauer himself became more and more convinced toward the end of his life, for transcendental idealism banishes all plurality of individuals into the realm of mere illusions, and makes all changes of the phenomenal, such as life and death, action and inaction, moral and immoral, a matter of complete indifference. On the other hand, if some one were to give a pluralistic interpretation of the Schopenhauerian will-metaphysics then concrete-monistic ethics would at once plunge back into the fallacy of individual-eudemonistic pseudo-morality. Von Hartmann gives no specific reference in his *System*, vol. VI, pp. 191–192, concerning the alleged theory of Schopenhauer. In all probability he has in mind Schopenhauer's doctrine on the monistic nature of the will, and as such, its attribute of "indestructibility" (*Unzerstörbarkeit*), in opposition to its manifestation in the world which are many, since they come under the conditions of individuation, i.e., are affected by the categories of space and time.[1]

Having left behind the ruins of theism, and finding the nucleus of true solution to his problem in Schopenhauer's ethical system, von Hartmann considers "genuine morality" as expressed in the principle of the substantial identity of individuals. Von Hartmann is convinced that as long as the individual regards himself as essentially and substantially individual, he has no motive to trouble himself with anything beyond himself; he must, in other words, be an absolute egoist. But as soon as he becomes aware of himself as only a phenomenal objectivation of the one absolute substance, he will also grasp immediately that whatever he does to another, whether good or evil, he does it to the same substantial essence (*Wesen*) which resides in him. This thought is best realized in Brahmanism and expressed in the famous axiom: "That art thou," i.e., every one is essentially identical with you, and is different and separate merely in appearance.[2] The greater is the metaphysical realization of the essential identity of the individuals the more will eudemonological egoism vanish. Realizing the subjective phenome-

---

[1] *Arthur Schopenhauer's Sämmtliche Werke*, ed. by P. Deussen and A. Hübscher (München: R. Piper and Co., 1911–1912), vol. II, pp. 23–27; vol. III, pp. 30–38, pp. 473–572.
[2] *Op. cit.*, p. 192.

nality of the ego egoism is fatally wounded at its very root, for the care to promote the well-being of the absolute essence, which simultaneously is my essence too, cannot be rightly labelled egoistic, for as absolute subject and universal essence, it is not ego any longer.

Although the moral necessity of the substantial identity of all individuals with each other and with the absolute has been established, the question is still open as to how can I serve best the well-being of the all-one essence and through it of all the other individuals in the phenomenal world? The answer cannot be given in the social-eudemonistic sense of the "greatest possible pleasure to the greatest possible number," since the exclusive application of this principle leads inevitably to the quietism of despair and practical nihilism. Thus the climb must continue in search for the ultimate moral principle, and von Hartmann hopes to find it in the religious moral principle of the essence-identity of all with the absolute.

This essence-identity of the individuals with the all-one, however, is not to be taken in a pantheistic sense. Von Hartmann's concrete monistic system upholds the distinction between God as essence and man as illusory or phenomenal individual. This distinction is supported by a twofold consideration; first, every single man is only one among the many illusory (phenomenal) individuals, thus cannot be identical with the real all-one; secondly, God as essence always remains something else than the mere sum-total of his appearances, the phenomenal world. This distinction notwithstanding, he maintains that all which is essence in me is not "I" but God; the self which finds in my ego one of its many mirrored reflections is no longer individual but supra-individual, all-encompassing, that merely operates in me in a special manner.[1] The conscious realization of this fact is the source and foundation of any and all true morality. Equipped with this truth, man rejects any conflict as nonsensical between his own will and the will of the absolute. This truth annihilates any alienation of God and man, and brings about man's absorption into the divine life, into a divine manner of feeling, thinking, willing, and acting. For as long as the absolute is understood as a "being at rest," as an abiding substance, the individual cannot deify his own individual life otherwise than by seeking to participate in the death-like immobility of the absolute. It is only when the absolute is comprehended as real, rational activity, and the union of the absolute idea and will is expressed as absolute teleology, that the deification of the individual's life can be sought in the participation of the

[1] *Ibid.*, p. 199.

absolute activity by submitting the self-will to the service of the absolute aim, purpose.

The results of these investigations can be summarized in the following principles: (1) the absolute essence and my essence are one and the
same essence; (2) the absolute essence is teleological in nature.
With the help of these truths we are now in the position to formulate
the absolute moral principle, which can be declared as the "moral
principle of the absolute teleology as that (teleology) of our own essence" (by virtue of the essence-identity of all with the absolute).[1]
This supreme moral principle of concrete monism does not abolish the
distinction between God as essence and man as phenomenal-individual,
it merely intends to emphasize the fact that in view of his substantial
identity with the absolute man's special aim as a phenomenon, i.e., the
pursuit of his individual happiness, must give way to the absolute aim,
which is also his own from the higher standpoint of his substantiality.
So if culture-development is assumed to be the teleological aim of the
absolute, it follows at once that should a conflict occur between this
culture-development and eudemonism the latter must give place to the
former.

Absolute teleology is, therefore, the ultimate principle of von Hartmann's ethical system. Its real content, however, is still hidden and
unknown to us. What can the absolute aim be? What is the purpose,
the final aim of all? What is the ultimate reason for and explanation
of the burning "why" of all suffering, despair, and desolation? Von
Hartmann's answer is simple but shocking. Eliminating the possibilities
of a positive-eudemonistic absolute aim as well as a negative-eude-
monistic one von Hartmann concludes:

It remains, therefore, that (the absolute aim) is a privative-eudemonistic aim,
i.e., the deliverance of the absolute from his transcendental misery, and the
return to his painless peace, by the means of the immanent torment of the
world-evolution.[2]

To accelerate this deliverance, as far as in him lies, is the duty of each
individual. But in order to make men realize and urge them on to
accept their share of responsibility in the process of this universal salvation, certain conditions must be fulfilled. First, and above all, they
must be resigned to a pessimistic *Weltanschauung* and consent to the
idea of self-effacement for the sake of the absolute unconscious.

[1] *Ibid.*, p. 204.
[2] *Ethische Studien*, p. 189. Cf. also *System*, vol. VI, p. 208.

In view of recent opinions concerning this problem,[1] which seem to hold that von Hartmann has abandoned his metaphysical pessimism in his ethics and has overcome the negative value-judgment concerning life's worth the following passage is of paramount importance:

All moral education must be aimed at the acceptance of the inevitability of self-denial and at making clear to all men that *they have no right to be happy* (here or hereafter) and they have not been born to be happy but to fulfill their cursed duty and obligation... In the masses... the optimistic illusions and egoistic demands must give place to a pessimistic conviction and a self-sacrificing devotion together with a desire for salvation. And when it is further understood that for the individual his true self-salvation is attainable only as a universal-salvation, through his moral cooperation in the furthering of the culture-process then the thought that the content of the absolute aim is the absolute salvation will at once become most comforting as well as stimulating. Then the desire to help to expiate a heavy and oppressive evil will be of greater motivating force than the craving for individual happiness. For an eudemonological pessimist who does not seek his own any longer, but who is, at the same time, a teleological evolutionist, the moral principle of the deliverance (of the absolute) must be the highest thinkable motivation to morality.[2]

In this morality pessimism is still the highest motivating force, and the suffering of the ego and the world is transformed into the suffering of God, and love of God is replaced by sympathy with God. The world can be saved only when God is delivered from suffering, and God can be delivered from his suffering only through the world-process which he orders as a means to his salvation, and through the morally-conscious souls who bring this culture-evolution to its culmination and fulfill-ment. For this reason men must place all their trust in God, for only through his salvation can men find their own liberation; similarly, for the same reason has God put his whole trust in humanity, because only through men can he bring to a completion the supreme metaphysical act of his existence: his self-deliverance.

Thus the final call to morality is issued by pessimism. It is our duty to remain in life and to continue the human species in order to alleviate the transcendental misery of the absolute, which is also our own misery, by our constant and interminable sufferings. In some mysterious man-ner evolution of all kinds, whether cosmic, organic, or intellectual, has a tendency in this direction. Evolution, progress, culture-development must be promoted at the cost of misery, pain, and suffering to the indi-vidual as well as to the whole race. The final dictum therefore is to develop culture and endure happily our unhappy lot until deliverance

[1] Kurt F. Leidecker in his article on von Hartmann in *The Dictionary of Philosophy*, ed. by Dagobert D. Runes (New York: Philosophical Library, 1942), states that von Hartmann "in ethics transcended an original pessimism... in a qualified optimism." p. 122, col. 2.

[2] *System*, vol. VI, pp. 213–214.

is attained and all return to the original unconsciousness of the absolute.

To gain a unified view of the value of von Hartmann's ethical philosophy it is more advantageous to bypass the errors of his gnoseological position, which make all his proofs and contentions *a priori* questionable, and focus attention upon his professedly inductive method in service of morality. It is immediately obvious that from the beginning his endeavors labor under two difficulties.

First he places the objectivation of ethical activity in general fundamentally in the unconscious, that is, in character and in the alogical will. But character and the nature of will are first known to us through their activity and operation, and not prior to them. Moreover, moral motivation always appears to us as conscious presentation, as is verified by our constant internal experiences, whereas for von Hartmann it is completely unconscious, thus, excluded from the realm of free action. Consequently, morality in its true significance is reduced to a mechanical execution of fatalistically determined actions, in other words, to a mere illusion. Only a will that deliberates freely and knowingly can serve as foundation of a true, genuine morality.

We believe that this position is in complete harmony with the mind of Aristotle. For him moral action necessarily involves choice, and choice in turn:

... necessarily involves both intellect or thought and a certain disposition of character... Hence choice may be called either thought related to desire or desire related to thought; and man, *as an originator of action*, is a union of desire and intellect.[1]

St. Thomas follows the Philosopher in demanding free deliberation for a truly genuine moral action:

When it (the will) is inclined to something as absolutely necessary to the end, it is moved to it with a certain necessity; but when it tends to something only because of certain befittingness, it tends to it without necessity... for the voluntary need be neither natural nor violent.[2]

And again:

... an action is called voluntary when the principle of that action is in the agent himself (whereby violence is excluded), in such a way, that the agent himself *knows* the singular circumstances which concur for the performance of the action (whereby ignorance is excluded which is the cause of an involuntary action).[3]

---

[1] *Eth. Nic.* bk. VI, ch. II, 405. Cf. also *ibid.*, bk. II, ch. VI, 15; bk. III, ch. I, II, V, VIII, IX, XI.
[2] *C. G.*, I, ch. V, 2.
[3] *In Eth. Nic.*, bk. III, ch. IV, 1.

Something is said to be voluntary not merely because it falls under the act of the will, but because it falls under the power of the will; in this sense even the act of not-to-will is called voluntary, because it is within the powers of the will, to will or not-to-will, to perform or not to perform an act.[1]

For actions of this kind obviously there is no place in von Hartmann's ethical system, since his moral determinism is a logical inference from his metaphysical determinism. This once more necessitates the perpetuation of moral evil in the phenomenal as well as in the noumenal world. In view of the actual existence of evil on one hand, and the doctrine of substance-identity of all with the absolute on the other, the origin of evil once more is necessarily placed in the unconscious absolute. Whence follows that evil not only happens to be, but it is impossible for it not to be. For this reason von Hartmann could never hold for a world without evil, for it is a metaphysical necessity within the monistic process itself which in the ethical realm becomes phenomenally objectivated. Thus insurmountable and final pessimism is transcendentally welded to the ethics of von Hartmann.

The second comment arises from a logical analysis of his deduction of the content of the moral judgment. Correctly, but inconsistently within his own system, the moral motive always appears as conscious presentation. In spite of such recognition von Hartmann insists that the origin of this motivation, considered formally, is the unconscious logical categorical function. Thereby implying clearly, that the conscious moral presentation is but a product of the unconscious, and the moral act is an unconscious realization of a logical relation devoid of any deliberation. How does our consciousness become aware of these unconscious logical functions? How does it come to know these sub-ethical principles of actions? The answer received is that our consciousness is passive and as such it cannot produce anything of itself; both content and form of any presentation must derive from the unconscious. But moral evaluation is not one of the functions of the unconscious, how could then the unconscious communicate it? On the basis of this consideration the conclusion cannot be avoided that the fact of the moral phenomenon remains unexplained. Moreover, how can von Hartmann account for the inner conviction that we act freely, consequently morally? The presentation of individual freedom cannot come from the unconscious as such for it is unknown to it, nor could it come from consciousness, for consciousness as such is a mere accidental givenness (*Gegebenheit*). The lack of solution remains one of the many riddles of von Hartmann's paradoxes.

[1] *De Malo*, bk. II, a. 1 ad 2.

In view of this double failure to remove deterministic pessimism from his ethical doctrine, and to give any rationally acceptable explanation for the moral prerequisite, viz., freedom, it may be thought that there is nothing more to say about the ethical studies and observations of von Hartmann. This is not the case. We would do injustice to him if we were to neglect to mention the wealth of his profound and keen scrutiny of moral phenomena, which is undeniably a witness to an impressive interest in him concerning ethical problems. Similarly, we would rightly be accused of prejudice if we ignored the admirable spirit of dedication that urged him on to gather a treasury of concrete facts for study by subsequent generations of moralists. The fact we sincerely deplore – and this more because of him than because of us – is that all this unselfish work is not what it should be, because it was not at the very outset what it ought to have been, i.e., a dialectic in the Aristotelian sense of the term. Any true, genuine moral study must be an unprejudiced search for and gradual systematization of ethical principles on the basis of immanent criticism. Von Hartmann's ethical system is more like the execution of a carefully arranged blueprint. The end is already firmly established, and the empirical material is not judged on its own merit, but in light of a preconceived view, and is molded to fit into a prefabricated pattern. The rules of a pure scientific induction are betrayed; in this von Hartmann is greatly influenced by Hegel in so far as in spite of the empirical phenomena morality is exhibited as the self-evolving of the moral idea from the most primitive and lowest stages of the moral phenomenon to its culmination in its highest form of concrete monism. This evolutionist treatment of morality is of paramount importance for it is devised to support in an inductive manner the metaphysics of the unconscious.

Beginning with eudemonism and rejecting it after its examination as a morally unworthy mode of behavior, ethical consciousness manifests itself in higher and higher forms, revealing thereby an underlying process of evolution. This evolution of morality is, of course, merely a portion of the universal evolution von Hartmann believes to have been proved from experience. But neither von Hartmann, nor any other evolutionist for that matter, can explain the absolutely binding character of morality if it is merely the result of different evolutionary stages. What comes by degrees may disappear by the same degrees or can be superseded by newly developing higher stages, and if this is the case, the concept of the "absolute" no longer has meaning. Furthermore, such a concept of evolution involves great intrinsic difficulties. How can a first moral concept arise at all and how can an ethical system develop from it without an original, innate predisposition toward them? In this latter view morality is naturally given in its fundamental outline in men, and the explanation of morality through an absolute development from submoral or amoral strata of the unconscious becomes not only unnecessary but impossible. That von Hartmann is forced to assume such a development is due to his notion of consciousness which is completely passive and void of substantiality.

Ethical self-awareness does not originate, therefore, from coarse egoism, as von Hartmann presupposes it. There may be agreement with him when he labels such morality unworthy of man, at least in so far as it is earth-bound, sensuous, and purely negative. But it is just as unethical, untrue, and unpsychological when he thinks that any search for happiness and peace of mind, whether here or hereafter, must be rejected. Morality is the acceptance and preservation of the order of objective values in the light of man's absolute, inner dependence.[1] The aspiration and search for happiness within the limits established by this order is certainly not immoral, to say the least, and even less so when the sought for happiness belongs to the order of temporal or eternal spiritual goods. To label this as a sort of "base egoism" is nonsensical. For spiritual goods, on the basis of their universal value and content, presuppose as a condition of attainment the repression of egoism. Moreover, our innermost being yearns for truth, goodness, and beauty, and to seek after and find them belongs to our very existence. Once found, it is most natural that we enjoy the inner happiness they can provide. In its highest form, this is preeminently true of spiritual, transcendental beatitude with God, who as the source of the soul, and fountain of all spiritual good is longed for in his most perfect reality. Morality can be based only upon the cultivation and furthering of objective values which in turn will bring about happiness and peace. Hence it is a short step to the conclusion that possession of God as the greatest absolute value is the highest form of morality and the greatest possible enjoyment of happiness.[2] That such complete happiness with and in God is metaphysically possible is evident from von Hartmann's own investigation, but with the all-important difference that while for him, because of his metaphysical misconceptions, this transcendental union is one of suffering here below, and annihilation hereafter, for us it is a union of beatitude here and eternal life hereafter.

[1] *S. Th.* I. q. 44, a. 1; q. 45, a. 2 and 5; q. 46, a. 1; q. 47, a. 1 and 2.
[2] *S. Th.* I. II. q. 3, a. 8.

A final notion that demands discussion and possible clarification, i.e., the notion of heteronomy. After disposing of the eudemonistic pseudo-morality von Hartmann insists upon discarding heteronomy in morality as well. Whether this is the only reason for rejecting heteronomy, or his *a priori* conviction necessitates such repudiation, is irrelevant here, what is certain is his belief that morality can be only one kind, that of autonomy. He constantly reminds us that heteronomy does not create morality but merely legality. Heteronomy is the surrender of freedom to violence, of the inner-self to outer influences, it is a submission to alien forces and power regardless of the content of the command.

It appears to us that in his hasty generalization von Hartmann unduly extends his own description merely of certain possible aspects of legal heteronomy, thereby showing disregard for the basic rules of logic. Man can follow and execute a command from without because he sees and judges it to be true and good. The point in question is not heteronomy but rather the moral judgment of the individual. In the case of carrying out the commands of external authorities, such as the family, State, Church, and customs, the individual does not act by heteronomous authority alone. For the conviction is always implied in our judgment that the laws of these external authorities, at least in their essential features, are effected with complete accordance of rational moral values, therefore, to comply with them, even without a full understanding from the individual's part, cannot be called immoral. Man first leaves the realm of morality and enters that of legality when he obeys a stronger power against the dictate of his reason and without the inner acceptance of a command. The above-mentioned authorities, even if not all in the same extent and in the same manner, are the embodiment and representatives of necessary supra-individual values; to reject them in principle would be contrary to reason, and therefore, immoral.[1]

The more reason and will, and consequently their content, truth and goodness, are represented by an authority, the more that authority deserves the submission of our reason and will to its command, and, as a result, the more perfect is the interchange between heteronomy and autonomy. The fullest expression of this is a personal God, absolute truth and goodness, thus absolute authority. His laws are the reflections of his essence: intellect, goodness, perfection, and sanctity. The human soul as likeness of the divine is capable to reflect upon and e-

[1] *S. Th.* I. II, q. 90, a. 1c. and ad 3.

valuate these laws, thus it is a dictate of *our own* moral judgment to comply with the laws of God. Where the divine precepts surpass our understanding and reach beyond human reasoning, we are still fully conscious of the fact that they are expressions of the absolute intellect and sanctity, and as such, of perfect morality and not the whimsical violence of an oppressive power. Heteronomy and autonomy are thus once more reconciled with the absolute and entitative dependence of all created autonomy as well as all just and rightful secondary heteronomy in the incomprehensible unity of "he who is."

God, then, is the ultimate moral principle and the fundamental resolution of any egoism. As the nourishment and strength of every soul, he is to be sought not only by the individual for the individual, but by all for all. All men are children of one Father, and in their unified totality they preeminently constitute the kingdom of God. From this point of view even evil can be understood and evaluated in its own manner. Its explanation will serve for its theoretical conquest and a proof for the moral principle.

Sin is the deliberate violation of the order of values, and is therefore a partial or total rejection of the ultimate norm and value, i.e., God. It is the preference of the sensile over against the spiritual and of the finite over against the infinite values. Its reparation consists in contrition as the restoration of order, and in change of purpose as an attempt of new re-evaluation.[1] This is not at all, as von Hartmann thinks, a debasement, dejection, and disintegration of the inner man, but his recognition of fault, return to truth, and re-establishment of the genuine order of values. To anchor morality in God does not imply moral heteronomy; on the contrary, it is the only humanly acceptable foundation of a rightly interpreted moral autonomy. Only on the assumption of a personal creator is moral freedom possible for only then can we speak of individual evaluations and responsible decisions. Our moral decision is not a judgment made under the influence of an alien, and therefore heteronomous set of standards, but a revelation and actual evaluation of our own worth or lack of worth in light of the known and inwardly accepted highest moral principle.

Finally, as is evident from these critical considerations, the metaphysical difficulties of theism of which von Hartmann speaks, are essentially imaginary. As our inductive investigations of the moral phenomenon at hand show, they lead to a self-conscious, personal God, and not to an unconscious absolute. Von Hartmann cannot reconcile

---

[1] *S. Th.* I. II. q. 71. a. 2 and 6.

and justify moral facts and his own postulates. In opposition to Hegel, who retains the absolute as revealed in the moral norms and being its own self-aim, he recognizes no individual as reaching beyond personal moral norms but only judgments of individuals of higher consciousness-stages. In this relation to the end he finds ethics purely subjective and treats it merely as a means to nowhere. For the ultimate end unveils itself finally in the return of all existence into non-existence. This is von Hartmann's final answer for the soul's longing for happiness; this is the ultimate pessimistic stage of the teleological evolution. Such a theory of morality is not only prejudiced and arbitrary, but it negates morality as well as all other activity of the spirit. It annihilates prior to commencement every kind of striving, hope, joy, and expectation. According to such a doctrine, it is totally irrelevant and immaterial how men live in this life. Saint or sinner, hero or traitor, will equally share in the same self-annihilating absorption into the unconscious. Together with all distinctions between different value judgments morality itself is abolished.

The conclusion is inevitable: genuine morality is possible only on the assumption that the absolute, the source as well as the final aim of morality, is the self-conscious possessor of infinite existence. As such he cannot be a god of dissolution and eternal annihilation, but only the God of eternal life.

CHAPTER VIII

PHILOSOPHY OF RELIGION

Was Christentum sei, darüber besteht bekanntlich durchaus keine Einigkeit. Das Wort bezeichnet einen ganz verschiedenen Inhalt im Urchristentum des ersten Jahrhunderts, in der griechischen Kirche des sechsten, in der römischen des sechzehnten Jahrhunderts, und im zwanzigsten Jahrhundert ist der Streit über das Wesen des Christentums von neuem entbrannt.[1]

The last statement of this quotation can hardly be applied with more truth to anyone than to von Hartmann. His ardor for religious polemics[2] is apparent in the first edition of the *Philosophy of the Unconscious*, where a lengthy chapter is dedicated to a comparative study of the unconscious and the God of theism,[3] and this interest in religious problems remained with him throughout his entire life. In 1870, shortly after the first edition of the *Philosophy of the Unconscious*, he published his *Briefe über die Christliche Religion*, the first of a long line of successive works devoted to the study of various aspects of religion.[4] The work claims to give an objective presentation of Christianity as it is found in the New Testament. It foreshadows in an outline the core of von

[1] *System*, vol. VII, Vorwort, p. V. "As to what is Christianity there is obviously no unanimous answer at all. The meaning of the word is entirely different as it is applied to the Christianity of the first century, or to the Greek Church of the sixth century, or to the Roman of the eleventh century, or to the evangelical of the sixteenth century, and the debate regarding the essence of Christianity is aflame anew in the twentieth century."

[2] The terms "religious," "religion," and similar ones describing man's relation to the absolute being are used in most unusual and unorthodox senses by von Hartmann. Formal expressions of the Christian religion are retained in his religious terminology but their meaning is altered, modified, or completely reversed to suit the demands of the religion of the unconscious, as we intend to show in the course of this chapter.

[3] *Philosophy of the Unconscious*, "The Unconscious and the God of Theism." Vol. II, chap. VIII, pp. 245–276. For the sake of clarity we want to note here that henceforth when the text refers to the God of the Old and New Testament the name is spelled by the capital letter, whereas if it denotes the god of von Hartmann's religion the small letter is used.

[4] *Briefe über die Christliche Religion* (Berlin: Carl Dunker, 1870). In publishing this work von Hartmann used the pseudonym F. A. Müller, in order not to interfere with the success of his first publication of the *Philosophy of the Unconscious*, since the *Briefe* show a hostile attitude toward Christianity. It attracted little attention at the time and later on it was enlarged and published under the title: *Das Christentum des Neuen Testaments* (Bad Sachsa Hermann Haacke, 1905).

Hartmann's twofold problem with regard to the Christian religion: first, whether we can still be called Christians according to the norms of the New Testament, and secondly, what can the old, historical Christianity offer to the religious consciousness of modern man.

To answer the first question, von Hartmann proceeds to a criticism of modern Christianity in the form of liberal Protestantism.[1] Liberal Protestantism is the consequence of the Reformation and, as such, it has destroyed faith in the infallibility of the Scriptures as well as in that of the Church, thereby, simultaneously destroying the positive content of Christianity itself. In this sense, Protestantism became the grave-digger of Christianity. Intended to restore the original beauty and simplicity of Christian religion, liberal Protestantism is in reality a meager theorem with an essentially negative content. With each succeeding sentence von Hartmann's criticism grows bolder, and he does not hesitate to label liberal Protestantism irreligious. For, he contends, each religion necessarily postulates some metaphysical principles, but all that liberal Protestantism has in this regard is a feigned appearance of a long surpassed metaphysics with its outmoded principles of the existence of a personal God and individual immortality. In fact, this is but a modern sort of naturalism with ridiculous superstitions. Modern consciousness can have nothing in common with such a religion.

The answer to the second question yields similar results. In analyzing the value of historical Christianity for the contemporary mind, von Hartmann follows closely the thoughts of Hegel, Feuerbach, Stirner, and Strauss. The ruling idea of the times, viz., evolution, came into its own in matters of religion also, and made these protagonists of evolution view Christianity as a thing of the past, a reminder of ancient times. The immanent idea through its self-realization in history brought forth new, more vigorous branches from the old trunk, and to cultivate these is not liberal only ultra-reactionary.[2]

If von Hartmann ever plays havoc with historical facts, it is with regard to the historical arguments of the foundation of Christianity that he shows this trait of his character most patently. Without the slightest attempt to substantiate his statements he writes:

Jesus was a Jewish sectarian who never made a promise to form a new religion. The entire traditional literature concerning the Life of Jesus rests upon additions of later times, so also the events which preceded his death. Jesus was no genius,

[1] The same problem is treated more extensively in a later work of von Hartmann, *Die Selbstzersetzung des Christentums und die Religion der Zukunft* (Berlin: Carl Dunker, 1874), 2nd ed.

[2] *Das Christentum des Neuen Testaments*, Vorwort, p. VIII.

merely a talented man, who, however, because of his complete lack of a history of culture-development could produce only something very mediocre which is vulnerable at many points and which labors under many serious errors and misconceptions. He is a fanatic and a transcendental dreamer, who, in spite of an innate love for men, hates and despises the world and everything earthly, and denounces any striving except after the transcendental values. He is a lovable and unassuming young man, who through a remarkable concatenation of circumstances is caught by the contagious idea of his time, and believes that he is the promised Messiah, and he is accepted by his followers as such.[1]

This hatred of the world and the belief in the approaching end of time is the most common idea of all the books of the New Testament in von Hartmann's opinion, and he views it as a combination of earthly pessimism and transcendental optimism. All the inevitable consequences ensuing from such a *Weltanschauung* such as transcendental eudemonism, belief in miracles, and misinterpretation of prophecies support the fact that the common basic outlook of the New Testament is thoroughly contradictory to the ideals of modern culture-development. The Christianity of Christ is completely useless for modern man; a renovation of Jesus's teaching is utterly impossible and impracticable.

The task of giving the world a new religion falls upon the philosopher, and von Hartmann believes himself equal to the calling. His mission consists in working:

... with zeal and loyalty... in order to offer the future a store of ideas as rich and valuable as possible, from which the eventual new religion can one day be formed.[2]

But von Hartmann is too impatient to wait for this day in idle expectation, and he offers his plan for action in a new work entitled *Die Krisis des Christentums in der Modernen Theologie*.[3] In it he sidetracks Schleiermacher's fashionable theology of mediation, and declares his own creed: Christianity belongs to the dead past, and there:

... rises against it as a free philosophy of religion, a new pantheistic (pessimistic) religion of the future, which places the results of speculative philosophy at the command of the highest possible degree of the fully liberated religious consciousness.[4]

The full enfolding of the principles of this new religion is the duty of the philosophy of religion. Von Hartmann undertakes this yet in another monumental work, his greatest historical endeavor, *Das Religiöse*

---

[1] *Ibid.*, p. 72.
[2] *Die Selbstzersetzung des Christentums und die Religion der Zukunft*, p. 94.
[3] *Die Krisis des Christentums in der Modernen Theologie* (Berlin: Carl Dunker, 1880), 2nd ed.
[4] *Ibid.*, p. 68.

Bewusstsein der Menschheit im Stufengang seiner Enwickelung.[1] He wrote this treatise with the intention of giving a solid historical foundation to his own philosophical position.

The underlying principle of von Hartmann's historical investigation is the theory of evolution which, applied to the field of religious consciousness, discovers beneath the successive series of chaotic appearances of the religious phenomena a self-realizing rational force or the idea. In its drive to achieve a new and higher degree of development von Hartmann recognizes the progressively evolving trend of a religious consciousness. Particular historical religions are placed within this line of evolution as component elements of the entire process, each containing a partial truth which will be embodied in a higher synthesis of elevated moments in a new religion.

Von Hartmann describes in great detail this development from its very first beginnings to its fullest consummation in the religion of the unconscious. In its naturalistic stage of development, the idea reveals itself first as henotheism. The most primitive form of henotheism is its anthropomorphic stage as we find it in the beliefs of the Greeks, Romans, and Teutonic tribes. In its more elevated development the same trend appears theologically systematized, as in the religion of the Egyptians and Persians. At this point the idea reaches an essentially different stratum of development, inasmuch as pure naturalism is sublimated into supra-naturalism. The first stage of this supra-naturalistic manifestation of the idea is abstract monism, as found in the religion of the Brahmans and Buddhists. The next phase is theism in its primitive monotheistic form, as it is realized in the legalistic religion of the Jews. The various attempts at reforms within Judaism produced Christianity, which in turn brought forth the realistic religion of redemption in the form of concrete monistic pantheism of von Hartmann.[2]

The theoretical exposition and gradual development of this new religion is the task of a number of von Hartmann's works.[3] The common

---

[1] *Das Religiöse Bewusstsein der Menschheit im Stufengang seiner Entwickelung* (Bad Sachsa: Hermann Haacke, 1906), 3rd ed.

[2] This anti-historical attitude and arbitrary interpretation of facts should not surprise us, since we have already encountered it. Von Hartmann is not interested in employing the exoteric and esoteric criteria of scientific historical investigations. His only concern is to show that evolution proves the truth of his religious doctrine. As is his wont, in his religious theory also, historical impartiality is sacrificed to his polemical spirit.

[3] Apart from *Das Religiöse Bewusstsein*, the following are of importance: *Die Religion des Geistes* (Bad Sachsa: Hermann Haacke, 1907), 3rd ed. *Etische Studien* (Leipzig: Hermann Haacke, 1898), No. I, V, and VIII, pp. 1–33, 109–125, 199–240. His comprehensive work, *System*, vol. VII; *Grundriss der Religiösen Philosophie* (Bad Sachsa: Hermann Haacke, 1909). In addition von Hartmann has a long line of articles published in various magazines. The most noteworthy: *Gegenwart*, "Das Wesen des Christentums," No. 1, 14, 15, 22, 1901; *Gegenwart*,

characteristic of these works is a systematic analysis of the religious phenomenon from three different points of view: psychological, metaphysical, and ethical.

In the psychological analysis von Hartmann gives first a detailed description of the religious function considered exclusively from the viewpoint of man as this function reveals itself in mental presentation. In other words, the religious phenomenon is actually realized only in man as a psychological fact. This phenomenon of man's consciousness necessarily demands an object to which it is related. The object must be incomparably superior to the subject of phenomenon, reasons von Hartmann, if we are to avoid once more eudemonism, moralism, aesthetism, and other false notions of religion. He finds that the term of this relation from the subject to the object of religious phenomenon is what is commonly called god. Thus the concept of god is not scientific, but merely a religious concept. Religion is the relationship of man to god, "and the name has no further content and meaning."[1] The nature of this god-presentation in the religious function of man will be the same as the forces which shaped this religious phenomenon. But whatever these forces may have been, primarily they must be transcendental in nature. In other words, we must believe that the object presented in consciousness has an independently existent correlative beyond the confines of consciousness itself, otherwise there would be no distinction between religion and illusion. The religious object cannot be merely the postulate of man's religious needs, but must be verified through cognition. Man's religious outlook must be in agreement with his theoretical views in general, and even if the two do not completely coincide in every detail, yet they may not contradict the common root of presentation. On the contrary, the two presentations, the religious and the scientific, must support one another. From the eventuality of an accidental disagreement of religion with scientific knowledge or certainty, there immediately follows the impossibility of an absolutely true religion, which, in turn, demands the necessity of the fact of tolerance. Any dogmatism, or claim to absolute truth in religion, would arrest the development of the idea on some historical, intermediary step of its evolution, thereby making it a mere propaedeutic to a philosophy of

"Zur Geschichte der Christlichen Religion," No. 9, 1900; *Illustrierte Deutsche Monatshefte*, "Die Anfänge der Religion," vols. 83, p. 495; Dezember 1897; *Türmer-Jahrbuch*, "Gedanken über den Individualismus," pp. 216–220; *Preussische Jahrbücher*, "Dorners Religionphilosophie," vol. 114, 1903; *Tag*, "Was wissen wir von Jesus?" No. 347, 349, 351, 1904. The following portion of our study will be a parallel summary exposition of von Hartmann's later works based primarily on the VIIth volume of his *System*. Cf. Vorwort, p. VII. footnote.

[1] *System*, vol. VII, p. 1.

religion, or a crypto-philosophy of religion. A true philosophy of religion, on the one hand, makes the latest and presently highest stratum of religious consciousness its object of scientific investigation. Thus presentation is an indispensable aspect of the religious function, but by no means the only one. Genetically it must be the first in order to serve as the key to the solution of the entire religious function, although it is obviously related to it as means to the end.

In the religious function man returns to himself and is entirely with himself after a meaningful contact with the religious object. He does not let the effects of this exchange fade away, but, on the contrary, refers the object to himself and himself to the object, draws god into his own consciousness and builds therefrom his relationship to god.[1]

This state, "being-with-him" and "remaining-in-him" of man and god is the religious feeling, the second moment, the innermost core and focal point of the religious function which lends to it all its warmth and intimacy. It may externalize itself in sheer sentimentality, in aesthetic expression, or in mysticism. The first is indicative of a purely eudemonistic outlook, the second runs the danger of vanishing in mere artistic practices. The most profound and properly religious sentiment is the mystical. It is indeed the living fountain of all piety without the disturbing interference of the purely sensory and aesthetic feelings. Unfortunately, mysticism has its shortcomings for other reasons. Although it is the most valuable of all feelings, it is, at the same time the most obscure and least determined of them. It contains all religious truth in itself, but only as an unconscious cause of conscious feelings.

As a conscious reflection of the highest religious truth it is the richest feeling, yet it is also the poorest; for it does not possess the truth in complete consciousness. This explains its insufficiency and its need for knowledge which reveals presentation as its unconscious cause. Without such knowledge mysticism could easily deteriorate into a self-sufficient pseudo-mysticism, which is only a step from subjective, arbitrary fancy, or religious phantasmagory. This possibility of different aberrations in religious feelings indicates that feelings alone are inept to bring about the religious function. Its true value consists in showing the unconscious process of motivation whose response in consciousness is the transformation of religious feeling into a definite willing. Religious feeling is called the best of all sentiments because it contains stability which aids greatly the task of presentation to perfect the religion of feeling into a religion of will.

[1] *Ibid.*, p. 8.

Will forms the principal substance of presentation. In its unconscious state it is the source of presentation, as conscious will it is the final aim. Without unconscious religious drives there would be no religion, without yearning for individual and social realization of the content of subjective religious consciousness religion would forever remain fruitless as well as aimless. Thus, the "will-to-action" determines the value of the religious function, and also the significance of the religious presentation and feeling. The religious drive achieves its fulfillment in conscious will as efficacious consciousness-content. In it the religious process returns to its starting point in order to begin a new phase. This result of the conscious will strengthens and refines the unconscious drive so that each subsequent process takes place on a higher degree of development.

At this point von Hartmann makes it clear that it is a grave mistake to divorce the will from its psychological surroundings and make it an independent religious function. For in that case, either it will be allowed to subsist independently in spite of a religious outlook, and then the influence of religion upon the will is reduced to a minimum, as in the case in Spinoza's system; or, we have to search for the motivating presentation in the will itself, as does Kant, in which eventuality all other cognitive manifestations will be judged simply illusory. In this latter case religion becomes morality and every religious perspective will be dealt with as the "transcendent projection of the immanent idea-content of morality."[1] But in this interpretation the true rapport between religion and morality is reversed. Historically all morality derives from religion. The certainty of the moral will is a sheer delusion unless it is founded upon a psychological, religious, and metaphysical basis. If religion is made dependent on morality, it becomes barren and lifeless. Religious moralism can presume to furnish the entire content of religion only when itself is unconsciously rooted in a religious-moral principle. The certainty of the religious-moral consciousness, that is, the religious moral conscience is the product in all stages of its development of the religious processes of presentation, feeling, and will.

Presentations, feelings, and acts of the will are deemed religious in so far as they are related to some religious situation or condition. Presentations are religious either because they are known to be adapted to objects of a religious situation, or because they *motivate one*. Feelings are called religious if they *manifest*, externally or internally, such an adaptation, motivation, or cultivation of a religious situation. Finally the acts of the will are religious in so far as they *follow* from such an

[1] *Ibid.*, pp. 15–16.

adaptation, motivation, or cultivation. The unconscious drive expresses itself as yearning after the divine in order to produce a religious
situation. It is that factor which accepts or rejects the presentation as
adapted or not to the religious or irreligious nature of the motive. The
entire wealth of the religious presentation is already contained, at least
implicitly and unconsciously, in religious feeling. From this enfolds
religious willing in a manner which is not totally perceivable in
consciousness. In this imperceptible manner is conscious religious
spiritual life present in its unconscious antecedents, which are the
hidden springs of its activity.

The unifying religious function encompassing presentation, feeling,
and will is called faith. Von Hartmann describes faith as the:

... trustful surrender of the self to the religious object and confidence in the
righteousness of his will, containing simultaneously the practical conviction in
the transcendental reality of the religious object.[1]

It is evident from this description that a genuine religious relation
presupposes not merely the reality of the religious object, but the reality of its relation to the subject as well. A unilateral religious relation
is inconceivable. The very possibility of religion demands that it be a
reciprocal, divine and human function, in which the divine is the term
or correlative of the human. From man's point of view this function is
faith and its corresponding divine function is grace, "... a gratuitously
given gift of god, through which god accepts the self-surrender of the
believer and raises it to the strength of the true religious relation."[2]
Faith and grace are one and the same function, they differ only in
points of view, and because of this unitary nature of the function it is
the real bond between man and god, and this bond establishes between
them a living relationship.

In the concluding part of his psychology of religion, von Hartmann
presents a summary of the different kinds of grace and faith and their
mutual relationships. Considered from the standpoint of religious
presentation, faith is intellectual, or the practical conviction of the
transcendental reality and truth of religious presentations; understood
from the divine standpoint, faith is revelation. Intellectual faith is not
fully conscious revelation; it becomes such through the external revelations of god in nature and history, which are ultimately directed to
the end of having this inner, individually experienced disclosure of god
conscious to the soul.[3] The sum of individual revelations produces then

[1] *Ibid.*, p. 18.
[2] *Ibid.*, p. 19.
[3] *Ibid.*, p. 21.

mankind's common religious consciousness, which serves as a basis for a new stratum in the development of the idea. If we turn to the sphere of religious feeling, we find that the source of man's basic ontological difficulty, his self-alienation, stems from his dependence on and attachment to the world. The resultant feelings of dependence and insufficiency manifest themselves in eudemonistic consciousness as evil and in moral consciousness as guilt.

Caught in the web of eudemonism man seeks deliverance from evil here on earth first by the help of god and renunciation of the goods of this world, and then in the hope of sharing in a better world after death. When man realizes that his present unhappy situation is the result of attachment to the world and that betterment may be hoped for only in the world to come, death and the annihilation of the world assume a religious significance for him as the real deliverance from evil. But meanwhile there is an ideal redemption attainable which consists in the inner detachment of man's petty striving for happiness. To be sure even then he will encounter evil, but it will appear to him as insignificant and trifling. The feeling of guilt arises from the fact that man has relapsed from the moral stratum of self-denial into the depths of seeking his own individual happiness. Redemption from guilt consists, therefore, in acquiring a state of mind, or inner conviction which cannot be swayed any longer by eudemonistic motives. To arrive at this stage man needs the influence of the supernatural power called redemptive grace.

Redemption consists in the fact that in the process of his becoming-conscious man feels his radical, metaphysical dependence upon god, elevated above the peripheric, endlessly divided and multiplied phenomenal dependence on the world.[1]

To this grace of redemption corresponds on man's part emotional faith, or consent of his emotions to seek aims contrary to the drives of natural eudemonism. From this resignation results god's peace in man. The grace that aims to reach the will is called sanctifying grace and in it the will recognizes the divine aim as its own. Reciprocal action on man's part is practical faith, which places all of man's religious activities, presentation, feeling, and will, directly in the service of the divine aims.

This whole view of salvation depends on the fact that man feels inadequate to save himself from evil, i.e., from his eudemonistic evaluation of life through merely natural means. Only on the presupposition of a pessimistic world-view is a religion of redemption thinkable. Opti-

[1] *Die Religion des Geistes*, p. 94.

mism makes religion, at least redemptive religion, superfluous and meaningless in the sense that it endeavors to convince man that happiness is attainable by natural means in this life.

Here von Hartmann reaches in his religious investigations what he calls the metaphysics of religion. In the introduction to it he explains the difference between theoretical and religious metaphysics. The first takes its point of departure from observable facts and proceeds by scientific induction to attain its ultimate principles, whereas the second draws its inferences from the postulates of religious consciousness. However, von Hartmann finds the confines of religious consciousness too narrow and too subjective to defend itself scientifically against the possible objection that the entire realm of religious consciousness is a mere psychological illusion. To amend this inner weakness of religious consciousness he deems it necessary to draw upon theoretical metaphysics to supply the scientific basis for the defense of this doctrine.

The first task of theoretical metaphysics in support of religious consciousness is the clarification and elaboration of the proofs for the existence of god, the object of religious consciousness. Man encounters god in his consciousness as "the conquering moment of his dependence upon the world." In this intuitive introspection man has immediate certainty of god's existence; consequently there is no need to prove it. For a detailed knowledge of its essence we must follow the path of intellectual scrutiny and rational analysis found in the traditional proofs for the existence of God.

Thus the study of the ontological argument discloses the notion of god's absoluteness. This attribute is arrived at by the knowledge that god conquers in consciousness man's relative dependence on the world through the consciousness of an absolute dependence of man and everything else upon itself. The traditional cosmological proof shows god as the absolute source and cause of all relations displayed in the natural world-order. The theoretical teleological argument proves this absolute source of all cosmological relation-complexes to be rational and purposefully operative, or as the immanent teleological reason of the universe.

A more detailed study of these proofs discloses further determinations of god's essence, or, what can be called its various attributes. Thus the ontological proof yields the notions of substantiality and identity. Substantiality is the mark of god's eternity; identity guarantees the permanence of its sameness. In the cosmological proof god's excellence is manifested in the extra-spatial, extra-temporal, and immaterial aspects of its essence. But god is also all-spatial, all-temporal, materially all-efficient, and therefore dynamically omnipresent, according to its operations. Through these attributes religious consciousness acquires assurance that man is in god's hand everywhere, at all times, and in all circumstances, and can never escape its power. It follows, furthermore, that god is the absolute source of the world, i.e., that god is omnipotent, and the primary cause of the world-order, and therefore rational. Rationality is even more apparent from the teleological proof. God is revealed here as the all-pervading wisdom, or omniscience, which continually attains its aims through the choice of the most proportionate means. From this determination of the divine essence we must conclude to another one, namely to all-knowing.[1] In his attempt to remove any and all traces of supernatural value from these attributes von Hartmann explains that reason alone can know each moment of the world as the realization of god's actually present logico-teleological thought. The future is already causally predetermined in the present, and god's foreknowledge is a simultaneous consideration of the future in and through the present. Only these conditions can vouch for the possibility of a genuine predestination as well as salvation. The teleological proof demands, therefore, the existence of a god who through its operations is immanent within the world.

In the second phase of the metaphysics of the religious object von Hartmann's investigations disclose the fact that god abrogates man's dependence on the world and replaces it with absolute dependence upon itself. This latter is said to be immediate from the standpoint of the subject, and mediate from the point of view of the object. These two aspects make up the notion of dependence. The objective dependence is effected through the sum of the ideal influences from the part of the world and it is manifested in the epistemological-ideal proof. The subjective dependence reveals itself in the religious content, and it is expressed in the psychological proof.

The epistemological-ideal proof concludes to god in the following manner: the ideal world of presentation as perceived in consciousness presupposes a logical-dynamic transcendental world, in other words, an objective-real unconscious content of presentation which is incessantly being realized through the activity of the absolute will. This objective-world determining our cognition postulates the existence of an absolute spirit as its carrier. Thus our dependence upon the world is transferred to the absolute spirit and will, thereby effecting the re-

---

[1] *System*, vol. VII, p. 30.

demption of the ego from the dependence upon the world through dependence upon god.

The psychological proof discloses immediately the spirituality of god's essence. The transcendental source and foundation of man's personal psychic life must be spiritual, for it is manifested as such in conscious psychic phenomena. All formal differences notwithstanding the psychic essence of god must be homogeneous with that of man. The psychological proof commences within our consciousness, but it extends over the entire range of existence, human, irrational, organic, and inorganic.

These two proofs, the epistemologico-ideal and the psychological, are raised to a higher unity in the identity-philosophical proof. It shows us that the objective-real: external world, and consciousness: inner world, are only the two manifestations of the same transcendental source, therefore, existence and consciousness are interwoven in the whole world. The unity of religious consciousness, however, does not admit double dependence on the external and internal manner of realization of the absolute, but it postulates a singular root of the outer and inner dependence, otherwise there could not be any salvation from the relative through the absolute dependence.

From these arguments we gain further knowledge of the divine essence itself. The idealistic proof discovers the fact that the actual state of the world is the realization of the idea through the absolute will. The instantaneous present of any phase of the idea's historical development originates from the homogeneous act of the absolute will, although this act simultaneously encompasses the multitude of operations. The development or becoming of the idea takes place with logical necessity, which at one time appears as causality, at another as teleology. The idea does not contain reflexive or discursive elements, and all presentations are simultaneously will-contents as well, i.e., all thoughts are simultaneously produced. These inferences conclude to the fact that god's knowledge is intuitive. This further corroborates its previously discovered attributes of all-knowing and all-wisdom. The will effectively realizing the idea is its omnipotence. God's knowledge of the world is also its creation of the world. Were god to have the knowledge of another world outside of the creative world-idea, it would immediately result in the formation of a second world. Thus, von Hartmann concludes, that absence of another world is a further argument that god is unconscious.[1]

[1] "For god the world is not something independent, existing outside of him, as if his

The psychological proof reveals god as essentially spiritual in nature. Von Hartmann, however, warns us not to attach any notion to the god-spirit which are secondary properties of the human soul, such as memory, character, and feeling. Von Hartmann accepts as primary psychological functions in man: presentation, desire, and the sensation of pain. Accordingly, as primary attributes of god we must postulate will and presentation, and to them we must add a twofold aspect of unhappiness. The first aspect is finite, and its source is the unfulfilled longing of the partial wills of individual substances into which the divine spirit has diffused itself. The second is infinite, inasmuch as there is an infinite striving and longing in the divine will, whereas the actual content of the idea is finite, i.e., the phenomenal manifestation of the divine substance, so that there is an endless overflow of dissatisfied willing in the god-spirit. This objectless will is the inevitable and necessary source of eternal unhappiness in the divinity.

The third problem is that of freedom. Man can gain true freedom only if in spite of his egoistical strivings he subjects himself unreservedly to the absolute aim. He will be freed from his relative dependence upon the world when he sets his actions in conformity with the divine will, thereby divinizing his own actions and reconciling heteronomy with autonomy. In this manner the divine and human functions are interwoven: man shares in the divinity by the unity of wills, and the divine shares in our person, for it is in man that god achieves personality. The divine-human self arising from this unity must be distinguished from the self-seeking and self-asserting ego. The latter is a part of the world, selfish, disordered, and enslaved; the other is supra-natural, totally dependent upon god, yet feeling really one with himself, and therefore, free.

To lay the foundation of freedom, god must set supra-individual aims. These aims are found in the teleological order, which from man's standpoint is called the moral world-order. The latter is absolute and immanent in the world-process and spurs the objective moral order to the realization of its highest aim. This development is aided by all the actions of all individuals, whether good or evil.

productive function would find an opposition in it, as if he could divide and reflect upon himself in a centripetal fashion, so that from such a reflection an ideal mirroring could exist in him, a receptive presentation of the world beside a creative idea. Were such a thing ever to occur in god, his will would immediately seize it and realize it, then there would be two worlds instead of one. Only a *received* idea of the world could be *conscious* in god, which would come about through a centripetal reflexion on the creative activity; but such an occurrence is neither possible nor real. Thus the idealistic proof does not conclude to consciousness in god."
Ibid., pp. 41–42.

As absolute immanent idea, the moral world-order is not a law but an immanent aim. As objective moral world-order, it is immanent order. It will become a truly autonomous moral law when man recognizes in the objective moral world-order the absolute moral world-order, the absolute divine aim operative in him as redemptive grace, and accepts this order and its aims willingly. With its acceptance the autonomous moral law becomes the source of man's inner freedom. There is a reciprocity between the two orders of morality inasmuch as the objective makes the emerging of the subjective possible; whereas the subjective is man's inner evidence for the existence of the objective as the divine order, and submits to its realization and promotion. In this mutual cooperation the efficacy of the moral world-order is shown.

These three orders help us to gain further insight into god's essence. The objective moral world-order discloses objective justice, sanctity, and grace as found in man's conscience in the form of an autonomous law of binding value. Finally, the absolute moral world-order shows absolute justice, sanctity, and grace, as long as god is not conceived as a person beyond the absolute world-order.

The moral world-order becomes the realization of grace, the religious order of salvation. The subjective world-orders become fully understood in the absolute world-order, when they are perceived as the historical manifestations of the absolute. This manifestation takes the form of immanent grace in the subjective world-orders. Thus the third ethical proof shows the absoluteness of grace and the unifying resolution of the subjective and objective world-orders in the absolute. From man's point of view the absolute world-order is the same as the teleological, it is the revelation of the divine essence in nature. The teleological world-order discloses the universal immanence of god in the world, whereas the moral world order proves god's immanence in man. This explains the identity of god and the absolute moral world-order as far as religion is concerned. The latter is but the logical enfolding of god in the world as it is brought about by the absolute will.

In this sense is god the absolute order of salvation, and consequently absolute grace. God is also the absolutely holy order of all things and, therefore, absolute holiness. Finally, god is absolute justice. These attributes are man's assurance that god has placed him into the right conditions of life, that his efforts will reap their just reward, that the subjective world-order will be sanctioned by objective acceptance, and that he can contribute to the absolute order of redemption which aims at universal salvation. Briefly, these divine attributes are man's guarantee of being saved from the world and be free in god.

From the problem of the religious object von Hartmann proceeds to the question of the religious subject and investigates it first from the standpoint of his need of and capacity for salvation. He calls this section of his philosophy of religion "religious anthropology."

Von Hartmann's axiological evaluation of life came to a negative conclusion and this negative conclusion becomes now a necessary postulate of religious consciousness. Without suffering and the feeling of guilt man would have no longing for salvation and sanctification, and without this longing and need for salvation there can be no true religion. Revelation alone is not religion, but merely an abstract metaphysics without practical value.

Religion presupposes a continuing, permanent evil from which it constantly redeems itself. Furthermore, religious consciousness demands the reality of evil and man. From these postulates von Hartmann concludes to the reality of responsibility as well. Responsibility requires the consciousness that I could have acted differently, had I considered a different motive for my action. This non-consideration is imputable to the will inasmuch as the will neglected it under the influence of other, more appealing egoistical motives. If I reflect upon my action and can say that I could have acted differently under the given circumstances, this is all that is required and necessary for responsibility.

Any possible objection at this point against the illusory nature of human responsibility by virtue of von Hartmann's own principle of the identity of divine and human wills would be countered by pointing to the twofold motive of human actions: the egoistical or evil, and the evolutionistic or good. A man led by the evil principle alone is incapable of moral actions, for his disposition is in opposition to genuine morality. This explains the lack of moral responsibility in an egoist. Moral responsibility presupposes the presence in the agent of both principles, good as well as evil. When we have the moral longing to place all our actions in the service of the objective aims, and possess the moral sentiment, which asserts itself as practical faith in the religious consciousness, then can we speak of moral responsibility. For all practical purposes, there are no purely natural, exclusively egoistic, unethical men. Thus all men are morally responsible. Adding our psychological self-determination to the ethical sentiment we are all capable to take up the struggle against all evil, external or internal.

For von Hartmann the moral sentiment is the definitive triumph over egoism, which sentiment assumes the presence of the moral will in man. But man alone cannot account for the development of his moral will precisely because of his egoism, therefore, the assumption of a given moral instinct is necessary. This assumption is also feasible on the basis of an analysis of human behavior which readily discloses the traces of an immanently operative moral world-order in man. Genuine moral sentiment shows itself first in those human actions where the good or the objective aim is intended and willed for its own sake. This will-act presupposes the presentation of good, whereas its opposite the presentation of evil. However, man gains a true understanding of evil not merely from its presentation but rather from its actual perpetration and consequences. Man himself must have done evil in order to acquire the sentiment of evil, responsibility, and guilt. The actual evil is a necessary stage of transition for the engendering and development of the actual moral will. All men are predestined to actual evil, but also to its victorious conquest. The promise of victory is carried within each man in the form of grace. Grace is the immanent moral world-order resident in each man. It is the *conditio sine qua non* of the need and capacity for salvation. The hereditary moral dispositions are auxiliary mechanisms of grace and are called hereditary graces. It is through actual grace that god is vitally present in man. Thus grace is simultaneously divine and human only if god and man are neither absolutely different nor identical. Man must be a constant source of partial-functions in the absolute will, and conversely, god is in man in a limited and individual manner. God-likeness comes to its rightful domain in man.

This consciousness of identity with god is not yet fully sufficient for salvation. The evil man is also one with god, for the bond of ontological identity between god and man is indissoluble. The longing for salvation will become irresistibly alive when man realizes in his innermost being, that he is destined not merely for an ontological unity with god, but also, even in a more eminent degree, for a teleological unity. It is grace that brings about this realization and unity, and for this reason it is in a most proper sense a divine function. Grace divinizes our nature and prepares it for salvation. Through grace man is raised from the narrow confines of his phenomenal ego to the ontological heights of his true self, where not the ego, but the unconscious, apersonal, absolute spirit reigns alone whose universal aims will replace the egoistic ones of the phenomenal individual. In this manner will man be delivered from evil and guilt. The desire for personal happiness must be abandoned forever, since it is the mark of the unholy, phenomenal will. To hope for it from god is in vain, for god has no happiness, and consequently he cannot give it to others.

With the inner realization of his divinity man's positive interest in immortality ceases. Immortality is a metaphysical postulate of a theistic religious outlook which promises man a future transcendental beatitude, in order to sooth his earthly unhappiness and to ease the fear of death of the egoistical will. But religious consciousness is not deceived by the illusions of egoism, and rejects its demands. Religious consciousness is also aware of the fact that with the continuation of personality, evil, suffering, consequently pessimism, would equally continue to exist. Furthermore, if the focal point of religious life were placed in an existence hereafter, man would neglect to perform his religious tasks in this life. It is the intention of the teleological world-order to replace the tired and weary warriors of the idea with new combatants who will promote with greater zeal and increased hereditary grace the enfolding of the world process. True piety is always willing to carry the burdens of life even through the gates of natural death, if it is in the interest of the universal aims of the absolute unconscious spirit. Those who labor for the advent of this new religion consider natural death as the well deserved rest after the long and hard toils of life, which will bring about their real salvation in addition to the ideal. Just as death is a welcome friend for the individual, so the entire universe yearns for deliverance through a cosmic death or annihilation. It is a firm belief in the teleological development of the world-process that prevents the individual from seeking directly his self-destruction. On the contrary, it spurs him on to dedicate his entire life to the task of universal salvation by carrying on the cause of the idea.

The problem of universal salvation takes us to the field that is called "religious cosmology" by von Hartmann.[1] Its analysis begins with the realization that the world is god's work, god rules it and logically determines it. It is a finite real world and with its realization through the actuality of god, time came also into existence.

Like bubbles in a champagne glass, time arises from the ocean of eternity only to burst again into oblivion. The infusoria, namely, men, who live and die in this bubble need not worry whether the absolute process produces only one or more of these bubbles.[2]

[1] *Ibid.*, pp. 54–70.
[2] *Ibid.*, pp. 70–79.

For them life is a constant struggle and sacrifice upon the altar of the idea that will be consummated by the individual's self-annihilation at the moment of death. This conception of life is extended by von Hartmann to the entire cosmos and is described as its inescapable tragedy. The redemption of the world, i.e., the triumph of the idea, can occur only through universal annihilation. The return of the spatio-temporal phenomenon into the eternal unconscious absolute is the universal redemption. The entire world-process reveals itself as an immense tragedy, in which the only actor, the unconscious absolute, plays all the roles, and fully partakes in all the torments and agony of each individual. After it has found its tragic end and total disillusionment in each assigned role, the show is over, and the curtain is rung down to end the absurdity of existence. A return into the undisturbed unconscious of the absolute is the highest aim of the world-process to which all existents must contribute their share.

The idea at the basis of these bizarre doctrines of von Hartmann is his belief that god itself must be redeemed from the bondage of finiteness. This occurs simultaneously with the redemption of the world, for by its return into the unconscious absolute, god is also relieved from its world-immanence and self-tormenting sufferings. The end of the world-process means also the end of god's transcendental unhappiness which came about by the self-assertion of the divine will.

In this way the tragedy of the world-process becomes a divine tragedy, in which the idea achieves its greatest triumph by the annihilation of that which ought-not-be.[1]

But because god delays the moment of universal redemption, it must be said, that in spite of his omnipotence, he cannot bring it to fulfillment as yet. This will be accomplished when the infinite will has realized all its finite presentations, thereby marking the end of the world-process.

Von Hartmann's last problem is the ethics of religion.[2] The treatise begins with the study of the subjective and objective processes of salvation. The subjective aspect is individual redemption by means of sanctification, whereas the objective aspect encompasses the sum of sanctifications by means of universal redemption. The former is an incessant process, and only through continuous toiling and persistent striving can man be partaker in grace, but he can never fully possess it. He must wage a permanent struggle in order to acquire his spiritual

---

[1] *Ibid.*, p. 76.
[2] *Ibid.*, pp. 80–101.

essence, and he must continually place himself at the service of the absolute aim.

Religious education is the greatest help in the development of the subjective process of sanctification. It is von Hartmann's conviction that religious instruction should begin only when the child reaches a certain degree of maturity, otherwise it will be a communication of a set of meaningless principles and uninspiring information. For the actualization of grace it is also of paramount importance that man perform occasional exercises, some difficult act, or take an unjust blame. These acts of voluntary sacrifice hasten the moment of illumination. Illumination begins with the recognition of guilt, followed by the feeling of guilt which acknowledges as evil the inclinations of the individual will. These are the preliminary preparations prior to the actual acquisition of grace. They effect the rejection of egoism and self-dedication to the cause of the idea. With the rejection of egoism grace simultaneously takes over and the regeneration of man's religious sentiment is at hand. This regeneration delivers man from his previous guilt and brings about a real unity with god, which is the expression ot the most perfect religious relation between god and man. The most significant practical result of the union is the sanctification of man's will.

The fruit of grace in man is moral improvement. Each step forward in the increase of grace is also the assurance of a higher place in the struggle for the victory of the idea. Cooperation with the objective process of salvation is the objective fruit of grace. All our obligations to god are in the service of this highest aim individually as well as collectively. Consequently, the obligations of different social institutions must be also deduced from the philosophy of religion, and this means that State as well as Church are obliged to promote the objective process of salvation. This obligation is indirect as far as the State is concerned, direct in regard to the Church. Von Hartmann is also convinced that no one single Church can ever undertake the role of representing god's kingdom on earth. The furthering of the cause of religious life through a Church may occur in three ways: Church-discipline, common cult, and preaching, or service of the word. Eventually, the first demands total separation of State and Church; the second requires the application of all branches of art to divine service. The service of the word in its highest degree of development will be a simple return of religious consciousness to itself. When the religion of the immanent spirit permeates larger regions of humanity, von Hartmann hopefully assumes, it will by then have an appropriate set of symbols at its disposal. At any rate, it is not expedient to pour new wine into old wineskins.

The service of the word can be most effectively developed in the family. Thus, the clerical class will lose its significance, and will be replaced by a religious laity. From the ranks of this new *sacerdotium* numerous individuals will step forward on given occasions, and through their inspired words the inner cult will be elevated to its highest possible form. Von Hartmann adds, that his philosophy of religion is only an ideal, but to help mankind to attaining this ideal is everyone's solemn obligation.

Religion in von Hartmann's system recalls the words of Jean Rostand:

> We refine God away, we simplify him, strip him of his attributes, relegate him to silence and inactivity... All we ask of him that we keep his name.[1]

Having assessed man's religious situation, all von Hartmann has left to offer man is a call for declaration of loyalty to an abstract notion; which is devoid of any objective content and represents no positive value in the order of being. For von Hartmann religion has little or no bearing upon the everyday life of the greatest part of mankind, and like everything else in his hands it becomes synonymous with science. This is not surprising in a man whose philosophical endeavors are guided by the principle that science begins where life ceases. Being consistent with his own principle, induction is claimed to guide him in constructing the new religion, when actually facts are molded to fit his preconceived historical and metaphysical assumptions. Pessimism is further justified in this pantragic religious outlook as he declares that only a pessimistic philosophy of life can give a permanent incentive for genuine religious striving. The notion of the unconscious receives a new, religious ratification by virtue of the psychological proof for the existence of the religious object. The analytic exposition of this proof yields the result that all imperfections, including personality, must be removed from the notion of the absolute in order to bring its unconsciousness into a clearer perspective. On the one hand, von Hartmann insists on man's identity with god through the unity of the divine and human wills; on the other hand, any resemblance between god and man, even analogical is denied, for god may not have love, mercy, or compassion for us. Von Hartmann's god is not the God of love, "who has shown love for us first;"[2] his god is the unconscious presentation and blindly raging will of a transcendental pessimism.

[1] Jean Rostand, *Pensées d'un Biologiste* (Paris: Stock, 1939), p. 37.
[2] I. John, 4: 10.

When one reflects upon the more important tenets of von Hartmann's philosophy of religion in greater detail, it appears inconsistent for von Hartmann to retain the notion of unconscious for the absolute after demanding spirituality as one of its attributes. Consciousness and spirituality are reciprocal notions, but in spite of this von Hartmann affirms the one and denies the other of the same object. The inconsistency is explained away simply by saying that these two notions are inseparable only according to our human manner of thinking and that basically this identification is false.

From conscious psychic life we must eliminate all that cannot be attributed to god, so that the remaining basic psychic functions cannot be considered conscious, merely such as *under certain circumstances* productive of consciousness.[1]

Since the first of these circumstances, the primary requisite of consciousness, according to von Hartmann, the material organism, is absent in god, the possibility of consciousness must also be excluded from it.

The alleged falsity of the identification of the two perfections of consciousness and spirituality is an unsubstantiated assumption of von Hartmann. It has been shown previously [2] that unless we are willing to commit with him the formal fallacy of assuming the greater in the lesser, and the metaphysical fallacy of confusing condition with cause, we have to reject his assertion that consciousness necessarily requires matter. It is inconceivable within a philosophical outlook based on reason that one can admit spirituality and deny consciousness in the same reality. Thus von Hartmann either has to deny spirituality in his absolute, or he must admit that it is pre-eminently self-conscious. To have it both ways is absurd and contrary to sound reasoning.

As far as the first part of our statement is concerned we are supported by the mind of St. Thomas:

... an incorporeal substance virtually contains the thing with which it comes into contact, and it is not contained by it: for the soul is in the body as containing it, not as contained by it.[3]

Therefore, whatever perfections the soul will communicate to the body it contains that same perfection virtually in itself prior to its communication. Thus to designate the material organism as cause of consciousness is to confuse condition with cause.

Substantiating the second part we must affirm that there is no real

---

[1] *System*, vol. VII, p. 42.
[2] Cf. Ch. III, pp. 57–60 of this book.
[3] *S. Th.*, I. q. 52, a. 2 c.

distinction in God between his attributes and essence.[1] If God has the attribute of spirituality, as von Hartmann admits, then his essence is *a fortiori* spiritual. If it is spiritual it is also intelligent. Intelligence, in turn, purports self-knowledge or consciousness. This is the teaching of St. Thomas commenting on the *De Anima* and *De Causis* of the Philosopher.

Hence, ... forms according as they are more immaterial, approach more nearly to a kind of infinity. Therefore it is clear that the immateriality of a thing is the reason why it is cognitive; and according to the mode of immateriality is the mode of knowledge. ... Since God is the highest degree of immateriality as stated above (Q. 7, a. 1) it follows that he occupies the highest place in knowledge.[2] ...those cognitive faculties which are subsisting, know themselves; hence it is said in *De Causis* that, *whoever knows his essence returns to it.* Now it supremely belongs to God to be self-subsisting. Hence according to this mode of speaking, he supremely returns to his own essence, and knows himself.[3]

Thus he who knows himself in a supreme manner cannot be unconscious of this knowledge, nor can he acquire it vicariously and implicitly through its phenomenal manifestations. If he is, he is his knowledge.

With similar logic we disagree with von Hartmann's assertions that God is not a person and the attribute of personality cannot be predicated of him. If we analyze St. Thomas' above conclusion carefully it is evident that the argument equivalently contains God's personality. Inasmuch as self-knowledge presupposes an intelligent nature and God's individuality is understood in the incommunicability of his being, God is a person since he is "the incommunicable existence of the divine nature."[4]

These considerations also aid us to realize the impossibility of unhappiness in the absolute and to see the inconsistency of demanding a negative evaluation of the life of the absolute and concluding to a transcendental pessimism.

Von Hartmann explained that of the twofold root of unhappiness in the absolute the first is the unfulfilled desires of the phenomenal substances which affect god's happiness inasmuch as the phenomenal substances are the spatio-temporal manifestations of god's own substance. If this is so, if god through its substance-identity with all things shares in the identity of its phenomena to the extent that the phenomenal will influences god's own state of being and produces some-

---

[1] *Ibid.*, q. 41, a. 4 ad 3.
[2] *Ibid.*, q. 14, a. 1 c.
[3] *Ibid.*, q. 14, a. 2 ad 1.
[4] *Ibid.*, q. 29, a. 3 ad 4.

thing very real in it, the conclusions of von Hartmann's cosmological and psychological proofs cannot be defended and accepted. If the relation between the phenomenon and the noumenon is reciprocal, in the sense that this reciprocity affects both terms of the relation, then the absolute cannot be extra-spatial and extra-temporal as the cosmological argument states. The presence of finite unhappiness in the absolute is explained as the spatio-temporal phenomenon's effect upon the noumenon. But the possibility of efficient operation demands that cause and effect belong to the same order, or at least, that the effect cannot belong to a higher order than its cause. In von Hartmann's assumption the phenomenal will is the principle of action toward the noumenon, which would necessitate that the effect in the noumenon must belong to the same or a lesser order than its phenomenal cause. If this proportion for an efficacious action is necessary in the order of causality, it is *a fortiori* necessary in the order of being. From which we must infer that either the cosmological proof is ineffective, i.e., god is not extra-spatial or the first source and reason of unhappiness in god must be eliminated.

Because the acceptance of the first of two alternatives would conclude to pantheism, which von Hartmann rejects, at least intentionally, the second alternative is to be accepted, and this would eliminate the source of pessimism in god. Furthermore, if the absolute is affected by the unhappiness of the phenomenal will, then the affirmation of the psychological argument cannot be valid either. The psychological argument states that god can have no mercy or sympathy for us. It is to be thought of exclusively as logical idea and senselessly tormented and tormenting will. But if god is affected by man's unhappiness, and shares in the suffering phenomenon's woes, as *ex hypothesi* it does, then this very fact is itself sympathy in contradiction to von Hartmann's psychological proof.

The second reason von Hartmann gives to justify pessimism in god, on a closer examination seems to defeat the aim and efforts of his epistemologico-ideal proof. In this proof he concludes to the intuitive knowledge of god and to the attributes of all-knowing and all-wisdom which follow from it. In spite of attributing this knowledge to god von Hartmann maintains that the source of transcendental unhappiness in it is the disproportion between the finitude of conscious divine knowledge, i.e., the self-knowledge of phenomenal manifestations of the god-substance, and the infinite striving of the divine will that becomes dissatisfied and, consequently, unhappy in lack of a proportionate object, i.e., a conscious infinite idea-content, to be pursued. However, if god's knowledge is intuitive, in the sense of being all-embracing, the knowledge of the divine essence cannot be lacking from it without contradiction. This all-embracing knowledge, or infinite idea, possessing all phenomenal as well as noumenal values, is an equivalent good for the infinite will to pursue. In this case the will has no excess power left for aimless striving and objectless longing which is the source of its transcendental suffering and discontent. As St. Thomas expresses it:

Just as God understands things apart from himself by understanding his own essence, so he wills things apart from himself by willing his own goodness.[1]

Whence it is logical to conclude that either von Hartmann's epistemologico-ideal argument is devoid of any meaning or transcendental pessimism cannot be reasonably accepted as justified or justifiable.

None of these pretensions of von Hartmann, unconsciousness, lack of personality, pessimism, can be justified in the absolute on the authority to which he has the final appeal. Man's religious consciousness does not represent a God-image, as von Hartmann depicts it. In his search for self-fulfillment and in the hope of finding his ontological moorings man does not turn toward a lifeless notion, an impersonal and unintelligible image devoid of positive values. Religious consciousness affirms more in the absolute than the victory of the logical over against the alogical, the triumph of the idea over the will, a triumph which is consummated in the extinction of knowledge, love, and happiness. It is not the existentially worthless and absolute nihil which man's religious consciousness affirms, it is rather the absolute Thou, the living God whom man addresses directly as a person in the hope that he will be his light, his truth, and his life, just as he was for Abraham, Isaac, and Jacob. This religious affirmation of God is not engendered by the hope of ultimately relieving the absolute from its transcendental misery, rather it surges from a judgment of value proclaimed with our whole being. It springs forth from an act of trust, and love to a God, regarded as the supreme perfection and value of all existence. Man's inner hopes and expectations yearn for an intelligent and all-comprehensive dialogue with a personal God who will resolve the mystery of mysteries of the human soul: the value and destiny of my existence.

Philosophy alone cannot have the final word and definitive answer concerning the existential quest of man. The longing of our religious consciousness to find a meaningful answer to the existential mystery

[1] *Ibid.*, q. 19, a. 3 ad 2; q. 19, a. 4 c.

reaches to regions that transcend the limits of natural reason and it trustfully hopes for enlightenment from the supernatural object of this consciousness itself. Man's religious consciousness would be but a blind groping, an empty search, if on God's part there were nothing to correspond to it, or, to be more precise, if God would not have taken the initiative and revealed himself to be man's final aim and eternal beatitude.

Such things as spring from the will of God alone, over and above what is owed to every creature, can be known by us only insofar as they are revealed in Sacred Scripture, through which the divine will is made known.[1]

Were philosophy to take the prerogative of fashioning God's image within itself it would not only violate religious consciousness but it would ignore historical facts as well. Von Hartmann's philosophy of religion is guilty of such usurpation and in it we find its greatest folly. As a consequence all the notions employed in his theory of religion are stripped of their true meaning and set within the limits of a purely naturalistic and pantheistic frame of mind. Faith is nothing but the recognition that man's actions must be placed in the service of the aims of the self-evolving idea, which is the corresponding term of man's religious consciousness. When this recognition becomes a guiding norm for the individual's actions, god's self-revelation is accomplished for that individual. On god's part grace is simply that idea's evolution in the teleological world-order, from man's part it is the conscious realization of god's presence in the universe. God-likeness is the efficacious functioning of man's will in the divine and of the divine will in man for the purpose of realizing the final deliverance of all existence. Salvation in von Hartmann's religion is: that all may be one in the redemptive oblivion of an eschatological nihilism.

Von Hartmann wishes to write a theology not only for the phenomenal manifestations of god but also for god itself. The god-image we are presented with by him shows a more pitiable condition than the unhappy lot of the entire phenomenal creation.

The beginning of life in god is also the beginning of the interminable misery which is due to its impotence to resist the innate drives of its own unbridled will. As a result it hurls itself fatalistically into a dreadful agony from which it is unable to save itself. Being helpless against itself, it brings relentlessly other innumerous beings into a most abject suffering in order to selfishly save itself through their misery and death. It partakes in the sufferings of all other beings, it is true, but it does so not by a free choice of its will but by an inevitable and irresistible force

[1] *S. Th.*, III, q. 1, a. 3 c.

of fate. This circumstance may incline us to judge its situation more deplorable without, however, absolving it of the guilt of being satanical in its action. In von Hartmann's religion god will never conquer evil, rather is forever helplessly subjected to it, and the only means to escape evil's yoke is by annihilating itself together with all existence. The ultimately victorious power, therefore, is not a perfect, loving, and good God, but rather a negative, hateful, and evil force.

It may be stated in conclusion that the final reason for von Hartmann's impingement upon the true nature of man's religious consciousness is the fact that he discounts completely the historical event of objective revelation in which God has communicated to us his true image. Von Hartmann has never undertaken a serious study of scriptural exegesis, among his numerous publications not one work is dedicated to a scientific discussion concerning the authority of the sources of revelation. Despite his lack of competence in this matter, he dismisses with a simple stroke of his pen not only the authority of the immediate sources of revelation, but the labors of the best exegetical scholarship of nineteen centuries as well.[1] For this kind of bias and intellectual provincialism there is no place in the realm of genuine dedication to the discovery and presentation of integral truth. Had he not been a slave to his own personal prejudices and the pseudo-scientific pretentions of his time, he would have been able to find for himself, as well as to transmit to posterity, a God-image which had been truly expressive of man's inner longings and religious consciousness. Had he been filled with the spirit of humility of a true philosopher, like Plato, in view of the enormity of the mystery he faced, and had he been a "man of God," instead of preferring the spirit of Dionysius, the pseudo-scientific attitude of "being stuffed with second-hand opinions,"[2] he could have also found the path leading to the true solution of the mystery of the beginning, reason, and end of all existence.

Of the beginning of existence, which gushes forth from the boundless divine love toward us; from a love, which remains the perennial *Leitmotiv* of every new stroke in the perfection of the divine image in man's religious consciousness. Of the reason of existence, which helps us to realize that all things are arranged in this life so that God's love for us may be manifested in sending his only begotten Son to atone, suffer, and die for our sins. Of the end of existence, that Jesus Christ's divine

---

[1] Cf. footnotes 2, p. 140; 1, p. 141; and 2, p. 142.
[2] *Thirteen Epistles of Plato*, ed. by L. A. Post (London: Oxford University Press, 1925). Quotation is taken from Epistle VII, paragraph 1.

love may redeem us from the sufferings and anguish of our earthly existence and exchange the abounding evil of this life into everlasting joy and happiness with God.

Now this is everlasting life that they may know Thee, the only true God, and him whom Thou has sent, Jesus Christ.... I am in them and Thou in me; that they may be perfected in unity, and that the world may know that Thou hast sent me, and that Thou has loved them even as Thou has loved me.[1]

---

[1] John, 17; 3 and 23.

CONCLUSION

An objective evaluation of von Hartmann's philosophy and historical importance is not an easy task. He was a controversial figure during his life and remained such after his death. His friends and admirers were understandably influenced in his evaluation as a philosopher by their personal appreciation for him as a man. This fact may question their objectivity in the mind of an impartial observer. On the other hand, his professional opponents were eager to seize every opportunity to belittle his endeavors and positive contributions to the cause of philosophical research under the guise of objective criticism. This makes them equally suspect with regard to a genuine representation of his philosophical significance. To find the balance between the two extremes and to present a realistic value-judgment concerning von Hartmann's philosophical system is the obligation of the unbiased student of history if he wishes to serve the truth.

In finding the proper premises for this evaluation it is necessary to keep in mind, first of all, that von Hartmann is personally involved in the struggle between two diametrically opposed philosophical and cultural views concerning the value of life. In his natural proclivities, in his innermost self, he is an idealist, but, at the same time, he cannot detach himself completely from the taints of materialism which played a decisive role in the formation of the culture of the nineteenth and early twentieth centuries. He dedicates his scientific endeavors to the resolution of these antagonistic forces and in this he finds his singular calling in life. The motivating force beyond his laboriously spent years is his firm conviction that it is his historically appointed task to bridge the chasm between idealism, with its neglect of reality, and the empirical sciences, with their scorn for any immaterial absolute. In the sublimated unity of the two lay the foundation of a new philosophy of culture.

It is not lack of enthusiasm that prevents him from fulfilling his intended aim. It is rather a misconceived approach and, as a result, an inept metaphysical ultimate which jeopardizes the philosophical value of his doctrine, for his philosophy neither saves genuine idealism nor does it overcome materialism. His zeal is indefatigable in constructing a new idealistic philosophy of culture, but he never succeeds in proposing an acceptable metaphysical principle as the foundation of his philosophical novelties. His whole life is witness to an uncommon dedication to the service of his intended aim, but in fact he remains forever prisoner of an irrational naturalism.

The task of the reconciliation of idealism and materialism, which in fact is a reconstruction, or rather the construction of his own philosophical system, begins with a detailed criticism of the classic methods as tools for the foundation of a philosophical system. Thus, von Hartmann dissociates himself first from the method of dialectics in its Aristotelian as well as in its Hegelian form since dialectics in either interpretation is incapable of providing the mind with a positive content of knowledge. Pure Platonic intuition is rejected because of its failure to establish real contact with transsubjective phenomena. Cartesian deduction, by equating thought with being, can never attain reality, and the knowledge it communicates is purely formal, lacking real objective content. The remaining alternative is inductive empiricism. Von Hartmann is firmly convinced that this method is the only source of true, scientific knowledge, and no philosophy is worthy of the name unless it is built on empirical data. The ratio between philosophy and inductive empiricism is direct, for the more philosophical, i.e., metaphysical, a system is, the wider its empirical foundation must be. Although the method of empiricism is necessary and indispensable for the philosopher, it is only the beginning. The philosopher's task commences after the collection of empirical facts. To obtain the greatest possible certitude that the proper method is employed for the discovery of the metaphysical principle in the collected empirical data, von Hartmann finds it expedient to devise his own method. He calls his newly constructed method criticism. It is an amalgamate of empiricism, speculative inductivism, and probabilism, and it is designed to bring forth von Hartmann's preconceived claims concerning the nature of his metaphysical noumenon. In the description of von Hartmann's criticistic method there is a deceivingly insignificant and almost unnoticeable adjective, viz., "speculative"; yet it is the key to the enigma of von Hartmann's philosophy. To the question as to how can von Hartmann expect to gain speculative results from exclusively empirical data the answer is to be found in the "speculative" aspect of his criticistic method. The term in its actual usage and employment means "clairvoyant intuition," which in turn means that the analysis of the phenomena is undertaken according to a predetermined view in mind leading inevitably to the discovery of the unconscious.

Von Hartmann makes no effort to hide his preference for this kind of intuition, and it is not surprising that his method of criticism soon ceases to be empirical or inductive, and becomes exclusively intuitive. It is through clairvoyant intuition that man partakes in the mystical vision of the absolute, and in this knowledge man's mind is unified with the metaphysical all-spirit. By virtue of it man shares the intuitive omniscience of the unconscious. Equipped with this kind of vision von Hartmann can now proceed and expound systematically the predetermined plan in the idea for its self-realization in the world of phenomena. With the aid of his clairvoyant intuition, he sees in the idea all its logically necessitated movements prior to their actual occurrence. The idea, or the metaphysical ultimate, is not discovered because of its phenomena, but rather its phenomena are explained according to their inner determination in the idea. According to our estimation there is one slight difficulty with this explanation, i.e., to call this noetic procedure empirical or *a posteriori* is either self-deceit or intellectual dishonesty.

Once this arbitrary nature of von Hartmann's noetic theory is realized it will come as no surprise that regardless of the phenomena analyzed the conclusion is always the same. Thus he discovers in the study of the structure, as well as in the instinctive and emotive actions of organic life, the activity of the universal unconscious will as the realizing force of the unconscious idea in nature. So also the minute and careful scrutiny of the intellectual, volitional, moral, aesthetic, and religious life of the human individual will ultimately necessitate, in von Hartmann's opinion, the assumption of the unconscious spirit. The study of the history of the human race yields the same result. Every successive stage of its development is an infallible witness to the purposive striving of the unconscious in its process of self-realization. Pressing his clairvoyant vision to its final absurdity von Hartmann explains even phenomenal consciousness as the reverted and inwardly accumulated intensity of the unconscious primordial atoms. This consciousness then in turn serves to show the path for the objective-real and the subjective-ideal worlds back to the consummate unity of the uncon-

scious spirit. It is evident, therefore, that von Hartmann's epistemological position whereby he discovers his metaphysical absolute, the
unconscious, is not only contradictory to the principles of his own
method of criticism, but also outside of the realm of rationality. Consequently its philosophical value is nil.

This same noetic background supports also his universal pessimism
in axiology. In von Hartmann's view the underlying principle of all
activity in the world and, consequently of all suffering, is the blind and
senseless striving of the absolute will or the alogical principle in the unconscious. But because by this principle alone the logical moment, the
teleological evolution of the world-process, cannot be explained, he is
forced to postulate another principle, the logical or the absolute idea.
The duality of these two distinct principles is resolved then in the
substantial unity of the absolute unconscious. The mutual interaction
of will and idea determines the purpose of the world, namely, the solution of the contradiction in the activity of the will through the influence of the logical idea. When this reciprocal action ceases, due to the
finite content of the idea that can be realized by the infinite will, the
end of the world-process is at hand, and everything returns into self-
annihilating unconsciousness.

In this assumption it is the alogical will which comes to grips with
itself, and in order to resolve its self-created contradictions, it needs the
aid and direction of the logical idea. However, it is inconceivable,
without a clairvoyant intuition, how a homogeneous, unitary principle
can become involved in contradictions with itself and senselessly rage
against itself. The blind will initiates its own movement, without being
externally aroused, and in this unsolicited drive it creates its own misery.
A *definite* tendency of the will without idea, however, is a chimera,
and to maintain that prior to its contact with the logical it can engage
in a purposive search for its rest and peace is unreasonable. In a con-
joint operation with the idea, the will cannot commit the mistake of
seeking its relief in the wrong objects, consequently it is not necessitated to bring about pain and suffering. If von Hartmann accepted the
logical view of the natural relation of will and idea at the very outset of
his philosophical investigations, the source and reason for his pessimistic evaluation of existence would disappear. But then, there could
be no philosophy of the unconscious.

It is hardly necessary to point out that von Hartmann's axiological
position is not arrived at either inductively or deductively, and it is
in need of proof as is the system itself that is built upon it. But, granting

for the sake of discussion, that he is correct in his pessimistic evaluation of the world, his conclusion concerning the necessary annihilation of all existence is still indefensible. For there is no necessary causal connection between a temporal ought-not-to-be and a future universal non-existence. In view of the inferences of a rational consideration of the value of existence, evil and suffering in the world are not irrevocably and unavoidably negating. As we endeavored to show in our discussion on pessimism, evil manifests itself in us either as painful feeling, or as subjective value-judgment of impressions and experiences, and, as such, it belongs primarily to the sphere of subjectivity. In this respect it may attest to a personal misfortune, or to an impediment in the process of the individual's self-realization; in either case, it is a sign of the ontological insufficiency of the individual. Evil, understood in this light, instead of being destructive of objective ontological values, actually enhances them. Instead of defacing reality, it can be a most valuable stimulus in man's search for greater and higher values. This view of evil coordinated to higher aims gives it a soothing, even welcome effect in the life of man. Von Hartmann must deny this interpretation of evil for it does not fit in his system. The *Philosophy of the Unconscious* is in no position to account for those values which show the subordinate nature of evil. On the grounds of his clairvoyant explanation of empirical facts and his metaphysical postulates von Hartmann has no other answer for the problem of evil than a definite annihilation of all existence. This conclusion, however, is not only inconsequential according to the rules of logic, but also lacks sufficient justification in the order of values.

In his ethical system von Hartmann intends to carry out further his philosophical avocation by forcibly reconciling antagonistic theories. He attempts to resolve and weld together realism and illusionism, eudemonological pessimism and teleological evolutionism in the union of the highest moral principle: the deliverance of the absolute. But contradictories admit no union, merely mutual destruction, and as a result, the curse of an eschatological nihilism looms threateningly over all human actions in his ethical analyses. The fact that von Hartmann uses traditional terms in expounding his moral views may give a faint appearance of morality to his system, but mere words are inept to salvage it from absurd consequences in psychology as well as in morality itself.

Von Hartmann demands the impossible from the phenomenal individual when he assigns the annihilation of his self-identity as his highest moral obligation through which the realization of the self-destructive end of the absolute unconscious is attained. The rational human agent can strive only for positive aims and real values. The basic condition for all morality is the sound hope of self-fulfillment and completion. Only a further assertion of our potential-self by the acquisition of positive values, and ultimately, a union with the source of all values, can motivate us for action and not the negation of these values. When he demands that man conduct his entire life by the ideal of the final extinction of all conscious existence, and for the sake of this end he is duty-bound not only to endure but to seek all suffering, pain, and misery, he demands the psychologically and morally impossible from man. In our opinion von Hartmann loses at this point all contact with rationality and reality. It seems that the entire theorem gravitates toward a gnostic myth bereft of all common sense and intelligibility.

If possible, von Hartmann's view of the value of existence is even more disconsolate considering the axiology of the absolute itself. The ordinary norms of positive perfections are not applicable to the absolute of the philosophy of the unconscious. Conscious intellectual activity, perfection of self-identity, possession of happiness, are unknown to it and debarred from its nature. Only the unhappiness of a blind and senseless groping is its share, and it can call its own only the sorry lot of carrying the consummate suffering of all existence. There is one dimly flickering ray of hope, although as yet unrealized, in this woeful state of things: the eventual extinction of all existence and return to non-existence.

Such an axiological position concerning the absolute, or ultimately God, is not only repulsive to man, but it entails simultaneously the denial of all positive values whether metaphysical, moral, or religious. The image of a God which has neither being nor worth in itself, yet suffers endless misery as a result of an unknown and mysterious chance, and which in order to attain its own deliverance is ready to hurl innumerable creatures into the abyss of hopeless suffering, can hardly be said to answer the innate yearnings of the human heart for perfect self-realization. A theory of religion which has for its absolute a pseudo-entity claiming only the lowest of human passions as its own, such as boundless egoism, blind urge and cruel insensitivity, a God who sows evil and reaps woes, who marches irresistibly through corpses to his own relief in pure nothingness, can be labelled with only one word: mono-satanism.

The notion of the absolute by virtue of its nature demands that it contain a sufficient explanation of the world as well as of itself. Anything less than an unlimited fullness of being, an ontologically intensive and virtually extensive infinity, is unsatisfactory and cannot be accepted. Conceived in this manner it is evident that such an absolute is ultimate perfection, consummate fullness of being. The primary possession and foremost attribute of such a being is consciously perfect beatitude, uninterrupted and uninterruptible happiness. The divine happiness does not require any antinomies in order to exist; it does not need external objects to attain its aim, nor is its happiness merely negative in the sense of being freedom from suffering, as von Hartmann teaches. It is its own reason and explanation as conscious fullness of infinite being, it is the endless possession of all values, of all truth, beauty and goodness. A proper understanding and interpretation of the terms "infinity" and "happiness" inescapably contain also the notion of self-awareness and personality. Without any of these values there were not only an essential imperfection in the notion of the absolute being, but we could find no rational explanation for the absolute's self-sufficiency, and consequently, no reason for the presence of teleology and values in the world. All positive values must be thought of as present in the absolute to the fullest measure of their reality since they are the highest forms of finite existence and must, therefore, eminently and without measure belong to the source of all existence.

Von Hartmann deprives his absolute of these values, for they are mere logical relations for him and his divinity stands above all relations. But such a being is an absolute impossibility for it is unthinkable. The solution of the problem will not be attained by denying all relations in God, but rather, by showing that all relations do not involve an ontological dependence, thus there being no necessity to assume change and multiplicity in God. Von Hartmann deprives his absolute of all relations because it must be beyond all change and particularity. Yet despite this, von Hartmann brings forth all evil and suffering from the will-potentiality of his absolute, from a will which lacks essence and content. This is one more of von Hartmann's paradoxical statements according to which the absolute does not have a will, yet it does have a will from which it can bring forth only evil and misery, thus forcing us to conclude to the nature of a diabolical will in his absolute.

To restate our position: an absolute will is a perfect will replete with infinitely positive values. Such a will cannot create a senseless world in which, pursuing blindly its selfish motives, the only thing it has to offer to its creatures is an interminable series of hopeless woes and wails, as does the unconscious of von Hartmann. We have to disagree with the conclusions of a philosophy which demands an imperfect and suffering god as the postulate of religious consciousness. An image of god represented in this manner is repulsive and contrary to man's inherent desire for God. The philosophy of the unconscious cannot present logically any other image of God, for in this philosophy everything revolves around the blind selfishness of a pseudo-god instead of the self-diffusive perfection of the true God.

God can be the fulfillment of man's yearning and the end of his thinking only if he is subsistent perfection without any shadow of imperfection; if he is absolute goodness who gratuitously shares his unfathomable riches with man and guarantees an unending enjoyment of his own infinite beatitude for man. This is the image of God arrived at through a serene, unbiased, unpretentious scrutiny of the world without and the postulates of man's consciousness within.

To substantiate these conclusions no better authority can be appealed to than the teaching of Aristotle, which professes in no uncertain terms that the world has its final principle in God,[1] who is the good *per se* [2] and the end toward which all things tend. In accordance with his metaphysical principles, he relates morality to the end or good, and unequivocally maintains that the aim of all moral action is happiness or eudemonia.[3] This happiness results from the performance of that characteristic activity which belongs to man as man.[4] This act is not merely living, for plants also live; nor the mere pleasures of sensations, for they are also shared by animals, but that exclusive activity of man which places him above all creation and distinguishes him from the rest of created beings. This is none other than his rational activity which, at the same time, is honorable and virtuous.[5] Thus pleasure is united with eudemonia, and exists in the highest degree in connection with that highest eudemonia which derives from the attainment of man's rational self-realization.[6]

It is this realistically founded proper proportion or order of things to their ultimate end that inspires St. Thomas to choose Aristotle's philosophy as the classic antecedent of his own. He also finds the basic reality, intelligibility, and value of things in that order which exists

---

[1] *Met.*, bk. XII, ch. 7.
[2] *Ibid.*, *loc. cit.*, ch. 6.
[3] *Eth. Nic.*, bk. I, 1. 2.
[4] *Ibid.*, *loc. cit.*, 1. 6; bk. X, 1. 7.
[5] *Ibid.*, bk. II, 1. 5.
[6] *Ibid.*, bk. X, 1. 7.

among them and of all creation to its ultimate cause.[1] Reality is not a
chance happening, the incalculable self-dichotomy of an unconscious
will, but the creatively thinking and teleologically ordering activity of
the personal God.[2] Things have real existence, consequently value,
intelligibility, and purpose, because they have been brought into being
by the creative thought of God. This creative fashioning of things is
simultaneously the reason of their ontological value as well as their
insufficiency, or the determining factor of their true creaturely situation.[3] This situation entails their inner goodness, inasmuch as they
represent God's infinite essence as well as their own defects, for no
creature can mirror completely the unfailing perfection of God. This
possibility of failure in creatures becomes an unhappy reality in the
case of man, who through his original and subsequent personal diso-
bedience to this divine plan endangers the very foundations of this
divine-human relation. Evil, sin deliberately perpetrated by man, is
not only an injury to God's creation but also a menace to man's true
reason for being, namely, his eternal happiness with God.[4] Taking man's
truly human situation into consideration, St. Thomas approaches the
penetration into the mystery of evil, to the extent this is possible to the
human mind, not only from its temporal and immanent aspect, but
more significantly, from its eternal and transcendental meaning.[5]
Placing it in this perspective, his final evaluation of the presence of evil
in creation is that of confidence, faith, and hope, which add sufficient
incentives to man's strivings to fulfill his often hard tasks in life, for
everything is ultimately ordered to the unending fulness of life with the
source and end of life.

It is hoped that these concluding thoughts mirror essentially correctly and objectively the value of von Hartmann's philosophy in light
of the truths of man's existentially given situation. In the course of this
analysis we arrived at a final value-judgment concerning the philosophy
of the unconscious, which evaluating conclusion is, at the same time,
also our main reason to disapprove this philosophy in itself, in its *a
priori* assumptions and consequent implications. This value-judgment
succinctly expressed asserts that von Hartmann's philosophy is unacceptable because its total outlook is basically irrational, and as such,
negative. In this regard it is the logical outcome and final culmination

---

[1] *S. Th.* I. q. 15, a. 2.
[2] *Ibid.*, I. q. 95, a. 6.
[3] *De Ver.* q. 1, a. 2.
[4] *S. Th.*, II. II. q. 9, a. 4.
[5] *C. G.*, bk. IV, ch. 42.

of that historical cycle which begins with the scepticism of Kant, continues its decline through the blind voluntarism of Schopenhauer and oppressive idealism of Hegel, culminates in its total destruction in the irrational nihilism of von Hartmann. This is the end-result of the Kantian philosophical scepticism, and it was inevitable that the twilight of the gods of philosophical romanticism should have come to pass. Man demands his rights and refuses to be enslaved any longer by the visionary makers of illusory worlds. What he demands is more reason and not less, more positive values and not less, more being and not less. Philosophical theorems that are unable to satisfy this natural hunger of the human agent for more truth, good, and beauty fall by the wayside. Because the philosophy of the unconscious is conceived of an existential starvation, it has nothing to offer to those who seek the living waters of all values. Von Hartmann's haughty aspirations for immortality notwithstanding, the philosophy of the unconscious is a fruitless end, a sterile fossil in the warehouse of the history of philosophy. Yet, the parting thought is that of gratitude to von Hartmann in the spirit of Aristotle and St. Thomas, for even if he was:

...wrong about the truth, he bequeathed to his successors the occasion for exercising their mental powers, so that by diligent discussion the truth might be seen more clearly.[1]

---

[1] *In Met.*, bk. II, 1. 1.

APPENDIX

The following letters present for the first time in English translation, abridged and summarized, the correspondence which took place between von Hartmann and Ernst Haeckel during the years of 1874–1876.

It was the 50th anniversary of von Hartmann's death, June 5th, 1956, that occasioned their first release by his daughter, Mrs. Bertha Kern-von Hartmann of Bonn. Haeckel's correspondence with her father is in her possession, while von Hartmann's original letters are preserved in the Haeckel-Archives in Jena. The cooperation of Dr. Hübscher, curator of the Haeckel-Archives, has greatly facilitated Mrs. Kern-von Hartmann's efforts to gain access to her father's original documents.

The initiative to enter into an exchange of ideas through personal contacts came from von Hartmann in the form of his first letter on October 30, 1874. This letter, however, intimates that there has been already some previous exchange of publications between the two men. Von Hartmann by his gesture hoped to eliminate, or at least reduce as much as possible the ideological differences between Haeckel and himself, between the respective *Weltanschauungen* they individually stood for.

The correspondence bears witness to an historical encounter of two opposed value-judgements on life, whose main protagonists endeavored to resolve their differences within an ideological framework larger and more comprehensive than their own personal positions. For it seemed most paradoxical to von Hartmann, that although both, Haeckel as well as himself, professing basically a monistic philosophical outlook, should be so far apart, and their respective views so antinomical as the actually existing opposition between mechanism and idealism of the 1870-ies. Von Hartmann was firmly convinced, that there must be a door for reconciliation, if only the right key could be found for it. He was determined to find this right key. "They (the mechanists) say, that there is nothing to look for beyond the mechanism of the atoms; I say, it is there where things first really begin!"

With sincere belief and staunch conviction in his cause he repeatedly pleaded with Haeckel, as the most authoritative proponent of the mechanistic view of life, to join and aid him in his search for this point of contact between the natural sciences and philosophy. For once found, it will benefit not only the two respective sciences, but will also give a "unity to our progress of culture."

The letters whose excerpts follow were published under the title METAPHYSIK UND NATURPHILOSOPHIE, Briefwechsel zwischen Eduard von Hartmann und Ernst Haeckel, herausgegeben von Bertha Kern-von Hartmann, Bonn; in the KANT-STUDIEN, vol. 48, no. 1, 1956/1957, pp. 3–24.

FIRST LETTER

Von Hartmann's letter. Berlin, October 30, 1874.

Von Hartmann begins the correspondence by conveying his most sincere gratitude to Haeckel for sending him the second edition of his *Natürliche Schöpfungsgeschichte*,[1] with which Haeckel has initiated between them a friendly exchange of publications. He also thanks him for the valuable *Anthropogenie*,[2] about which he agreed to write an article for the *Deutsche Rundschau*, comparing in it this new work with Haeckel's previous publications. In order to make this article factual as well as interesting he asks Haeckel to supply him with some biographical data and reviews of the *Anthropogenie* he may have received from its critics.

Then he inquires whether Haeckel has read his latest work, *Wahrheit und Irrtum im Darwinismus*,[3] in the 3rd and 4th numbers of the quarterly *Literatur*. His interest is so much the greater, since he would like to have Haeckel's reaction regarding a polemic, which is directed against him in the last chapter of this work. Von Hartmann avows that Haeckel's theory of descendence is not touched in itself as a result of his new evaluation of the relation between descendence and idealism. The only change is an external one, inasmuch as, instead of being opposed to it, as was the case before, henceforth it is integrated into the sphere of idealism. "That I could convince you, that your mechanistic outlook on life is a thing which has nothing to do with your task as a scientist, and it is only erroneously welded to it, I hardly dare to hope." On his part von Hartmann is convinced that as far as they are opponents both of them transgress *unnecessarily* their specific field of competence, but their *positive* endeavors serve a common interest.

SECOND LETTER

Haeckel's reply. Jena, November 4, 1874.

Haeckel expresses his appreciation for the interest von Hartmann shows toward his work, and assures him that he himself follows eagerly the philosophical activity of von Hartmann as far as he is capable of following him into the realm of the speculative (soweit ich überhaupt befähigt bin, Ihnen auf das speculative Gebiet zu folgen). Thanks von Hartmann for sending him the fifth edition of the *Philosophie des Unbewussten*,[4] and tells him that his opinion about the work has not changed since he first expressed it in the *Preface* to the fourth edition of his *Natürliche Schöpfungsgeschichte*. Nor has he revised his agreement with the anonymous critic who censured severely von Hartmann's notion of the un-

---

[1] Ernst Haeckel, *Natürliche Schöpfungsgeschichte*; 2nd. ed. Berlin, 1868.

[2] Ernst Haeckel, *Anthropogenie oder Entwicklungsgeschichte des Menschen*; Leipzig, 1874.

[3] Eduard Von Hartmann, *Wahrheit und Irrtum im Darwinismus*; first appeared in the third and fourth numbers of the quarterly *Literatur* in 1874; then was published as a book in 1875; finally in 1890 it became part of the third volume of the tenth edition of the *Philosophie des Unbewussten*.

[4] Eduard von Hartmann, *Philosophie des Unbewussten*. 5th revised and enlarged edition; Berlin, 1873.

conscious in the treatise *Das Unbewusste vom Standpunkt der Physiologie und Descendenztheorie*.[1]

Making closer references to their own respective positions he agrees with von Hartmann, that antagonistic as they may be, regarding monism, evolution and Darwin's theory of descendence, there is no disagreement between them. In this sense Haeckel feels a greater affinity with von Hartmann's views than with the views of those scientists of nature who reject the theory of evolution, and abuse him daily for upholding it. He labels them "gross empiricists," and wastes little effort in calling their chief spokesman, Adolf Bastian, an "ethnologic Coripheus."[2]

Next he reminds von Hartmann that in his upcoming review of the *Anthropogenie*, he should particularly stress the fact, that it is the first attempt to revitalize the old theory of ontogenesis by the theory of phylogenetic causal connection, and in its overall view it is a search for the "strictly scientific causal explanation of genetic phenomena." Although, Haeckel admits, that he may be wrong in some details, he has no doubt as to the general value and correctness of his theory.

For the rest Haeckel singles out certain chapters of the *Anthropogenie* which might be of particular interest to von Hartmann, encloses in his letter the requested biographical data and a long list of publications. He appends to each his remarks regarding the reaction the work received at its publication from the authorities of the day.

THIRD LETTER

Von Hartmann's reply.   Berlin, November 4, 1874.

Von Hartmann thanks Haeckel for the friendly answer and the materials received to complete his pending article. He assures Haeckel that he has read the *Anthropogenie*, with great interest from beginning to end.

Under request of discretion von Hartmann discloses to Haeckel that he himself is the author of the anonymous critique of the unconscious, *Das Unbewusste vom Standpunkt der Physiologie und Descendenztheorie*, etc. In writing this work he wanted to make, on the one hand, several corrections concerning the mechanical manner of mediating and interpreting teleological tasks in his main work, which he could not very well accomplish in a new edition without destroying the structural unity of the whole; on the other hand, he wanted to show that he is well versed in the mechanistic interpretation of Darwinism, that he is not afraid of their objections, and that he is fully convinced of the correctness of his own teleological position. He bemoans the fact that the stupid public, "das dumme Publikum," misunderstood his motives and thought it to be nothing else but a mere senseless sophistry.

In the remainder of the letter he overtly reminds Haeckel as to what are the chances of converting him to the mechanistic interpretation of nature and reality in general. With regard to their special relationship his foremost intent is "not to deny what you have established, rather to establish something you have denied,

---

[1] *Das Unbewusste vom Standpunkt der Physiologie und Descendenztheorie;* Eine kritische Beleuchtung des naturphilosophischen Teils der Philosophie des Unbewussten aus naturwissenschaftlichen Gesichtspunkten. Berlin, 1872. (At its first publication von Hartmann published it anonymously).

[2] Adolf Bastian, ethnographer and ethnologist, 1826–1905, a frequent critic and opponent of Haeckel. Cf. his "Open letter to Herr Professor Dr. Ernst Haeckel," 1874.

i.e., to go beyond the limits you have fixed arbitrarily." ..... "You say, beyond mechanism, beyond the empirically observable material atoms there is nothing; I say, there is where things really begin." (..... da fängt es erst recht an).

Haeckel's reply.   Jena, November 7, 1874.

The disclosure of the fact that von Hartmann is the anonymous critic of his own work, although surprised him, it did not come totally unexpected. What perplexes him more is the paradoxical stand he finds between von Hartmann's critique and his latest publication in the *Literatur*.[1] Since he shares the views expressed in the critique, the acceptance of the inferences drawn in the second work is next to impossible for him. He emphatically reminds von Hartmann, that in his new work, as in all similar works, the recurring fundamental question is the "unity of organic and inorganic nature", which, from his part, must be considered closed on the basis of the facts he offered as proofs in his *Generelle Morphologie*.[2]

The key to the understanding of these questions is his own doctrine of the "Moneren." He suggests that von Hartmann dedicate a thoroughgoing study to these "most important and most interesting 'organisms without organs'." He offers to send a copy of his *Monographie der Moneren* to von Hartmann to facilitate his study.[3] He is convinced that the conclusions he has drawn from all the available and carefully collected facts are as simple as are apodictic. He is compelled, furthermore, to these progressive views, if he wishes to bring light and challenging thought into the dreadful empirical chaos of his own science of biology. "The lack of thinking and intellectual density of the greater majority of the conceited 'exact' biologists is indeed appalling." In order to make his point he refers to the example of his *Anthropogenie*, p. 628, and to the celebrated controversy between discontinuous and gradual genetic development, (sprungweiser und allmählicher Entwicklung!!), *ibid.* p. 132.

He concludes his letter by asking von Hartmann whether he has read Alexander Wiessner's work *Das Atom*.[4]

---

[1] It is a reference to *Wahrheit und Irrtum...*, in which von Hartmann restates his own original views in opposition to the *Unbewusste...* It is a critique of the critique, as it were, which Haeckel read in the *Literatur*, erroneously thinking that von Hartmann sent him the articles.

[2] Ernst Haeckel, *Generelle Morphologie*. Allgemeine Grundzüge der organischen Formenwissenschaft, mechanisch begründet durch die von Charles Darwin reformierte Descendenztheorie. Vol. 1: Allgemeine Anatomie der Organismen; vol. 2: Allgemeine Entwicklungsgeschichte der Organismen. Berlin, 1866.

[3] Ernst Haeckel, *Monographie der Moneren*. Jenaische Zeitschrift für Naturwissenschaften. Vol. 4, 1868. *Monere (-n)* is Haeckel's term for his discovery which he discribes as "organisms without organs." They are considered to be the basic carriers of vegetative as well as animal life.

[4] Alexander Wiessner, *Das Atom*. Leipzig, 1875.

Haeckel's letter.   Jena, November 11, 1874.

Haeckel hastens to comply with von Hartmann's request and sends him his *Studien über Moneren*. He recommends the reading of certain passages to von Hartmann, so that he may gain a quicker acquaintance with the basic aspects as well as the overall view of the work.

As a supplement to his study Haeckel explains in the letter that the *Protamoeba* has lately been rediscovered in different places in sweet water and it seems to be thriving there just as well as the *Bathybius* in the sea. In the case of the latter he finds it particularly significant that its *protoplasma* or *plasson* is *not yet individuated*. "Every little particle lives and functions in exactly the same way in the smaller as in the greater complexes." Furthermore, he informs von Hartmann, that the repeated artificial dissection of the *Protamoeba* did not prevent any one of its particles either to keep on living undisturbedly. These results are "of utmost importance for the doctrine of individuation," which he was compelled to revise essentially on the basis of these findings in his *Monographie der Kalkschwämme*, vol. 1, pp. 89–124.[1]

Von Hartmann's reply.   Berlin, November 26, 1874.

Von Hartmann notifies Haeckel of the material he is returning to him, and thanks him especially for the annotated *Biologische Studien*.

He expresses his disappointment to Haeckel concerning his own new study which, due to the restrictions of space, is much less detailed than he wished to make it.[2] Thus he had to forgo a strong assertion of the philosophical standpoint against Haeckel's position, which his readers had every right to expect from him, he had no opportunity to call attention to Haeckel's newest publication, nor was he able to comply with Haeckel's wishes in emphasizing the importance of the *Morphologie*, which hitherto was hardly noticed. "Thus many things were left unsaid which I wished to discuss in detail." With factual simplicity he tells Haeckel that his critical exposé "next to the light shows also the shadows," hoping that this fact will not displease Haeckel, since he is well aware of the small number of those recommendations where there are no restricting reservations. All in all, von Hartmann believes, that his essay will reflect that warm objective and personal interest which Haeckel's efforts and endeavors have awakened in him in a steadily increasing manner.

He concludes his letter with an exchange of photographs, and with the hope that his manuscript will arrive in time for release in the January issue.

P.S. Von Hartmann wants to briefly answer a rebuttal by Haeckel in his *Anthropogenie*, pp. 132 sqq., because of his stand concerning the theory of discontinuous and gradual evolution. Since he treats of this matter in his latest writing, here he restricts himself to the following observations: first, he is in

---

[1] Ernst Haeckel, *Die Kalkschwämme* (Calcispongien oder Grantien). Eine Monographie und ein Versuch zur analytischen Lösung des Problems von der Entstehung der Arten. Berlin, 1868.

[2] Cf. footnote 1, p. 181 in following letter.

complete agreement with Haeckel as to the continuity of all ontogenetic evolution; secondly, he rejects Haeckel's inference therefrom as to the same nature of phylogenetic evolution also. He calls this reasoning an entirely unjustified *metabasis eis allo genos*. Furthermore, he is convinced that Haeckel's appeal to the individual growth-process of the third and fourth horns of goats in support of his theory is totally irrelevant in view of the facts his opponents point to as phylogenetic discontinuity and leaps in nature.

Continuing the argument von Hartmann reminds Haeckel that, in order to refute his opponents, he must prove that in the first ten generations of goats there is only a small protrusion of the skull, in the next ten there is an observable appearance of bone-growth, and that from the first generation through the line of successive generations the horns have developed in an ever increasing manner. But when one generation has only two, and the next four fully developed horns, the phylogenetic discontinuity is thereby irrevocably vindicated empirically.

Moreover, the ontogenetic development itself will show a morphological jump despite the steadiness of physiological growth, if we reflect, that in a definite moment a process of cell-division of diverse morphological value must step in in order to account for the additional two new horns. This moment, in which the morphologically heterogeneous progress of cell-division occurs must be considered as a jump in evolution, if not physiologically, at least morphologically. In the phylogenetic evolution of the type (class) the problem revolves, on the one hand, *only* around the morphological and not at all around the physiological continuity of evolution, and, on the other hand, the classes must be compared only on the *same* level of the ontogenetic development, in the case under consideration, the developed two-horned goats with the developed four-horned ones.

D. O.

SEVENTH LETTER

Haeckel's reply. Jena, December 8, 1874.

Haeckel assures von Hartmann of his gratitude for sending him the article *Anfänge naturwissenschaftlicher Selbsterkenntnis*,[1] which he has read with great interest. Von Hartmann's criticism of du Bois-Reymond's speach is of particular significance for him, since he also opposes his idea of the "double limit of cognition," although for different reasons than von Hartmann. As a scientist, Haeckel continues, du Bois-Reymond has rendered valuable service to neurophysiology, but his lack of appreciation of the history of evolution is regrettable.

He finds especially objectionable in du Bois-Reymond's latest statements the *Deus ex machina*-like appearance of consciousness, instead of a gradual evolution of it. This lack of understanding the problems of genetics is most striking when he treats the question of necessary connection between the soul and the nerve-substance. He conveniently ignores the fact that all lowest animals (protozoa, and a part of the zoophyta), which possess no nervous system, only indifferent cells, are just as well "animated" (*beseelt*), as are the others. In Haeckel's

---

[1] Eduard von Hartmann, *Anfänge naturwissenschaftlicher Selbsterkenntnis*. Wiener Abendpost, No. 33–35; reprinted in the *Gesammelte Studien und Aufsätze*, pp. 445–459.

opinion, this neglect of and contempt for the doctrine of evolution and everything that relies on it, like his own morphology, is greatly responsible for the onesidedness of contemporary physiologists and the stagnation of their own science.

In reference to von Hartmann's P.S. Haeckel agrees that his remarks concerning "discontinuous evolution" are quite correct, except for the fact, that von Hartmann uses the term "discontinuous" in an entirely different sense than the natural scientists do. They intend to deny by it the "continuation of what has progressed before," and want to describe by this term a new, unmotivated rise of the form, a marvel of new species (ein Wunder neuer Art), as an opposed theory to natural phylogenesis. Furthermore, in the case of these *seemingly* discontinuous geneses the laws of abbreviated and falsified heredity (*abgekürtze und gefälschte Vererbung*), play a significant role together with the homologous transition of cells.

In conclusion Haeckel promises to elaborate further on this problem whenever the occasion arises in the future.

EIGHTH LETTER

Von Hartmann's reply.   Berlin, February 24, 1875.

Von Hartmann apologizes for the long delay in answering Haeckel's last letter, but a misinformation concerning the early publication of his article in the *Deutsche Rundschau*, which he hoped to attach, held up his reply.[1] Since it is still indefinite when the article will be published, he hastens to dispatch two of his latest writings, the *Kritische Grundlegung des transcendentalen Realismus*,[2] and the *Wahrheit und Irrtum im Darwinismus*.[3] He asks Haeckel to read the parts which deal with the criticism of his philosophy in the first book, and the relation between the natural sciences and the philosophy of nature in the second book, with special attention.

Next he makes reference to Wiesner's work *Das Atom*, Haeckel previously asked him to read, and states rather frankly that he did not find it very impressive. However, this work led him to Pfeilsticker's *Kinet-System*,[4] which he thinks to be so promising and revolutionary that it signals the beginning of a new era in the field of molecular-physics.

Von Hartmann wonders whether Haeckel has read Klein's base personal attack against him in his periodical *Gäa*, which was reprinted from the *Grazer Tagepost*. Klein withdrew his accusations in the first issue of the year, and the libel suit against the *Grazer Tagepost* is currently pending. Von Hartmann cannot repress his astonishment over the fact that such irresponsible personal gossips can appear in respectable publications. He suspects that the cause and propagator of these slanderous rumors is the same Dühring who had to resign from the University of Berlin because of his scandalous attacks on Professor Wagner.[5]

---

[1] Cf. footnote 1, p. 184 in the eleventh letter.

[2] Eduard von Hartmann, *Kritische Grundlegung des transcendentalen Realismus;* 2nd enlarged edition of "Das Ding an sich und seine Beschaffenheit," Berlin, 1875.

[3] Eduard von Hartmann, *Wahrheit und Irrtum im Darwinismus*, eine kritische Darlegung der organischen Entwicklungstheorie. Berlin, 1875.

[4] Albert von Pfeilsticker, *Das Kinet-System oder die Elimination der Repulsivkräfte und überhaupt des Kraftbegriffes aus der Molekularphysik*. Stuttgart, 1873.

[5] Karl Eugen Dühring (1833–1921), who lost his right to lecture (venia legendi) in 1877

Haeckel's reply.   Jena, March 3, 1875.

Haeckel regrets that he has time only for a brief answer, because he is about to embark on a trip to Corsica and Sardinia to further his studies of the Gastraea-theory and the homologous nature of the seed-leaves. He also informs von Hartmann of his recent illness, which prevented him to read as yet his newest publications on Darwinism and transcendental realism.

Then he voices his fear that von Hartmann's thoroughgoing criticism of Wigand's book may have given it a status of respectability which it certainly does not deserve.[1] In his own opinion the whole work is completely non-sensical (... *völlig verbohrt*). The best critique he has seen of this book is M. Müller's review in the *Jenaer Literarische Zeitung*, 1874, No. 17, p. 250. As a natural scientist Wigand is a non-entity; he is recognized neither by the followers nor by the opponents of Darwinism. "He has not yet written one single decent work. He is a fanatic follower of Irving, and thinks he is one of the 12 angels."

Haeckel closes his letter by expressing his sympathy for the indignities von Hartmann had to suffer, and is firmly convinced that it was instigated by Dr. Dühring, whose "new philosophy" he has read briefly, and finds it very shallow and unscientific.[2]

Von Hartmann's reply.   Berlin, March 10, 1875.

Von Hartmann receives with sincere concern the news of Haeckel's illness, and expresses his hope that the trip to the Mediterranean will aid not only his scientific work, but will hasten the recuperation of his health as well.

In reference to Wigand's work, he explains, his foremost intent was to find the golden means of judicious reason in the raging cacophony of pros and cons. He is well aware that Wigand is anything but an original thinker, and in the field of natural sciences he will never create anything noteworthy. The only compliment he paid to the work was his admission that it is the most ambitious and common-place compilation of materials already treated in other works. He knows that the role of an arbitrator is a thankless one, yet he wanted to do his utmost to check both extremes in this controversy with objective calm and conscientious care, and open a path of *possible* reconciliation between the two warring camps. Whether he has succeeded in his attempt or not, let competent judges decide.

He concludes his letter by repeating his best wishes for Haeckel's health.

because of his open attack on the German University life in general, and on the Professors of the University of Berlin in particular.

[1] Albert Wigand, *Der Darwinismus und die Naturforschung Newtons und Cuviers*. vols. 3, Braunschweig, 1874–1877. (As a botanist he was one of the sharpest opponents of Darwin).

[2] Karl Eugen Dühring, *Kursus der Philosophie als streng wissenschaftliche Weltanschauung und Lebensgestaltung*. Leipzig, 1875. (It is described as "new philosophy" in reference to his earlier work: *Geschichte der Kritischen Philosophie von ihren Anfängen bis zur Gegenwart*. Berlin, 1869).

184 APPENDIX

Von Hartmann's letter. Bad Elster (Sachs), July 6, 1875.

Von Hartmann notifies Haeckel that he has mailed him the July issue of the *Deutsche Rundschau*, which contains his article about Haeckel.[1] Due to restrictions of space and Rodenberg's editorial insistence, the article will not appear in its original length. He intends to rectify this shortcoming in a collection of essays: *Gesammelte Studien und Aufsätze gemeinverständlichen Inhalts*, planned for publication in early 1876.

Next, wishing to bring Haeckel up on his literary activity since their last correspondence, tells him of his newest publications. *I. H. von Kirchmanns erkenntnistheoretischer Realismus* came off the press as a supplement to his *Kritische Grundlage des transcendentalen Realismus*, which could be of interest to Haeckel in its detailed exposition of the notion of causality.[2] In June he has finished another pamphlet: *Zur Reform des höheren Schulwesens*, which is slated for publication in the fall.[3]

In May he has completed yet another work: *Zur Physiologie der Nervencentra*, which follows closely the theories of Wundt and Maudsley, occasionally referring also to Haeckel's doctrine in the *Anthropogenie*. He asks Haeckel not to form a definitive judgement about his position with regard to the philosophy of nature without reading first this work. He plans to append it to the seventh edition of the *Philosophie des Unbewussten*, after its publication in the *Athenäum*.[4]

In conclusion he informs Haeckel of dropping the charges against the *Grazer Tagespost* after the editors withdrew their accusations.

Haeckel's reply. Jena, July 7, 1875.

Haeckel thanks von Hartmann for the objective appraisal of his scientific endeavors in the article published in the *Deutsche Rundschau*. He is especially gratified by von Hartmann's sensitive appreciation of his *Generelle Morphologie*, which is, indeed, the creed and life-program of his entire scientific activity. He has far-reaching plans for this work, which once completed, will be presented in a second edition.

As a result of his sojourn in Corsica his Gastraea-theory assumed its final shape, and to his amazement, it is rapidly becoming a "colossal success" among the experts. Also, while in Corsica, he found opportunity to follow closely the gastrula-formation in embryos of the most diverse kind of animals and conclude with certitude, that the existing differences among them can be reduced to one single basic-form.

[1] Eduard von Hartmann, *Ernst Haeckel*. Deutsche Rundschau, No. 4, pp. 7–32. Reprinted in *Gesammelte Studien und Aufsätze*, pp. 460–496.
[2] Eduard von Hartmann, *I. H. von Kirchmanns erkenntnistheoretischer Realismus. Ein kritischer Beitrag zur Begründung des transcendentalen Realismus*. Berlin, 1875.
[3] Eduard von Hartmann, *Zur Reform des höheren Schulwesens*. Berlin, 1875.
[4] Eduard von Hartmann, *Philosophie des Unbewussten*. 7th enlarged edition in 2 vols. Vol. 1: Phänomenologie des Unbewussten, (with the added new appendix: Physiologie der Nervencentra); vol. 2: Metaphysik des Unbewussten, Berlin, 1875.

In the following he informs von Hartmann that he is working on the third edition of the *Anthropogenie*, and conveys his gratitude for the helpful insights he gained regarding the revision of this work by reading von Hartmann's *Wahrheit und Irrtum im Darwinismus*. He regrets, however, that von Hartmann pays only a token notice to the "theory of selection," (while he himself, perhaps, too much). Concerning the question of teleology, the kind that is compatible with mechanism, he believes, they could come to terms. The great difficulty is, in his opinion, that the teleological public wants absolutely no part of this kind of teleology!

In conclusion he asks von Hartmann whether he is acquainted with Fritz Schultze's book *Kant und Darwin*,[1] and wishes him a successful stay at the spa in Bad Elster.

THIRTEENTH LETTER

Von Hartmann's reply.   Elster, July 9, 1875.

Von Hartmann is greatly gratified by Haeckel's appreciation of his article in the *Deutsche Rundschau*, and also by the fact, that Haeckel found his *Wahrheit und Irrtum...*, stimulating and thought-provoking. He does not aspire to any recognition, he is satisfied to know that he is of assistance through his endeavors to others in clarifying and bringing problems closer to solution. Unfortunately, this was not the case until now. His efforts were either ignored as so much philosophical phantasmagories, or labeled as unscientific arrogance by other scientists.

With a shade of disillusion in his words he complains to Haeckel, that although he has many critics, who sneer at his attempts and openly ridicule him, there is hardly anyone who would appreciate his efforts to bring the historical development of philosophy and the natural sciences in a closer, and mutually beneficial relationship. This situation reminds him of his earlier rapport with the theologians, who also ignored or ridiculed him first, now they watchfully follow him as a dangerous opponent.

Von Hartmann is delighted to hear that Haeckel has found new conclusive evidence for his Gastraea-theory. As far as he is concerned, he always had great confidence in this theory, for through the gastraea the process of evolution receives as simple an explanation as is most befitting nature.

Then suddenly, von Hartmann voices a frank disagreement with Haeckel's opinion, that the public wants no part of teleology that is reconcilable with mechanism based on the laws of nature. On the contrary, he is convinced that as soon as the mechanists cease to spread their belief, that the teleological view is irreconcilable with the mechanistic, the protagonists of the teleological outlook will also lose interest in combatting the mechanists, and will show willingness to listen to the voice of those who labor indefatigably to bring about a resolution of their onesided truth in a higher synthesis. "The struggle of the teleologists against your mechanism is unfortunately a reaction against your opposition to teleology, which you have inherited from the materialism of the natural sciences of the fifties."

In order to support his stand further, i.e., that the impass between teleology and mechanism is not insurmountable, von Hartmann makes reference to the

[1] Fritz Schultze, *Kant und Darwin*. Jena, 1875.

work of an orthodox Lutheran,[1] and a speculative Calvinist.[2] He believes his diagnosis is correct in stating, that there is a feeling of uneasiness in the philosophically trained teleological public exactly because of this cleavage between the teleological and mechanistic outlook, and it ardently hopes for a *reconciliation* with the natural sciences. Whether there will be steps taken *soon* on the part of the scientists toward this direction, depends in definitive measure on Haeckel as leader of the natural-philosophical trend. It is von Hartmann's hope, that his own work, *Zur Physiologie der Nervencentra*, will assist Haeckel in taking the initiative toward this unity, the eventual realization of which is only a matter of time.

"It is in your hands to hasten by a decade or more, the peace between the forward-pressing sciences of nature and the philosophical enterprise at large, and thus, safely securing the unity of our culture-progress spare many minds and hearts from heavy concerns and wearisome struggles. The early realization of this truce seems to me so much the more important, because the victory of culture over ultramontanism must be fought out in the next decade *for the whole world* in Germany, and to this end *all forces* of German science must cooperate. Should Germany succumb to Rome, Rome's victory is secured for the next century in all parts of the world."

Notifying Haeckel that he has not yet heard of Schultze's work *Kant und Darwin*, and thanking Haeckel's gracious offer to send it to him, von Hartmann concludes his letter.

FOURTEENTH LETTER

Von Hartmann's letter.   Berlin, December 28, 1875.

Von Hartmann sends his best wishes to Haeckel on the occasion of the New Year, and greatfully acknowledges the beautiful Christmas present he received from Haeckel via Reimer's publishing-house.

In the continuing controversy between Haeckel and His, von Hartmann ventures to voice the views of a disinterested outside observer. Although incompetent, according to his own admission, to offer a judicious statement in the matter, his remarks about the formal method could be of interest to Haeckel.

As an introduction he questions Haeckel's right to dismiss *a priori* His' method as fruitless and useless, on the sole ground that it is opposed to his own stand on the basic law of biogenetics. Although, von Hartmann is willing to admit, that the possibility is not excluded that in His' way, seen only *a posteriori*, no results of any significance will turn up, and the factual value of his efforts can be left out of consideration. Yet, the problem still remains, that when the line of ancestry is the causal impact upon the ontogenetic evolution of a germ, this influx cannot be explained by some sort of magic or mystery, rather it must be laid down in the given molecular conditions of the germ, from which the ontogenetic development issues forth according to purely mechanical laws. Be this so, then it remains an open enterprise for anyone to search for an explanation of these mechanical processes of growth in the germ. For whatever must be termed, on the one hand,

---

[1] Adolf Lasson, *Mechanismus und Teleologie*. Verhandlungen der Philos. Gesellschaft zu Berlin, Heft 1. Leipzig, 1875.
[2] Alois E. Biederman, *Christliche Dogmatik*. Zürich, 1869.

as individual resumption of the pre-history of the seed, must also, on the other hand, have its accuracy as pure mechanical process. "Both are but different aspects of consideration, which *temporarily abstract* from one another, but *on the long run* they cannot mutually *exclude* each other, on the contrary, they clarify and supplement one another."

Since Haeckel is certainly not opposed to the second standpoint, he can, perhaps, judge more leniently the methodical tendency of a researcher who has decided to abstract, for the time being, from the first view, and consequently gives a onesided emphasis to the importance of the second.

In conclusion he lists the works he sent Haeckel lately, the supplements to the seventh edition of the *Philosophie des Unbewussten*, and two pamphlets, *Zur Schulreform*, and *Kirchmanns Realismus*. He will also present him his *Gesammelte Studien und Aufsätze*, as soon as it comes off the press.[1] Reich's review, the *Athenäum*, will publish, beginning next year, his newest writing, *Die sittliche Freiheit*.[2]

FIFTEENTH LETTER

Haeckel's reply.   Jena, December 30, 1875.

Haeckel acknowledges von Hartmann's letter, and welcomes his frank critical remarks. Formally speaking, he believes that von Hartmann's criticism has its merits, although, Haeckel injects, were von Hartmann more familiar with the works and objectives of His, he would have no difficulty in agreeing with Haeckel, at least, materially. Haeckel readily grants, that His' method cannot be rejected a priori, nor does he do this, since he has already acknowledged it as an attempt at a "physiology of growth."

Any expert in the field, however, could have foreseen, that if His' efforts bring any results, it will be in spite of and not because of his method. In addition, His' pretended "explanation" (which in fact contains no causal-impact) gave dangerous ammunition to the empiricists, who will feel supported by His' views in their own crude mechanical explanation of phenomena.

At any rate, Haeckel concedes, that he himself is not very happy with his polemics against His' *Ziele und Wege* either. In the heat of the battle he has gone much too far, and he is glad that he has not completed the second part of the same work. In this part he planned to compare the views of von Hartmann, as laid down in the *Philosophie des Unbewussten*, Alexander Braun, his friend and teacher,[3] and his own, concerning the history of evolution. Since this was not intended to be polemical, it would have been ill-fitting with the first part. Also, in the process of study he realized more and more his inadequate philosophical orientation in the matter and found it best to discontinue the project.

"The more I think about the philosophical problems of the history of evolution, the more I realize how much I am lacking in the necessary preparation, and how

[1] Eduard von Hartmann, *Gesammelte Studien und Aufsätze gemeinverständlichen Inhalts*. Berlin, 1876.
[2] Eduard von Hartmann, *Die sittliche Freiheit*.Reich's "Athenäum," no. 2, 1876, pp. 44–54, 193–203, 328–340. (Reprinted: Phänomenologie des sittlichen Bewusstseins. Prolegomena zu jeder künftigen Ethik. Berlin, 1879).
[3] Alexander Braun, (1805–1877), able systematizer and outstanding morphologist, unviersity professor at Karlsruhe, Freiburg im Br., Giessen, and Berlin.

far I am from a mature knowledge of the question." To be sure, he is constantly aware of the high aims that are set for any serious student in this particular field, yet, in his own estimation it was only in the latter years that he succeeded in approaching them. Thus he agrees, that von Hartmann's remarks made in this regard in his friendly review of Haeckel's efforts "are most correct, and should not have been made in vain."

Matters being as they are, the best he can do is to confine himself again "to a narrow empirical portion of the immense biological field," and with the help of his phylogenetic studies further his knowledge of the enormous amount of the empirical raw-material. Nothing can match the satisfaction he derives by working in this field, as his latest essay *Die Gastrula und die Eifurchung* proved it to him again. Not only is it gratifying, it is inviting to pensive reflection, which yields highly significant results for him, as well as for his fellow biologists.

In conclusion he thanks von Hartmann for the generous reading material he received, although, his immediate pre-occupation with the completion of the Gastraea-theory and other future plans will prevent him, he fears, for a considerable time from reading it.

Expressing his best wishes for the New Year, he terminates his last letter of their correspondence.

SIXTEENTH LETTER

Von Hartmann's reply.   Berlin, October 24, 1876.

Von Hartmann begins his letter with a sincere apology for the long delay in answering, and lists a number of personal misfortunes and family tragedies as excuses, among them the death of his father, and the serious illness of his only child.

Then he thanks Haeckel for sending him his new short work, *Perigenesis*,[1] in return he mailed him his earlier promised *Gesammelte Studien und Aufsätze*. Moreover, he has two other works in preparation, von Hartmann tells Haeckel; one already in the press, the other in the process of being completed. The first, *Neukantianismus, Schopenhauerianismus und Hegelianismus*,[2] contains several topics that may be of particular interest to Haeckel, like his treatise on F. A. Lange, which deals with the pseudo-reconciliation between philosophy and the natural sciences, and the polemics he directs against Bahnsen, Frauenstädt, and Rehmke. The second is a new, revised edition of his originally anonymous *Unbewusste*, this time being published under his name.[3] The preface of this latter book will elaborate further on his intimations and suggestions he projected in his letters, and he also hopes to make repeated references to Haeckel's *Perigenesis*.

---

[1] Ernst Haeckel, *Die Perigenesis der Plastidule oder die Wellenerzeugung der Lebensteilchen*. Ein Versuch zur mechanischen Erklärung der elementaren Entwicklungsvorgänge. Berlin, 1876.

[2] Eduard von Hartmann, *Neukantianismus, Schopenhauerianismus und Hegelianismus in ihrer Stellung zu den philosophischen Aufgaben der Gegenwart*. Second enlarged edition of the "Erläuterungen zur Metaphysik des Unbewussten." Berlin, 1877.

[3] Eduard von Hartmann, *Das Unbewusste vom Standpunkt der Physiologie und Descendenztheorie*. Second augmented edition of the anonymously published work in 1872, together with the writing of Oskar Schmidt: *Kritik der naturwissenschaftlichen Grundlagen der Philosophie des Unbewussten*. Berlin, 1877.

How justifiable was the anonimity of the first edition of the above work can easily be seen from such vitriolic and hateful attacks as J. Bahnsen's in the last chapter of the anonymously edited writing *Landläufige Philosophie und land-flüchtige Wahrheit*. Von Hartmann is confident that by next April he can present both of his works to Haeckel, so that his standpoint concerning the philosophy of nature may finally be clear to Haeckel in as complete an exposition as it can be expected. In doing this he nurtures no false hopes of converting Haeckel, merely wishes to convince him, that:

1) the difference between their respective views concerning the philosophy of nature is considerably less than it is generally believed;

2) this difference is *simply irrelevant*, as far as the natural sciences, their representatives, and their unhampered research is concerned;

3) his stand affords a more effective defense of practical idealism than Haeckel's, and due to this fact it is better qualified to bring into harmony the idealistic culture of Germany with the new findings of the exact sciences, thereby to bridge the gap which presently exists between the two.

As a conclusion to their entire correspondence, with a sense of anticipated failure, von Hartmann remarks: "Were I ever to succeed in moving you to the acceptance of these three points, it would be one of the happiest moments of my life."

BIBLIOGRAPHY

Von Hartmann's Works in Chronological Order

Über die dialektische Methode. Berlin: Carl Dunker, 1868. 2nd unaltered photo-copied edition, Darmstadt: Wissenschaftliche Buchgesellschaft, 1963.

Philosophie des Unbewussten. Berlin: Carl Dunker, 1869. [There are twelve editions all in all of this work. The first publication appeared in one volume and was in preparation from Christmas, 1864 until Easter, 1867. Von Hartmann was only 22 years old when he began the compilation of his best known work. By the beginning of 1870 all 1000 copies of the first edition were sold out, and by 1874 it reached its sixth edition. It was the seventh edition which appeared first in two volumes in 1876, the eighth and ninth in 1878 and 1884 respectively, and only the tenth edition reached the final form of three volumes in 1890. The eleventh edition published in 1904 is the reprint of the tenth with the addition of two new chapters in the Preface: *The Concept of the Unconscious,* and *The History of the Philosophy of the Unconscious.* The twelfth and last edition was edited under the supervision of Arthur Drews, which is an unchanged reprint of the eleventh, and was published in Leipzig by Alfred Kröner in 1923].

Schellings positive Philosophie. Berlin: Otto Loewenstein, 1869.

Das Ding an sich und seine Beschaffenheit. Berlin: Carl Dunker, 1871. [The second edition of the same work was published with a new title: *Kritische Grundlegungen des transzcendentalen Realismus.* Berlin: Carl Dunker, 1875; reprinted as vol. I of the *Ausgewählte Werke.* Leipzig: Hermann Haacke, 1889. Cf. also letter 8 of the Appendix].

Das Unbewusste vom Standpunkt der Philosophie und Descendenztheorie. [For the story of this work cf. letters 2 and 3 of the Appendix. In its final placement it was added, with two others, *Wahrheit und Irrtum im Darwinismus; Die naturwissenschaftliche Grundlagen der Philosophie des Unbewussten und die darwinische Kritik,* as the third volume to the tenth edition of the *Philosophie des Unbewussten*].

Gesammelte philosophische Abhandlungen zur Philosophie des Unbewussten. Berlin: Carl Dunker, 1872. Second edition of the same work appeared under the title: *Neukantianismus, Schopenhauerianismus, und Hegelianismus.* Berlin: Carl Dunker, 1877.

Anfänge naturwissenschaftlicher Selbsterkenntnis. [Part C, No. II, of the *Gesammelte Studien und Aufsätze gemeinverständlichen Inhalts.* Berlin: Carl Dunker, 1876. Cf. also letters 7 and 11 of the Appendix].

Ernst Haeckel als Vorkämpfer der Abstammungslehre. [Part C, No. III. of the *Gesammelte Studien...* Cf. letters 6, 7 and 11, of the Appendix].

Erläuterungen zur Metaphysik des Unbewussten mit besonderer Rücksicht auf den Panlogismus. Berlin: Carl Dunker, 1874.
Johann H. von Kirchmanns naiver Realismus. Berlin: Carl Dunker, 1875. Cf. also letter 11 of the Appendix.
Zur Physiologie der Nervenzentra. See in the *Ergänzungsband zur ersten bis neunten Auflage der Philosophie des Unbewussten.* Leipzig: Wm. Friedrich, 1889. Cf. also letters 11 and 13 of the Appendix.
Phaenomenologie des sittlichen Bewusstseins. Berlin: Carl Dunker, 1879. The second edition was published under the title: *Das sittliche Bewusstsein.* Leipzig: Hermann Haacke, 1889.
Zur Geschichte und Begründung des Pessimismus. Berlin: Carl Dunker, 1880.
Die Krisis des Christentums in der modernen Theologie. Berlin: Carl Dunker, 1880.
Das religiöse Bewusstsein der Menschheit im Stufengang seiner Entwickelung. Berlin: Carl Dunker, 1882.
Das Judentum in Gegenwart und Zukunft. Leipzig: Wm. Friedrich, 1885.
Philosophische Fragen der Gegenwart. Leipzig: Wm. Friedrich, 1885.
Der Spiritismus. Leipzig: Wm. Friedrich, 1885. Second edition, 1898.
Moderne Probleme. Leipzig: Wm. Friedrich, 1886.
Lotzes Philosophie. Leipzig: Wm. Friedrich, 1888.
Das Grundproblem der Erkenntnistheorie. Leipzig: Wm. Friedrich, 1889.
Kritische Wanderungen durch die Philosophie der Gegenwart. Leipzig: Wm. Friedrich, 1889.
Die Geisterhypothese des Spiritismus und seine Phantome. Leipzig: Wm. Friedrich, 1891.
Kants Erkenntnistheorie und Metaphysik. Leipzig: Wm. Friedrich, 1894.
Die sozialen Kernfragen. Leipzig: Wm. Friedrich, 1894.
Kategorienlehre. Leipzig: Hermann Haacke, 1896.
Ethische Studien. Leipzig: Hermann Haacke, 1898.
Geschichte der Metaphysik, 2 vols. Leipzig: Hermann Haacke, 1899.
Neue Tagesfragen. Leipzig: Hermann Haacke, 1900.
Zur Zeitgeschichte. Leipzig: Hermann Haacke, 1900.
Die moderne Psychologie. Leipzig: Hermann Haacke, 1901.
Die Weltanschauung der modernen Physik. Leipzig: Hermann Haacke, 1902.
Das Christentum des Neuen Testaments. Bad Sachsa: Hermann Haacke, 1905.
Das Problem des Lebens. Leipzig: Hermann Haacke, 1906.
Ausgewählte Werke. 12 vols. Leipzig: Hermann Haacke, 1889–1900.
    Kritische Grundlegungen
    Das Sittliche Bewusstsein
    Aesthetik
    Philosophie des Schönen
    Das Religiöse Bewusstsein der Menschheit
    Die Religion des Geistes
    Phaenomenologie des Unbewussten
    Metaphysik des Unbewussten
    Das Unbewusste und der Darwinismus
    Kategorienlehre
    Geschichte der Metaphysik – bis Kant
    Geschichte der Metaphysik – seit Kant
System der Philosophie im Grundriss. 8 vols. Bad Sachsa: Hermann Haacke.
    Grundriss der Erkenntnislehre, 1907.
    Grundriss der Naturphilosophie, 1907.
    Grundriss der Psychologie, 1908.
    Grundriss der Metaphysik, 1908.

Grundriss der Axiologie, 1908.
Grundriss der Ethischen Prinzipienlehre, 1909.
Grundriss der Religionsphilosophie, 1909.
Grundriss der Aesthetik, 1909.
Philosophie des Schönen. Ed. by Müller-Freienfels. Berlin: Volksverband der Bücherfreunde, 1924.
Metaphysik und Naturphilosophie. Briefwechsel zwischen Eduard von Hartmann und Ernst Haeckel. Ed. by Bertha Kern-von Hartmann. "Kant-Studien." Köln: Kölner Universitätsverlag. Vol. 48, No. 1. 1956/1957.

Translations

Hartmann, Eduard von. *The Philosophy of the Unconscious.* 2 ed. Trans. from the ninth German ed. by William Charles Coupland. London: Routledge and Kegan Paul Ltd., 1950.
— *Philosophie de l'inconscient.* 2 vols. Trans. by M. D. Nolen. Paris: G. Brailliere et Cie., 1874.
— *La filosofia del inconsciente.* 2 vols. Trans. by Suárez y de Urbina, José. Madrid, 1879.
— *La Verdad y el error del darwinismo.* Trans. by Sales y Ferré, Manuel. Sevilla, 1879.
— *La religion del porvenir.* Trans. by Zozaya y You, Antonio. Madrid: Imp. Helenica, 1935.
— *Religious Metaphysics.* Trans. by Thomas Hitchcock. New York: MacGowan and Slipper, 1883.
— *The Religion of the Future.* Trans. by Ernest Dare. London: W. Stewart and Co., 1886.
— *Spiritism.* Trans. by G. Fullerton. London: The Psychological Press, n.d.

Works Consulted

Albiol, Henry, C. M. *Spirit of Joy.* Trans. by B. T. B. Buckley, C. M. Westminster: Newman Press, 1956.
Aquinas, St. Thomas. *Opera omnia.* Leonine edition. 16 vols. Rome: Ex Typographia Polyglotta S. C. De Propaganda Fide, 1882–1948.
Vols. IV –XII. *Summa theologiae,* 1888–1906.
Vols. XIII–XV. *Summa contra gentiles,* 1918–1930.
— *In metaphysicam Aristotelis commentaria.* Edited by M.-R. Cathala. 3d edition. Turin: Marietti, 1935.
— *Basic Writings.* Edited by Anton C. Pegis. New York: Random House, 1945.
Aristotle. *Opera.* Ed. by Academia Regia Borussica. 4 vols. Berlin: Apud Georgium Reimerum, 1831–1870.
— *The Works of Aristotle.* Translated into English under the editorship of W. D. Ross. 12 vols. Oxford: The Clarendon Press, 1908–1952.
Arnou, Renatus, S.J. *De Quinque Viis Sancti Thomae ad Demonstrandam Dei Existentiam.* 2nd ed. Romae: Apud Aedes Pont. Univ. Gregorianae, 1949.
Augustine, St. "The Problem of Free Choice," *The Ancient Christian Writers.* Vol. XXII. Trans. by Dom Mark Pontifex. London: Longmans, Green and Co., 1955.
Bailey, Robert B. *Sociology Faces Pessimism.* The Hague: M. Nijhoff, 1958.
Barlow, James William. *The Ultimatum of Pessimism.* London: Kegan Paul, Trench, and Co., 1882.

Baynes, H. G. *Mythology of the Soul: A Research into the Unconscious.* London: Baillière, Tindall, Co., 1940.

Bolland, Gerard J. P. J. *Briefwechsel mit Eduard von Hartmann.* Den Haag: De Brauw, 1937.

Bonatelli, Francesco. *La filosofia dell'inconscio esposta ed esaminata.* Roma, 1876.

Bouyer, Louis. *Christian Humanism.* Trans. by A. V. Littledale. Westminster: The Newman Press, 1959.

Bowen, Francis. *Modern Philosophy from Descartes to Schopenhauer and Hartmann.* New York: Scribner, Armstrong Co., 1877.

Braun, Otto. "Eduard von Hartmann," Frommanns *Klassiker der Philosophie.* Ed. by Richard Falckenberg. Stuttgart: E. Hauff, 1909.

Brinkmann, Donald. *Probleme des Unbewussten.* Bern: A. Franke, 1943.

Bryar, William. *St. Thomas and the Existence of God.* Chicago: Henry Regnery Co., 1951.

Burnet, John. *Scriptorum Classicorum Bibliotheca Oxoniensis.* London: Clarendon Press, 1905–06.

Butler, Samuel. *Unconscious Memory: A Comparison Between the Theory of Dr. F. Hering and the Philosophy of the Unconscious of Dr. E. Von Hartmann.* 2nd ed. New York: E. P. Dutton Co., 1910.

Callahan, Leonard. *A Theory of Esthetic.* 2nd printing. Wash., D.C.: The Catholic University of America Press, Inc., 1947.

Caro, E. *Le pessimisme au XIXe siècle.* 2nd ed. Paris: Hachette et Cie., 1880.

Collins, James D. *A History of Modern European Philosophy.* Milwaukee: The Bruce Publishing Co., 1954.

— *The Lure of Wisdom.* Milwaukee: Marquette University Press, 1962.

Connolly, F. G. *Science versus Philosophy.* New York: Philosophical Library, 1957.

Copleston, Frederick, S.J. *Arthur Schopenhauer, Philosopher of Pessimism.* London: Burns, Oates and Washbourne, Ltd., 1947.

— "Augustine to Scotus," *A History of Philosophy.* Vol. II. London: Burns, Oates and Washbourne, Ltd., 1950.

Coreth, Emerich, S.J. *Das Dialektische Sein in Hegels Logik.* Wien: Herder, 1952.

Crousaz, Pierre De. *La Logic.* Luzern: no publisher, 1735.

Cudworth, Ralph. *The True Intellectual System of the Universe.* 3 vols. Ed. by J. Harrison. London: R. Royston, 1845.

D'Arcy, Martin C. *The Pain of this World and the Providence of God.* New York: Macmillan Co., 1935.

D'Avanzo, Luigi. *Il problema della storia nella filosofia dell'inconscio di E. di Hartmann.* Avella: Ferrara, 1958.

— *Il problema estetico nella filosofia dell'inconscio di E. di Hartmann.* Avella: Ferrara, 1959.

Dilthey, Wilhelm. *Gesammelte Schriften.* Stuttgart: G. G. Teubner, 1959.

Drews, Arthur. *Eduard von Hartmanns Philosophisches System im Grundriss.* Heidelberg: C. Winter, 1906.

— *Das Lebenswerk Ed. von Hartmanns.* Leipzig: Friedrich, 1907.

Drioton, E., Contenau, G., Dr., and Duchesne-Guillemin, J. "Religions of the Ancient East," *The Twentieth Century Encyclopedia of Catholicism.* Vol. CXLI. Trans. by M. B. Loraine. New York: Hawthorn Books, 1959.

Ebbinghaus, Hermann. *Über die Hartmannsche Philosophie des Unbewussten.* Düsseldorf: Fr. Dietz, 1873.

Erdmann, Johann, Z. E. *Grundriss der Geschichte der Philosophie.* 3rd ed. Berlin: W. Hertz, 1878.

Faggi, Adolfo. *La filosofia dell'inconsciente, metafisica e morale.* Contributo alla storia del pessimismo. Firenze: Successori Le Monnier, 1890.

Fischl, Johann. *Idealismus, Realismus und Existentialismus der Gegenwart.* Graz: Verlag Styria, 1954.

Gentile, Marino. *Il problema della filosofia moderna.* Brescia: La Scuola ed., 1950.

Gilson, Etienne. *The Unity of Philosophical Experience.* New York: Charles Scribner's Sons, 1950.

— *History of Christian Philosophy in the Middle Ages.* New York: Random House, Inc., 1955.

God, Man and the Universe. Ed. by J. de B. de la Saudee. New York: P. J. Kenedy and Sons, 1953.

Groddeck, Georg. *Exploring the Unconscious.* New York: Funk and Wagnalls, 1950.

Haeckel, Ernst. *Generelle Morphologie der Organismen.* 2 vols. Berlin: G. Reimer, 1866.

Hall, G. Stanley. *Founders of Modern Psychology.* London and New York: D. Appleton and Co., 1924.

Hartmann, Agnes Taubert von. *Philosophie gegen Naturwissenschaftliche Überhebung.* Berlin: C. Dunker, 1872.

Hartmann, Alma von. *Ed. von Hartmanns Konkreter Monismus,* in *Der Monismus dargestellt in Beiträgen seiner Vertreter.* 2 vols. Ed. by Arthur Drews. Jena: Diedericks, 1908.

— *Zurück zum Idealismus.* Berlin: C. A. Schwetschke und Sohn, 1920.

Hartmann, Wilfried. *Die Philosophie Max Schelers in ihren Beziehungen zu Eduard von Hartmann.* Düsseldorf: M. Triltsch, 1956.

Hawkins, D. J. B. *The Criticism of Experience.* New York: Sheed and Ward, 1945.

— *Crucial Problems of Modern Philosophy.* London: Sheed and Ward, 1957.

Haym, Rudolf. *Gesammelte Aufsätze.* Die Hartmann'sche Philosophie des Unbewussten, pp. 461–591. Berlin: Weidmann, 1903.

Hedge, Frederick Henry. *Atheism in Philosophy, and other Essays.* Boston: Roberts Bros., 1884.

Heyse, Christian W. L. *System der Sprachwissenschaft.* Berlin: Steinthal, 1856.

Horvath, Alexander M., O.P. *Studien zum Gottesbegriff.* Freiburg: Paulusverlag, 1954.

Huber, Max. *Eduard von Hartmanns Metaphysik und Religions-Philosophie.* Winterthur: P. G. Keller, 1954.

Humboldt, Wilhelm von. *Gesammelte Werke.* Stuttgart und Tübingen: Cotta, 1841–1872.

Hume, David. *Dialogues Concerning Natural Religion.* 2 vols. Ed. by T. H. Breen and T. H. Grose. London: Longmans, Green and Co., 1878.

Jessel, Otto. *Die induktive Methode bei Eduard von Hartmann.* Hamburg: Hartung et Co., 1907.

Jünger, Ernst. *Über die Linie.* Frankfurt A.M.: Vittorio Klostermann, 1950.

Kant, Immanuel. *Versuch einer Betrachtung über den Optimismus.* Königsberg: Hartung, 1759.

— *Versuch den Begriff der Negativen Grössen in die Weltweisheit Einzuführen.* Königsberg: Hartung, 1763.

— *Beobachtungen über das Gefühl des Schönen und Erhabenen.* Königsberg: Hartung, 1765.

— *Sämmtliche Werke.* 12 vols. Ed. by Rosekranz und Schubert. Leipzig: Baumann, 1838–1842.

Kapossy, Luczian I. *Hartmann Pesszimizmusa.* Esztergom: Egyetemi Nyomda, 1878.

Kappstein, Theodore. *Eduard von Hartmann.* Berlin: F. A. Perthes, 1907.

Kemeny, John G. *A Philosopher Looks at Science.* Princeton: D. van Nostrand Co., Inc., 1959.

Kenner, A. *The Sexes Compared.* London: Swan Sonnschein and Co., 1895.

Knox, I. *Aesthetic Theories of Kant, Hegel and Schopenhauer.* New York: Columbia University Press, 1936.

Köber, R. *Das philosophische System Ed. von Hartmanns.* Breslau: Köbner, 1884.

Krause, Ingrid. *Studien über Schopenhauer und den Pessimismus in der Deutschen Literatur des 19. Jahrhunderts.* Bern: P. Haupt, 1931.

Lange, Frederick A. *The History of Materialism.* 3rd ed. Trans. by E. Ch. Thomas. New York: The Humanities Press, 1950.

Leibniz, Gottfried W. von. *Opera Omnia.* 2 vols. Ed. by J. E. Erdmann. Berlin: G. Eichler, 1840.

Leidecker, Kurt F., Eduard von Hartmann. *The Dictionary of Philosophy.* Ed. by Dagobert D. Runes. New York: Philosophical Library, n.d. p. 122.

Lemaitre, Solange. "Hinduism," *The Twentieth Century Encyclopedia of Catholicism.* Vol. CXL. Trans. by J. F. Brown. New York: Hawthorn Books, 1959.

Lewis, C. S. *The Problem of Pain.* New York: The Macmillan Co., 1947.

Lichtenberg, Georg Ch. *Vermischte Schriften.* Göttingen: I. E. Dietrich, 1800–1805.

Maritain Jacques. *St. Thomas and the Problem of Evil.* Milwaukee: Marquette University Press, 1942.

— *The Range of Reason.* New York: Charles Scribner's Sons, 1952.

— *Approaches to God.* New York: Harper and Row, 1954.

— *An Essay on Christian Philosophy.* Trans. by E. H. Flannery. New York: Philosophical Library, 1955.

— *The Degrees of Knowledge.* Trans. from the fourth French edition by Gerald B. Phelan. New York: Charles Scribner's Sons, 1959.

Marcuse, Ludwig. *Pessimismus.* Hamburg: Rowohlt, 1953.

Maupertuis, Pierre Louis M. de. *Oeuvres.* Nouvelle ed. 4 vols. Lyon: Bruiset, 1756.

Mauriac, François. *Men I Hold Great.* Trans. by E. Pell. New York: Philosophical Library, 1951.

Miller, J. G. *The Unconscious.* New York: Wiley and Sons, 1942.

Moretti-Costanzi, Teodorico. *Kant, padre del pessimismo.* Roma: ed. Arte e Storia, 1950.

Mounier, Emmanuel. *Be Not Afraid.* Trans. by Cynthia Rowland. London: Rockliff Publishing Corp., Ltd., 1948.

Müller, Max Fr. *Chips From a German Workshop.* London-New York: Longmanns-C. Scribner and Co., 1866–1869.

Münsterberg, Hugo. *The Eternal Values.* New York: Houghton, Mifflin and Co., 1909.

McGill, V. J. *Schopenhauer, Pessimist and Pagan.* New York: Brentano, 1931.

MacIntyre, A. C. *The Unconscious.* New York: Humanities Press, 1958.

Northridge, William L. *Modern Theories of the Unconscious.* London: Kegan Paul, Trench, Ltd., 1924.

O'Brien, Thomas C., O.P. *Metaphysics and the Existence of God.* Washington: The Thomist Press, 1960.

Padovani, U. A. *Arturo Schopenhauer: L'Ambiente, la Vita, le Opere.* Milan: Vita e Pensiero, 1934.

Pieper, Joseph. *The End of Time.* Trans. by Michael Bullock. London: Faber and Faber, 1954.

— *Happiness and Contemplation.* Trans. by Richard and Clara Winston. New York: Pantheon, 1958.

— *The Silence of St. Thomas.* Trans. by John Murray, S.J. and Daniel O'Connor. New York: Pantheon, 1957.

Plato. *Quae Exstant Opera.* 5 vols. Ed. by Fredericus Astius. Lipsiae: Weidmann, 1819–1832.

— *The Works of.* Trans. by B. Jowett. 4 vols. New York: Tudor Publishing Co., n.d.

Plümacher, Olga. *Der Pessimismus in Vergangenheit und Gegenwart.* Heidelberg: G. Weiss, 1884.

— *Der Kampf um's Unbewusste.* Leipzig: W. Friedrich, 1890.

Post, L. A. *Thirteen Epistles of Plato.* London: Oxford University Press, 1925.

Rauschenberger, W. *Eduard von Hartmann.* Heidelberg: C. Winter, 1942.

Rice, Philip Blair. *On the Knowledge of Good and Evil.* New York: Random House, 1955.

Rostand, Jean. *Pensées d'un biologiste.* Paris: Stock, 1939.

Rozwadowski, Alexander, S.J. *De Optimismo Universale Secundum S. Thomam.* Rome: Gregorian University Press, 1936.

Ryan, John K. *Basic Principles and Problems of Philosophy.* Westminster: The Newman Press, 1954.

Salmon, Elizabeth G. *The Good in Existential Metaphysics.* Milwaukee: Marquette University Press, 1953.

Saltus, Edgar. *The Philosophy of Disenchantment.* Boston: Houghton, Mifflin Co., 1885.

Schelling, Friedrich W. J. *Sämmtliche Werke.* Ed. by K. F. A. Schelling. Stuttgart: J. C. Cotta, 1856–61.

Schmidt, Oskar. *Die Naturwissenschaftlichen Grundlagen der "Philosophie des Unbewussten."* Leipzig: Brockhaus, 1877.

Schnehen, Wilhelm von. *Eduard von Hartmann.* Frommanns *Klassiker der Philosophie.* Ed. by Richard Falckenberg. Stuttgart: E. Hauff, 1929.

Schneidewin, Max Dr. *Lichtstrahlen, Aus E. von Hartmanns Sämmtlichen Werken.* Berlin: C. Dunker, 1881.

Schofield, Alfred T. *The Unconscious Mind.* New York: Funk and Wagnalls Co., 1901.

Schopenhauer, Arthur. *Parerga und Paralypomena.* Berlin: Hayn, 1851.

— *Die Welt als Wille und Vorstellung.* 3rd ed. 2 vols. Leipzig: F. A. Brockhaus, 1859.

— *Sämmtliche Werke.* 16 vols. Ed. by P. Deussen und A. Hübscher. München: R. Piper und Co., 1911–1942.

Sertillanges, A. D., O.P. *Foundations of Thomistic Philosophy.* Trans. by Godfrey Anstruther, O.P. Springfield: Templegate, n.d.

— *Le problème du mal, la solution.* Paris: Aubier, 1951.

Sheen, Fulton J. *God and Intelligence.* New York: Longmans, Green and Co., 1925.

— *Religion Without God.* New York: Longmans, Green and Co., 1928.

— *Philosophies at War.* New York: Charles Scribner's Sons, 1943.

Sillem, Edward. *Ways of Thinking About God.* London: Darton, Longman and Todd, 1961.

Silva-Tarouca, Amadeo. *Thomas Heute.* Wien: Herder, 1947.

Siwek, Paul, S.J. *The Philosophy of Evil.* New York: Ronald, 1951.

— *The Enigma of the Hereafter.* New York: Philosophical Library, 1952.

Spiegelberg, Herbert. *The Phenomenological Movement.* A Historical Introduction 2nd ed. The Hague: M. Nijhoff, 1965.

Steffes, J. P. *Eduard von Hartmanns Religions-Philosophie des Unbewussten.* Mergentheim: Karl Ohlinger, 1921.
Steinthal, H. *Der Ursprung der Sprache.* 2nd ed. Berlin: Kummler, 1858.
Sully, James. *Pessimism: A History and Criticism.* London: Henry S. King and Co., 1877.
Taubert, Agnes. *Der Pessimismus und seine Gegner.* Berlin: C. Dunker, 1873.
Taylor, A. E. *Elements of Metaphysics.* 13th ed. London: Methuen and Co., 1952.
Tsanoff, Radoslav A. *The Nature of Evil.* New York: Macmillan, 1931.
Ueberweg, Friedrich Dr. *History of Philosophy.* 2 vols. Trans. by G. S. Morris. New York: Scribner, Armstrong and Co., 1876.
Vaihinger, Hans. *Hartmann, Dühring, und Lange.* Iserlohn: J. Baedeker, 1876.
Venetianer, Moritz Dr. *Der Allgeist, Grundzüge des Panpsychismus.* Berlin: C. Dunker, 1874.
Volkelt, Johannes E. *Das Unbewusste und der Pessimismus.* Berlin: F. Henschel, 1873.
Vyverberg, Henry. *Historical Pessimism in the French Enlightenment.* Cambridge (Mass.): Harvard University Press, 1958.
Weckesser, Albert. *Der empirische Pessimismus in seinem metaphysischen Zusammenhang im System von Eduard von Hartmann.* Bonn: Carl Georgi, 1885.
White, Victor Fr. *God and the Unconscious.* Chicago: H. Regnery Co., 1953.
Whyte, Lancelot, Law. *Unconscious Before Freud.* New York: Doubleday and Co., 1960.
Windelband, Wilhelm. *Die Hypothese des Unbewussten.* Heidelberg: Carl Winters, 1914.
— *Lehrbuch der Geschichte der Philosophie.* 14th ed. by Heinz Heimsoeth. Tübingen: J. C. B. Mohr, 1950.
— *A History of Philosophy.* 2 vols. Trans. by James H. Tufts. New York: Harper and Brothers, 1958.
Wrangel, Ewert H. G. *Eduard von Hartmanns Estetiska System i Kritisk Belysning.* Lund: C. W. K. Gleerup, 1889–1890.
Wundt, Wilhelm. *Vorlesungen über die Menschen und Thierseele.* Leipzig: L. Voss, 1863.
Zeller, Eduard. *Philosophie der Griechen.* 3rd ed. 5 vols. Leipzig: Fues, 1869–79.
Ziegler, Leopold Von. *Das Weltbild Hartmanns.* Leipzig: Fritz Eckhardt, 1910.
Zimmern, Helen. *Schopenhauer: His Life and Philosophy.* New York: Charles Scribner's Sons, 1932.

Articles

Bavink, B. "Eduard von Hartmann und die moderne Naturphilosophie," *Blätter für Deutsche Philosophie*, Vol. 16, pp. 162–166, 1942.
Braig, Carl. "Der Pessimismus in Seinen Psychologischen und Logischen Grundlagen," *Zeitschrift für Philosophie und Philosophische Kritik*, Vol. 82, pp. 249–262, 1883.
— "Der Pessimismus in Seinen Ethischen Grundlagen," *Zeitshrift für Philosophie und Philosophische Kritik*, Vol. 84, pp. 78–105, 1884.
Brandenstein, Béla von. "The Twentieth Century: Age of Despair?," *International Philosophical Quarterly*, Vol. III, No. 4, pp. 554–570, 1963.
Büsing, Max. "Eduard von Hartmann," *Geistige Arbeit*, Vol. 9, No. 4, 1942.
Caldwell, J. W. "Hartmann's Moral and Social Philosophy," *Philosophical Review*, VIII, pp. 465–483, 1899.
— "The Epistemology of Eduard von Hartmann," *Mind*, XVIII, pp. 188–207, 1893.

Dorner, L. von. "Von Hartmanns Pessimismus," *Zeitschrift für Philosophie und Philosophische Kritik*, Vol. 155, pp. 129–148, 1914.

Grapengiesser, C. "Kants Transcendentaler Idealismus und Eduard von Hartmanns Ding an Sich," *Zeitschrift für Philosophie und Philosophische Kritik*, Vol. 61, pp. 191–247, 1872.

Hartmann, Eduard von. "Die Allotrope Causalität," *Archiv für Systematische Philosophie*, Vol. V, no. 1, pp. 1–24, 1899.

— "Die Selbstzersetzung des Christentums und die Religion der Zukunft," trans. by A. Tuttle and J. A. Heinsohn, *Religio-Philosophical Journal*, Vol. XXIX, no. 26; vol. XXXI, no. 6.

— "Zum Begriff der Unbewussten Vorstellung," *Philosophische Monatsheften*, Vol. XXVIII, pp. 1–25, 1892.

— "A Critical Representation of the Theory of Organic Development," trans. by H. J. D'Arcy, *Journal of Speculative Philosophy*, Vol. XI, pp. 244–251; pp. 392–399, 1877; Vol. XII, pp. 138–145, 1878.

— "Das Kompensations-Aequivalent von Lust und Böse," *Zeitschrift für Philosophie und Philosophische Kritik*, Vol. 90, pp. 50–63, 1887.

— "Der Wertbegriff und der Lustwert," *Zeitschrift für Philosophie und Philosophische Kritik*, Vol. 106, pp. 20 sqq., 1895.

Korwan, Anton. "Zur Verteidigung des Pantheismus Eduard von Hartmanns," *Zeitschrift für Philosophie und Philosophische Kritik*, Vol. 126, pp. 44–60, 1905.

Lawrenny, H. "A New System of Philosophy: Philosophy of the Unconscious," *The Academy*, Vol. III, no. 43, pp. 90–93, 1872.

Leibniz, G. W. "Système nouveau de la nature," *Journal des Savants*, Vol. XXIII, pp. 444–462, 1695.

Marcel, Gabriel. "Philosophical Atheism," *International Philosophical Quarterly*, Vol. II, No. 4, pp. 501–514, 1962.

Mitchell, Ellen M. "The Philosophy of Pessimism," *The Journal of Speculative Philosophy*, Vol. XX, pp. 187–194, 1886.

Morse, William R. "Schopenhauer and Von Hartmann," *The Journal of Speculative Philosophy*, Vol. XI, pp. 152 sqq., 1877.

Nadler, K. "G. J. P. J. Bollands Briefwechsel mit E. von Hartmann," *Literaturblatt des Deutschen Kunstbladen*, Vol. 4, pp. 100–102, 1937.

Prufer, Thomas. "The Philosophical Act," *International Philosophical Quaterly*, Vol. II, No. 4, pp. 591–594, 1962.

Renouvier, C. B. "Notre pessimisme," *La Critique Philosophique*, Vol. I, No. 17, pp. 257–262, 1872.

Siwek, Paul, S.J. "Optimism in Philosophy," *The New Scholasticism*, Vol. XXII, No. 4, pp. 417–439, 1948.

— "Pessimism in Philosophy," *The New Scholasticism*, Vol. XXII, No. 3, pp. 249–297, 1948.

Volkelt, Johannes. "Über die Lust als Höchsten Wertmassstab," *Zeitschrift für Philosophie und Philosophische Kritik*, Vol. 88, pp. 233–259, 1886.